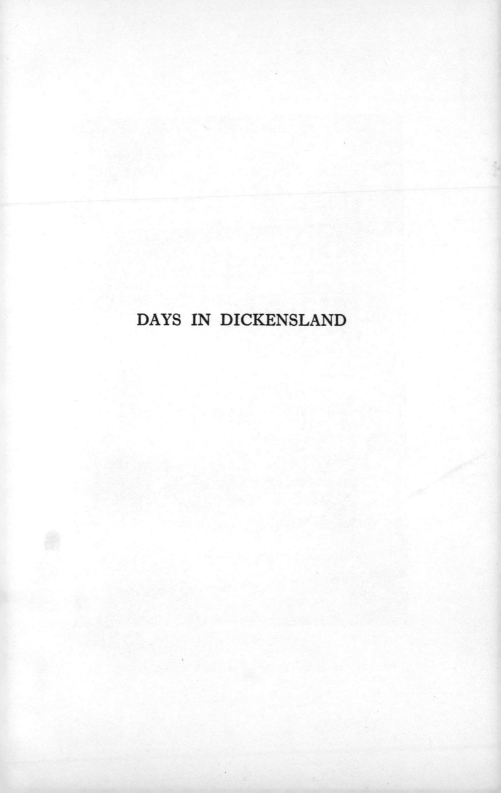

DAYS IN DICKENSLAND

CHARLES DICKENS'S HOUSE AT 48 DOUGHTY STREET

DAYS IN DICKENSLAND

BY

WALTER DEXTER

WITH TWENTY ILLUSTRATIONS

HASKELL HOUSE PUBLISHERS Ltd.
Publishers of Scarce Scholarly Books
NEW YORK, N. Y. 10012
1972

HASKELL HOUSE PUBLISHERS Ltd.

Publishers of Scarce Scholarly Books

280 LAFAYETTE STREET

NEW YORK. N. Y. 10012

Library of Congress Cataloging in Publication Data

Dexter, Walter, 1877-1944.
  Days in Dickensland.

  Reprint of the 1933 ed.
  1. Dickens, Charles, 1812-1870--Homes and haunts.
2. Literary landmarks--Great Britain. I. Title.
PR4584.D35 1972   823'.8 [B]   72-3610
ISBN 0-8383-1559-3

Printed in the United States of America

INTRODUCTION

SIR ARTHUR QUILLER-COUCH, speaking at a Dickens Birthday Dinner a year or two ago, said that Dickens created a world of his own and filled it with men and women. That is our Dickensland.

Its origin was probably—in addition to his native genius—the little shelf of books in his father's house, " the glorious host " that kept him company in the dull sad days of his childhood. " They kept alive my fancy, and my hope of something beyond that place and time," he tells us. " Every barn in the neighbourhood, every stone in the church, and every foot of the church-yard, had some association of its own, in my mind, connected with the books, and stood for some locality made famous in them. I have seen Tom Pipes go climbing up the church steeple ; I have watched Strap, with knapsack on his back, stopping to rest himself upon the wicket-gate ; and I *know* that Commodore Trunnion held that club with Mr. Pickle in the parlour of our little village ale-house."

Thus did the books he read appeal to Dickens ; and Dickens in his turn has so kept alive our fancy by his own books that pilgrimages to places associated with him and his stories are a regular feature of various literary societies and rambling clubs as well as with overseas visitors. Every reader desires to see the site of Garraway's Coffee House, from which Mr. Pickwick indited his famous chops and tomata sauce epistle to Mrs. Bardell ; to see the remains of the Marshalsea

Prison, and the church adjacent where Little Dorrit was married ; to see Fountain Court in the Temple, endeared to us by its association with the love-making of Ruth Pinch and John Westlock ; to see the Pump at Aldgate, and the Whittington Stone at Highgate ; to see the P.J.T. house in quaint old-world Staple Inn, where Mr. Grewgious lived ; to walk in the steps of Oliver Twist when he first made the acquaintance of London in company with the Artful Dodger ; to linger on Southwark Bridge (though it be not the Iron Bridge of the story) thinking of Little Dorrit and her meetings here with John Chivery and Arthur Clennam ; to walk from Blackfrairs to the Borough in the footsteps of young Dickens himself, on the way home from the blacking factory ; and to follow him in later years in what he called his "Uncommercial travels" through the streets of London.

And then to go farther afield to see the veritable house of his dreams at Gad's Hill near Rochester, and to linger in that city with the jolly Pickwickians, and perchance pay a visit to Mr. Pumblechook, the seed-merchant in the High Street ; or wander among the Cathedral precincts in an endeavour to solve the mystery surrounding Edwin Drood. And then on to the city of Canterbury, where Agnes Wickfield lived, and young David Copperfield went to school ; and then to Broadstairs, Dover and Folkestone, so intimately associated with both Dickens himself and his books.

All these desires may be satisfied by the reader of this book, in the compilation of which I have drawn largely upon my two earlier volumes, *The London of Dickens* and *The Kent of Dickens*, long out of print.

The best and most appropriate of Dickens's inimitable descriptions are quoted in the text ; readers who wish for further information are directed to the references to book and chapter at the end.

Photographs are included of only such places as are in existence at the present time. I wish to express my thanks to The Dickens Fellowship for the loan of the blocks from which some of these are printed.

WALTER DEXTER

April 1933

I am both a town traveller and a country traveller, and am always on the road. Figuratively speaking, I travel for the great house of Human Interest Brothers, and have rather a large connection in the fancy goods way. Literally speaking, I am always wandering here and there from my rooms in Covent Garden, London—now about the city streets, now about the country by-roads—seeing many little things, and some great things, which, because they interest me, I think may interest others.

(*The Uncommercial Traveller.*)

Mr. Jonas inquired in the first instance if they were good walkers, and being answered "Yes," submitted their pedestrian powers to a pretty severe test ; for he showed them as many sights in the way of bridges, churches, streets, outsides of theatres, and other free spectacles, in that one forenoon, as most people see in a twelvemonth. It was observable in this gentleman that he had an insurmountable distaste to the insides of buildings ; and that he was perfectly acquainted with the merits of all shows, in respect of which there was any charge for admission, which it seemed were every one detestable, and of the very lowest grade of merit.

(*Martin Chuzzlewit.*)

CONTENTS

ix

LIST OF ILLUSTRATIONS

Except where otherwise acknowledged, the illustrations are from photographs by the Author

DAYS IN DICKENSLAND

FIRST DAY

THROUGH LEGAL LAND TO ST. PAUL'S

TO begin our exploration of the London of Dickens and his works, there is no finer way imaginable than to take a stroll through the Inns of Court to the Temple; its secluded ways, unknown to many Londoners, are one of the many beauties the great city possesses; they are as foreign climes even to those people who pass and repass its very portals day after day. The great thoroughfares of Holborn, Fleet Street, and the Strand run through its centre; Theobald's Road and the Thames Embankment flank its farthest sides. Truly, as we shall see, entering these regions of repose is akin to putting cotton wool in our ears, as Dickens has likened it, so contrasting is the bustle of the street without with the silence reigning within.

Dickens's gallery of lawyers is by no means the least engrossing of the many types he has created for us; and, strangely enough, there is hardly a lawyer in that extensive list who had not his location in the legal district that runs from Doughty Street to the Thames Embankment. Dodson & Fogg, Sampson Brass and Mr. Jaggers are almost the only exceptions, and, outside London, we can but call to mind the firm of Wickfield & Heep.

The reason for the predominance of description given by Dickens to his legal characters is that from his very earliest days the power of the law had a really great meaning to him; his first occupation as a lad on leaving school was as office boy to a firm of solicitors when his fancy took free flight in the grass-centred squares and trim gardens of the Temple and Lincoln's Inn, in the subdued grey and red buildings, in the quaint Halls, the quainter and more secluded nooks and corners, in the narrow winding staircases, the little small-paned windows, and the deep and silent recesses. As a young man he occupied chambers in Furnival's Inn, and at the age of twenty-seven he entered his name as a student of Middle Temple— but he was never " called."

The Dickens House at 48 Doughty Street is our starting point. It was the first house rented by Dickens after his marriage, and here he lived from 1837 to 1839. Here *Pickwick Papers* was finished, *Oliver Twist* and *Nicholas Nickleby* written, and *Barnaby Rudge* commenced. It was purchased by The Dickens Fellowship in 1924 and vested in trustees. It contains a very fine library of Dickensiana, many autograph letters, the reading-desk which accompanied Dickens on his reading tours in this country and America, and many other pieces of interest.

Doughty Street leads into John Street, at the end of which Theobald's Road runs right and left.

On our left lies Gray's Inn Road, the place of residence of Mr. Mortimer (otherwise Wilkins Micawber). The patriarchal humbug Casby in *Little Dorrit* " lived in a street in the Gray's Inn Road, which had set off from that thoroughfare with the intention of running at one heat down into the valley and up again to the top of Pentonville Hill : but which had run itself out of breath in twenty yards, and had stood still ever since." Dickens adds, " There is no such place in that part now," which was quite true, as the streets had meanwhile been completed ; but investigation has proved that Acton Street was for many years only partially built, so we are not far wrong in supposing that Acton Street was in his mind when he referred to the street that stopped short.

The continuation of Gray's Inn Road on the right, leading into Holborn, was formerly called Gray's Inn Lane, and is briefly mentioned in *Pickwick* and one or two other books.

Before visiting Gray's Inn there is a little detour worth making. By the side of Holborn Hall at right angles to Gray's Inn Road runs Clerkenwell Road. Leather Lane on the right figures in the account of the riots in *Barnaby Rudge*.

The second turning to the right is Hatton Garden, where at No. 54 was the " very notorious Metropolitan Police Office," presided over by Mr. Fang : in reality it was the Hatton Garden Police Court, and a Mr. A. S. Laing was one of the magistrates there between 1836 and 1838. Oliver was brought here, " down a place called Mutton Hill, where he was led beneath a low archway and up a dirty court into this dispensary of summary justice, by the back way. It was a small paved yard into which they turned."

If we turn in at Hatton Wall we shall find the archway mentioned above, next a tavern, leading to a narrow passage called Hatton Yard parallel with the backs of the houses in Hatton Garden. This way, too, came Nancy, at the request of Fagin, tapping at the cell doors with her keys in the endeavour to trace Oliver. The backs of the houses have now been built over. No. 54 itself is the original building, although newly faced.

The Jellybys, in *Bleak House*, once lived in lodgings in Hatton Garden. " When Mr. Jellyby came home, he usually groaned and went down into the kitchen. There he got something to eat, if the servant would give him anything ; and then, feeling that he was in the way, went out and walked about Hatton Garden in the wet."

Mutton Hill is now known as Vine Street. Here

is Field Lane Ragged School, in which Dickens took a great interest.

Farther along Clerkenwell Road we reach Clerkenwell Green. It was near here that Mr. Brownlow, attentively reading a book at a stall outside a shop, was considered " a prime plant," as the Artful Dodger, Charley Bates, and Oliver Twist " were just emerging from a narrow court not far from the open square in Clerkenwell, which is yet called, by some strange perversion of terms, ' The Green.' "

The narrow court is said to be Pear Tree Court.

It was to the Clerkenwell Sessions House (now Avery House, the large square building surmounted by a dome) that Bumble was bound when he announced to Mrs. Mann he was going up to London. " And I very much question whether the Clerkenwell Sessions will not find themselves in the wrong box before they have done with me," said Mr. Bumble, drawing himself up proudly.

As in the days of *Barnaby Rudge* so it is now : there are " busy trades in Clerkenwell and working jewellers by scores." Then, Dickens tells us, " it was a poorer place with farm-houses nearer to it than many modern Londoners would readily believe, and lovers' walks at no great distance, which turned into squalid courts long before the lovers of this age were born."

" In the venerable suburb—it was a suburb once—of Clerkenwell, towards that part of its confines which is nearest to the Charterhouse, and in one of those cool, shady streets of which a few . . . yet remain," lived that honest locksmith, Gabriel Varden, at " a house not over-newly fashioned, not very straight, not large, not tall, not bold faced with great staring windows, but a shy, blinking house, with conical roof going up into a peak over its garret window of four small panes of glass, like a cocked hat on the head of an elderly gentleman with one eye. . . . A great wooden

GRAY'S INN

LINCOLN'S INN

emblem of a key, painted in vivid yellow to resemble gold, dangled from the house front, and swung to and fro with a mournful creaking noise, as if complaining that it had nothing to unlock."

Mr. Jarvis Lorry, in *A Tale of Two Cities*, " walked along the sunny streets from Clerkenwell, where he lived, on his way to dine with the Doctor " (Dr. Manette, who lived near Soho Square) ; and Mr. Venus, so we are told in *Our Mutual Friend*, lived in " a narrow and a dirty street " in Clerkenwell, at a little dark, greasy shop with a dark window with one tallow candle dimly burning in it, where he was visited by Silas Wegg, who " being on his road to the Roman Empire approaches it by way of Clerkenwell."

We now return to Theobald's Road, pass Gray's Inn Road, and find on our left the spacious gardens of Gray's Inn, where Flora, in her second wooing of Arthur Clennam, " considered nothing so improbable as that he ever walked on the north-west side of Gray's Inn Gardens at exactly four o'clock in the afternoon."

We pass along the gardens and turn in at the gateway on the left, by the side of Raymond Buildings, where at No. 1 Dickens was a clerk to a firm of solicitors in 1827. The desk at which he sat in the office is now to be seen in the Dickens House.

Beyond is Gray's Inn Square, where Mr. Perker had his chambers up " two pairs of steep and dirty stairs." The " old 'ooman " who opened the door to Mr. Pickwick and Sam, called herself " Mr. Perker's laundress," which gave rise to Mr. Pickwick's remark :

" It's a curious circumstance, Sam, that they call the old women in these inns laundresses. I wonder what's that for ? "

" 'Cos they has a mortal awersion to washing anythin', I suppose, sir," replied Mr. Weller.

" I shouldn't wonder," said Mr. Pickwick, looking at the old woman, whose appearance, as well as the condition of the office, which she had by this time opened, indicated a rooted antipathy to the application of soap and water."

" Gray's Inn, gentlemen. Curious little nooks in a great place like London these old inns are," said another character in *Pickwick*.

Gray's Inn is certainly attractive and belies the later description given of it in *The Uncommercial Traveller* as " the most depressing institution in brick and mortar known to the children of men. Can anything be more dreary than its arid square Sahara Desert of the law, with the ugly old tiled-topped tenements, the dirty windows, the bills To Let, To Let, the doorposts inscribed like gravestones ? "

There has fortunately been a change for the better since that day.

Passing through the archway of Gray's Inn Hall, we reach South Square, where Mr. Phunky had chambers. " Phunky's—Holborn Court, Gray's Inn. Holborn Court, by the by, is South Square now."

Traddles' address was " Holborn Court, sir, number two," where he " occupied a set of chambers on the top storey " ; and when David visited him he had to ascend " a crazy old staircase . . . feebly lighted on each landing by a club-headed little oil wick, dying away in a little dungeon of dirty glass."

His subsequent reception by his old friend Traddles, by Sophy and by all the Devonshire beauties (who had been playing Puss-in-the-Corner), was, however, a sufficient recompense.

Dickens was an office boy at No. 1 South Square with Ellis and Blackmore before they moved to Raymond Buildings.

Gray's Inn Gateway, referred to in *Pickwick*, leads into Holborn, where we turn left, passing the site of Gray's Inn Coffee House, at which David Copperfield stayed when visiting Traddles at his chambers.

His bedroom, he tells us, was " an old wainscoted apartment, over the archway leading to the inn," and here he dwelt on the pleasure his visit had given him. " If I had beheld a thousand roses in a top set of chambers in that withered Gray's Inn, they could not have brightened it half so much," he adds.

Holborn and the site of Furnival's Inn we deal with on our second day.

Opposite the southern end of Gray's Inn Road we see on the right a little group of picturesque houses, behind which lies Staple Inn, thus described in *Edwin Drood* :

" Behind the most ancient part of Holborn, London, where certain gabled houses some centuries of age still stand looking on the public way, as if disconsolately looking for the Old Bourne that has long run dry, is a little nook composed of two irregular quadrangles, called Staple Inn. It is one of those nooks the turning into which out of the clashing street imparts to the relieved pedestrian the sensation of having put cotton in his ears and velvet soles on his boots."

Entering the gateway we find ourselves in a veritable oasis : " It is one of those nooks where a few smoky sparrows twitter in the smoky trees, as though they called to one another, ' Let us play at country,' and where a few feet of garden mould and a few yards of gravel enable them to do that refreshing violence to their tiny understandings. Moreover, it is one of those nooks which are legal nooks ; and it contains a little hall, with a little lantern in its roof : to what obstructive purposes devoted, and at whose expense, this history knoweth not."

It was Mr. Snagsby, we remember, who, " being in his way rather a meditative and poetical man," delighted to walk in Staple Inn " to observe how countrified the sparrows and the leaves are."

Beyond the first courtyard is another, containing

the Hall of the Inn, and the house on the left, " presenting in black and white over its ugly portal the mysterious inscription :

P.

J.   T.

1747

In which set of chambers, never having troubled his head about the inscription, unless to bethink himself at odd times on glancing up at it that haply it might mean Perhaps John Thomas, or Perhaps Joe Tyler, sat Mr. Grewgious writing by his fire."

Here, too, was the scene of the " Magic Beanstalk Country " at Mr. Tartar's chambers : " The top set in the house next the top set in the corner, the neatest, cleanest and best-ordered chambers ever seen under the sun, moon and stars. No man-of-war was ever kept more spick and span from careless touch." And there was a neat awning " rigged over Mr. Tartar's flower garden, as only a sailor could rig it."

The far side of the Inn leads into Chancery Lane, where we turn to the left.

Chancery Lane figures largely in the novels. Mr. Pickwick went there on his way to the Fleet : John Rokesmith first saw Mr. Boffin there. " Old Tom Jarndyce in despair blew his brains out at a coffee house in Chancery Lane," and Mrs. Snagsby was " the high standard of comparison among the neighbouring wives a long way down Chancery Lane on both sides." Young Smallweed had " a passion for a lady at a cigar shop " here, and Mr. Bucket remarked to Esther that, " It looks like Chancery Lane and was christened so." Indeed *Bleak House* is the novel of Chancery Lane.

In Cursitor Street on the left is Took's Court, the original of Cook's Court, where " Mr. Snagsby, law stationer, pursues his lawful calling. In the shade of

STAPLE INN, P.J.T. HOUSE

Cook's Court, at most times a shady place, Mr. Snagsby has dealt in all sorts of blank forms of legal process ; in skins and rolls of parchment ; in paper —foolscap, brief, draft, brown, white, whity-brown, and blotting ; in stamps, in office quills, pens, ink, India-rubber, pounce, pins, pencils, sealing-wax and wafers ; in red tape and green ferret ; in pocket-books, almanacks, diaries and law lists ; in string boxes, rulers, ink-stands—glass and leaden, penknives, scissors, bodkins and other office cutlery."

Mrs. Snagsby's own domain, the drawing-room, com manded a view " of Cook's Court at one end (not to mention a squint into Cursitor Street) and of Coavinses', the sheriff's officer's back yard at the other," was regarded by her as " a prospect of unequalled beauty."

Cursitor Street itself sheltered Coavinses and his Castle.

Symond's Inn occupied the site of Lonsdale Chambers and the side of it backed on to Bream's Buildings. Dickens's first situation as an office boy was with Molloy, a solicitor, who had his offices here in 1827, and in *Bleak House* what in all probability were the same offices were assigned to Mr. Vholes. In that book Dickens describes Symond's Inn as " a little, pale, wall-eyed, woe-begone inn, like a large dust-bin of two compartments and a sifter. It looks as if Symond were a sparing man in his way, and constructed his Inn of old building materials, which took kindly to the dry rot and to dirt and all things decaying and dismal and perpetuated Symond's memory with congenial shabbiness. Quartered in this dingy hatchment commemorative of Symond, are the legal bearings of Mr. Vholes."

Behind was Rolls Yard and Chapel, where also Mr. Snagsby loved " to lounge about of a Saturday afternoon, and to remark (if in good spirits) that there were old times once."

Opposite Rolls Passage is Chichester Rents, at the far corner of which stood the Old Ship Tavern, the original of Sol's Arms, famous for its Harmonic Meetings—and its inquests. Next door was Krook's Rag and Bottle Warehouse ; " blinded by the wall of Lincoln's Inn," and the " little side gate " and " narrow back street " (Star Yard), mentioned in Chapter V of *Bleak House*, are easily identified. One of the lodgers at Krook's shop was Miss Flite, who " lived at the top of the house in a pretty large room, from which she had a glimpse of the roof of Lincoln's Inn Hall."

Returning to Chancery Lane and retracing our steps, we reach Lincoln's Inn Gateway, thus described by Esther in *Bleak House*, " We passed into sudden quietude under an old gateway and drove on through a silent square until we came to an odd nook in a corner, where there was an entrance up a steep, broad, flight of stairs like an entrance to a church. And there really was a churchyard, outside, under some cloisters, for I saw the gravestones from the staircase windows."

The Old Hall opposite us was the scene of the memorable trial of Jarndyce *v.* Jarndyce. " In Lincoln's Inn Hall, at the very heart of the fog, sits the Lord High Chancellor in his High Court of Chancery."

The Chapel, with gravestones underneath, is on the right, and a passage by the side leads to Old Square, in which Kenge & Carboy had their offices, where Mr. Guppy used to take a breath of air at the window and look out " into the shade of Old Square, surveying the intolerable brick and mortar." Here Serjeant Snubbin had chambers in *The Pickwick Papers*.

Lincoln's Inn Fields lie beyond us : somewhere hereabouts David Copperfield's aunt, being in mortal dread of fire, took lodgings for a week " at a kind of private hotel in Lincoln's Inn Fields, where there was a stone staircase and a convenient door in the roof." On the far side of the Fields is No. 58, the house of Dickens's friend and biographer, John Forster. This was the original of Mr. Tulkinghorn's house in *Bleak House*, " a large house, formerly a house of state." " It is let off in sets of chambers now ; and, in those shrunken fragments of its greatness, lawyers lie like maggots in nuts. But its roomy staircases, passages and ante-chambers, still remain ; and even its painted ceilings, where Allegory, in Roman helmet and celestial linen, sprawls among balustrades and pillars, flowers, clouds, and big-legged boys, and makes the head ache—as would seem to be Allegory's object always, more or less."

Here it was that Dickens was a frequent visitor, and here he read *The Chimes* in 1844 to a select circle of friends, before its publication, coming from Italy specially for the purpose.

Facing No. 58 we turn to the left and soon reach Portsmouth Street, when on the left is a quaint and picturesque piece of Old London, inaccurately described as " The Old Curiosity Shop, immortalised by Charles Dickens."

At the end of Portsmouth Street is the George IV Tavern, on the site of the original Magpie and Stump of *Pickwick*. The Insolvent Court and the Horse and Groom public-house were both in Portugal Street ; the latter is no longer in existence ; it was the scene of the meeting of the two Wellers with Mr. Solomon Pell.

Through Carey Street we reach Bell Yard, altered out of all knowledge since the day when it was a narrow alley in which the Neckett children lived over the chandler's shop. At the end of Bell Yard is a monument known as " The Griffin," marking the site of Temple Bar and dividing Fleet Street from the Strand.

What a fund of romance was lost to London town when Temple Bar was taken from us in 1878. Posterity had to bow its head to the exigencies of time, and a great Dickens landmark disappeared.

As Temple Bar stands to-day at the entrance to Theobald's Park, Middlesex, it is meaningless to us. No longer is it the gateway to the magic city of the giants, through which Dickens pictured himself passing when he " got lost one day in the City of London " and resolved to " try about the city for any opening of a Whittington nature." When he came to it, he tells us, in *Gone Astray*, it took him half an hour to stare at it, and he left it unfinished even then. " It seemed," he said, " a wicked old place, albeit a noble monument of architecture and a paragon of utility."

In the opening chapter of *Bleak House*, Temple Bar is not treated with quite so much respect, for we find it referred to as " that leaden-headed old obstruction, appropriate ornament for the threshold of a leaden-headed old corporation," and, again, in the same book, on the hottest day in the long vacation, it says, " Temple Bar gets so hot that it is, to the adjacent Strand and Fleet Street, what a heater is in an urn, and keeps them simmering all night."

The Prentice Knights of *Barnaby Rudge* " took an oath not on any account . . . to damage or in any way disfigure Temple Bar, which was strictly constitutional, and always to be approached with reserve."

Temple Bar was " headless and forlorn in these degenerate days " when Mr. Dorrit passed under it—also, like us, on the way to the city—and on a like mission David Copperfield and Dan'l Peggotty " came through Temple Bar into the City," whilst Tom Pinch actually had the temerity to stop inside Temple Bar itself to laugh heartily over the " beef-steak pudding made with flour and eggs, until John

Westlock and his sister fairly ran away from him and left him to have his laugh out by himself."

Crossing Fleet Street we reach Middle Temple Gate, mindful that it was Maypole Hugh in *Barnaby Rudge* who likewise crossed the road here for the purpose of visiting Sir John Chester, and " plied the knocker of Middle Temple Gate," only to be regarded suspiciously and told, " We don't sell beer here."

It was also at Middle Temple Gate that Mr. Fips arranged the meeting with Tom Pinch which led to his engagement at the mysterious chambers, of which we make mention later.

What is probably the best description of the charm of the Temple is to be found in *Barnaby Rudge* :

" There are still worse places than the Temple on a sultry day, for basking in the sun or resting idly in the shade. There is yet a drowsiness in its courts and a dreamy dullness in its trees and gardens. Those who pace its lanes and squares may yet hear the echoes of their footsteps on the sounding stones and read upon its gates in passing from the tumult of the Strand or Fleet Street, ' Who enters here leaves noise behind.' There is yet in the Temple something of a clerkly monkish atmosphere, which public offices of law have not disturbed and even legal firms have failed to scare away. In summer time, its pumps suggest to thirsty idlers springs cooler and more sparkling and deeper than other wells . . . and, sighing, they cast sad looks towards the Thames and think of baths and boats, and saunter on, despondent."

Passing through Brick Court and Essex Court we reach Fountain Court, where, as is said in *Barnaby Rudge*, " there is still the plash of falling water." But it is in *Martin Chuzzlewit* that Dickens made a romance for us round Fountain Court and its association with Ruth Pinch, her brother Tom, and John Westlock.

" There was a little plot between them that Tom should always come out of the Temple by one way ; and that was past the fountain. Coming through Fountain Court, he was just to glance down the steps leading into Garden Court, and to look once all round him ; and, if Ruth had come to meet him, there he would see her ; not sauntering, you understand (on account of the clerks), but coming briskly up, with the best little laugh upon her face that ever played in opposition to the fountain, and beat it all to nothing.

" Either she was a little too soon, or Tom was a little too late—she was so precise in general that she timed it to half a minute—but no Tom was there. Well ! But was anybody else there, that she blushed so deeply, after looking round, and tripped off down the steps with such unusual expedition ?

" Why, the fact is that Mr. Westlock was passing at that moment. The Temple is a public thorough-fare ; they may write up on the gates that it is not, but so long as the gates are left open it is, and will be ; and Mr. Westlock had as good a right to be there as anybody else. . . .

" Merrily the tiny fountain played, and merrily the dimples sparkled on its sunny face. John Westlock hurried after her. Softly the whispering water broke and fell ; and roguishly the dimples twinkled, as he stole upon her footsteps. . . .

" ' I felt sure it was you,' said John, when he over-took her, in the sanctuary of Garden Court. ' I knew I couldn't be mistaken.'

" She was *so* surprised.

" ' You are waiting for your brother,' said John. " Let me bear you company.' . . .

" Merrily the fountain plashed and plashed, until the dimples, merging into one another, swelled into a general smile that covered the whole surface of the basin. . . ."

On a later occasion we again find ourselves in Fountain Court when

" Brilliantly the Temple Fountain sparkled in the sun, and laughingly its liquid music played, and merrily the idle drops of water danced and danced, and, peeping out in sport among the trees, plunged lightly down to hide themselves, as little Ruth and her companions came towards it.

" And why they came towards the Fountain at all is a mystery ; for they had no business there. It was not in their way. It was quite out of their way. They had no more to do with the Fountain, bless you, than they had with—with Love, or any out-of-the-way thing of that sort.

" It was all very well for Tom and his sister to make appointments by the Fountain, but that was quite another affair. Because, of course, when she had to wait a minute or two, it would have been very awkward for her to have had to wait in any but a tolerably quiet spot ; but that was as quiet a spot, everything considered, as they could choose. But when she had John Westlock to take care of her, and was going home with her arm in his (home being in a different direction altogether), their coming anywhere near that Fountain was quite extraordinary.

" However, there they found themselves. And another extraordinary part of the matter was, that they seemed to have come there by a silent understanding. Yet, when they got there, they were a little confused by being there, which was the strangest part of all ; because there is nothing naturally confusing in a Fountain. We all know that.

" What a good old place it was ! John said with quite an earnest affection for it.

" ' A pleasant place indeed,' said little Ruth. ' So shady ! '

" O wicked little Ruth !

" They came to a stop when John began to praise it. The day was exquisite ; and, stopping at all, it was quite natural—nothing could be more so—that they should glance down Garden Court ; because Garden Court ends in the Garden, and the Garden ends in the River, and that glimpse is very bright and fresh and shining on a summer's day. Then, oh, little Ruth, why not look boldly at it ! Why fit that tiny, precious, blessed little foot into the cracked corner of an insensible old flagstone in the pavement ; and be so very anxious to adjust it to a nicety ! "

Pip in *Great Expectations* had his chambers at " the top of the last house in Garden Court down by the river. . . . Alterations have been made in that part of the Temple since that time, and it has not now so lonely a character as it had then, nor is it so exposed to the river."

Here it was that Magwitch revealed himself one stormy night, as the source of the great expectations.

Facing the river, we turn left to Middle Temple Lane and cross it, passing through Elm Court, reach Pump Court, the court " more quiet and more gloomy than the rest," where Tom Pinch was employed so mysteriously by Mr. Fips.

Descending the steps on the right beneath the Dining Hall of the Inner Temple, we reach Paper Buildings, where Sir John Chester had his chambers. They were then described as :

" A row of goodly tenements, shaded in front by ancient trees, and looking at the back upon the Temple Gardens. . . . Through the half-opened window the Temple Garden looks green and pleasant ; the placid river, gay with boat and barge and dimpled with the plash of many an oar, sparkles in the distance."

The original Paper Buildings were destroyed by fire in 1838.

Opposite is King's Bench Walk, dedicated to the

memory of Sydney Carton, who "turned into the Temple, and, having revived himself by twice pacing the pavement of King's Bench Walk and Paper Buildings, turned into the Stryver Chambers."

The Walk leads down to the River, and the site of Temple Stairs, where Mr. Tartar kept his boat and from which he rowed Rosa and Mr. Grewgious up the river. This landing-place also figures in *Great Expectations*, during the exploit of Pip and Herbert on the river as a prelude to getting Magwitch out of the country.

Returning along King's Bench Walk we find Whitefriars Gate on the right, through which Pip came one eventful evening. "My readiest access to the Temple was close by the riverside, through Whitefriars. . . . It seldom happened that I came in at that Whitefriars Gate after the Temple was closed."

Here, by the light of the night-porter's lantern, he read Wemmick's message, superscribed "Please read this here," containing the laconic instructions, "Don't go home."

This way came Mr. George in *Bleak House*, "by the cloisterly Temple and by Whitefriars" to the Bagnets in Blackfriars. Rogue Riderhood, after seeing "Governors Both" in the Temple, "pulled his drowned cap over his ears with both hands, and . . . went down the stairs round by Temple Church, across the Temple, into Whitefriars and so on by the waterside streets."

Reversing the steps of Rogue Riderhood we pass Paper Buildings and under the Inner Temple Dining Hall and so reach Temple Church. Beyond are the churchyard and Goldsmith Buildings, the latter built on the site of the old chambers occupied by Mortimer Lightwood in *Our Mutual Friend*.

"Whosoever had gone out of Fleet Street into the Temple . . . until he stumbled on a dismal

2

churchyard and had looked up at the dismal windows commanding that churchyard, until at the most dismal window of them all he saw a dismal boy, would in him have beheld . . . the managing clerk, junior clerk, common law clerk, conveyancing clerk, chancery clerk . . . of Mr. Mortimer Lightwood."

Through Inner Temple Gate, where Mr. Dolls, in one of his usual maudlin conditions, was conducted by Eugene Wrayburn, we reach Fleet Street, opposite Chancery Lane. Here it was that Bradley Headstone used to rest " in a doorway with his eyes upon the Temple Gate," waiting and watching for Eugene Wrayburn. " For anything I know he watches at the Temple Gate all night," said Eugene.

We turn right for a walk along Fleet Street.

What a crowd of characters did Dickens cause to pass along Fleet Street ! First Mr. Pickwick in the hackney-coach on his way to the Fleet. Then Mr. Stryver, " projecting himself into Soho while he was yet on St. Dunstan's side of Temple Bar bursting in his full-blown way along the pavement to the jostlement of all the weaker people." Then Mr. Boffin, " jogging along Fleet Street . . . when he became aware that he was closely tracked and observed by a man of genteel appearance," who was, of course, John Rokesmith. Then David Copperfield himself, who, when he had no money, " used to look at a venison shop in Fleet Street."

In later years David took his old nurse Peggotty " to see some perspiring waxwork in Fleet Street (melted I should hope these twenty years)." Probably these were Mrs. Salmon's Waxwork at No. 17, once the palace of Prince Henry.

The funeral cortege of the spy, as described in A Tale of Two Cities, found " an unusual concourse pouring down Fleet Street westward," and a similar concourse eastward is described in Pickwick when

Sam Weller got himself put into the Fleet to keep his master company. " Some little commotion was occasioned in Fleet Street by the pleasantry of the eight gentlemen in the flank who persevered in walking four abreast."

With all these thoughts crowding upon us, let us imagine we pass through Temple Bar into Fleet Street. Immediately on our right, No. 1 Fleet Street marks the site of the older premises which Dickens called Tellsons Bank in *A Tale of Two Cities*. " Tellsons Bank by Temple Bar was an old-fashioned place . . . It was very small, very dark, very ugly, very incommodious . . . the triumphant perfection of inconvenience. After bursting open a door of idiotic obstinacy with a weak rattle in its throat you fell into Tellsons down two steps, and came to your senses in a miserable little old shop with two little counters, where the oldest of men made your cheque shake as if the wind rustled it, while they examined the signature by the dingiest of windows. . . . In the musty back closet . . . Mr. Lorry sat at great books ruled for figures, with perpendicular iron bars to his window as if that were ruled for figures too, and everything under the clouds were a sum."

Outside the bank, Jerry Cruncher was wont to sit on the " wooden stool made out of a broken backed chair cut down," a character " as well known to Fleet Street and the Temple as the Bar itself—and almost as ill-looking."

A little farther along and on the opposite side of the road is Clifford's Inn, where the " tenant of a top set—bad character—shut himself up in his bedroom closet, and took a dose of arsenic," to be found by his successor some months later, as narrated at the Magpie and Stump in *Pickwick*.

Tip Dorrit found " a stool and twelve shillings a week . . . in the office of an attorney . . . in Clifford's Inn," and here " languished for six months." Clifford's

Inn is also referred to in *Bleak House* by Trooper George as the office of Melchisedeck, the legal agent of old Smallweed ; and, in the archway, Rokesmith made his secretarial proposals to Mr. Boffin.

" Would you object to turn aside into this place— I think it is called Clifford's Inn—where we can hear one another better than in the roaring street ? . . . Mr. Boffin glanced into the mouldy little plantation, or cat preserve, of Clifford's Inn, as it was that day. . . . Sparrows were there, cats were there, dry rot and wet rot were there, but it was not otherwise a suggestive spot."

Next to Clifford's Inn is St. Dunstan's Church. This was the church of *The Chimes*. " High up in the steeple of an old church, far above the light and murmur of the town . . . dwelt the chimes I tell of."

Outside the church was the beat of Toby (or Trotty) Veck, the messenger, and here he used to trot up and down taking consolation from the bells. The old church, with its clock and two giants—as seen by Maypole Hugh, and David Copperfield, and also by young Charles in *Gone Astray*—was pulled down in 1830.

On the opposite side of the street is Serjeant's Inn, mentioned in connection with Mr. Pickwick's journey to the Fleet Prison. Although the front is new, many of the old buildings are to be seen by passing through the gate-way.

At No. 166 Fleet Street is Johnson's Court, where were the offices of the old *Monthly Magazine* that published Dickens's first contribution to literature, the MS. of which he dropped " stealthily one evening at twilight, with fear and trembling, into a dark letter-box in a dark office up a dark court in Fleet Street."

The *Daily News* office farther along, on the right, reminds us that it was Dickens who started the paper in 1846. The present offices in Bouverie Street are

adorned with a head of Dickens carved in the stone-
work.

At No. 146 on the left is Wine Office Court, in
which is that famous tavern, the Cheshire Cheese.
Although never mentioned by name, so famous an
inn, with its associations with Dr. Johnson, must have
been well known to Dickens, and it is thought probable
that he had the Cheshire Cheese in mind when Sydney
Carton induced Charles Darnay to dine with him,
after the latter's acquittal at the Old Bailey of the
charge of high treason. They went " down Ludgate
Hill to Fleet Street, and so up a covered way into a
tavern."

In Whitefriars Street opposite is Hanging Sword
Alley where Jerry Cruncher lived with his better
half, addicted to " flopping." " Mr. Cruncher's apartments were not in a savoury neighbourhood, and were
but two in number, even if a closet with a single pane
of glass in it might be counted as one."

Mr. George, in *Bleak House*, paid particular attention
to this curiously named alley in walking from his
shooting gallery near Leicester Square to the Bagnets
in Blackfriars through " the cloisterly Temple and by
Whitefriars (though not without a glance at Hanging
Sword Alley, which would seem to be something in
his way)."

Fleet Street ends at Ludgate Circus ; to the right
is Blackfriars (see page 95). To the left runs Farringdon Street, formerly Fleet Market, on the right of
which, where Memorial Hall now stands, was once
the Fleet Prison, memorable from its associations with
Pickwick.

Just under the railway arch in Ludgate Hill and on
the left is La Belle Sauvage Yard where stood the
famous coaching inn which Tony Weller made his
headquarters : farther on, at No. 42, is what was once
the London Coffee House, where Arthur Clennam

sat on the Sunday of his arrival in London watching
the people sheltering from the rain in the " public
passage opposite, and listening to the bells ringing
' Come to church, come to church. . . . They *won't*
come, they *won't* come.' " The house still exists, little
altered in appearance structurally.

In the distance St. Paul's looms large as it appeared
to so many of Dickens's people. " There be Paul's
Church. Ecod, he be a soizable 'un, he be." Thus
John Browdie to his wife on their wedding trip. " Ralph
Nickleby . . . as he passed St. Paul's stepped aside
into a door-way to set his watch, with his hand on the
key and his eye on the Cathedral dial."

In *Master Humphrey's Clock* we have a long account
of a visit made to the clock turret ; and David Copperfield " varied the legal character of settling Peggotty's
affairs by going to the top of St. Paul's " : not that it
afforded that good creature much pleasure, for " from
her long attachment to her work-box it became a rival
of the picture on the lid, and was in some particulars
vanquished, she considered, by that work of art."

In St. Paul's Churchyard, David's aunt was accosted
by her husband, much to the surprise of David ; and
Eugene Wrayburn tracked the schoolmaster watching
them in this neighbourhood.

Dean's Court on the right leads to where what
Mr. Boffin called " Doctor Scommons " used to
stand. Doctors' Commons is described by Steerforth
as " a lazy old nook near Saint Paul's Churchyard . . .
a little out-of-the-way place . . . that has an ancient
monopoly in suits about people's wills and people's
marriages."

Here David worked for the proctors, Spenlow &
Jorkins. Here, too, in earlier years had come Jingle
for his marriage licence.

It was described by Sam Weller as " low archway
on the carriage side, bookseller's at one corner, hotel

on the other, and two porters in the middle as touts
for licences."

This prompted Sam Weller to tell the amusing tale
of his father's adventures with the touts who used to
infest the neighbourhood.

In " an upstairs room . . . of a certain coffee-house
which in those days had a door opening into the
Commons, just within the little archway in St. Paul's
Churchyard," David Copperfield had that momentous
interview with Mr. Spenlow and Miss Murdstone, as
narrated in Chapter 38.

An interesting association with this district is
that Dickens rented an office at No. 5 Bell Yard, off
Carter Lane, in 1831, whilst a reporter for one of the
offices in the Commons. How near we were to losing
Dickens as a novelist, at this period, is told in a letter
he wrote to Forster some years later :

" I wrote to Bartley, who was stage-manager of
Covent Garden Theatre, and told him how young
I was, and exactly what I thought I could do ; and
that I believed that I had a strong perception of
character and oddity, and a natural power of repro-
ducing in my own person what I observed in others.
This was at the time when I was at Doctors' Commons
as a shorthand writer for the proctors. And I recollect
I wrote the letter from a little office I had there, where
the answer came also. There must have been something in my letter that struck the authorities, for
Bartley wrote to me almost immediately to say that
they were busy getting up the ' Hunchback ' (so
they were), but that they would communicate with
me again in a fortnight. Punctual to the time another
letter came, with an appointment to do anything
of Matthews I pleased before him and Charles Kemble,
on a certain day at the theatre. My sister Fanny was
in the secret, and was to go with me to play the songs.
I was laid up when the day came with a terrible bad

cold and inflammation of the face, the beginning, by the by, of that annoyance in one ear to which I am subject to this day. I wrote to say so, and added that I would resume my application next season. I made a great splash in the gallery soon afterwards ; the Chronicle opened to me ; I had a distinction in the little world of the newspaper, which made one like it ; began to write ; didn't want money ; had never thought of the stage but as the means of getting it ; gradually left off turning my thoughts that way, and never resumed the idea. I never told you this, did I ? See how near I may have been to another sort of life."

At No. 29 Knightrider Street is the Horn Tavern on the site of the Horn Coffee House, to which Mr. Pickwick sent a messenger from the Fleet Prison, for a bottle or two (or " bottle or six ") of wine to celebrate Mr. Winkle's visit.

BLOOMSBURY AND HOLBORN TO THE CITY

NEXT to the Strand and Fleet Street, Holborn may justly claim to be the thoroughfare that is most replete with Dickens memories. But a greater change has come over the face of Holborn than over the other two great arteries; particularly at the beginning and the end, Kingsway and Newgate and Smithfield.

In writing of the district of Bloomsbury and of the great historic thoroughfare called Holborn, memories at once surround us of that part of Bloomsbury which housed the immortal Mrs. Gamp, and which was cleared away in 1905 when Kingsway was planned; of the Black Bull in Holborn, where she and Betsey Prig nursed " turn and turn about," swallowed up by Gamage's premises in about 1904 ; of Furnival's Inn, the birthplace of *Pickwick*, now covered by the offices of the Prudential Assurance Company ; of Snow Hill— a name only—of the Saracen's Head—whose memory is recorded—of Field Lane, happily gone ; of Holborn Hill, now spanned by a viaduct, and of Newgate Prison on the site of the present Sessions House at the corner of Newgate Street and Old Bailey.

But however dear memories may be there are fortunately preserved to us some few relics of the buildings that Dickens knew, on which we can feast our eyes in this journey of a couple of miles or so ; and a few detours into the Inns—Gray's Inn and Staple Inn (pages 5–7), with perhaps another place or two a little off the route, will enable us to pass most pleasantly a day in this enchanted land of dreams and realities.

The junction of Hart Street with High Holborn is

our starting point, on the edge of the Bloomsbury district, which figured in the early sketch by Boz entitled *The Bloomsbury Christening*, the Kitterbells living in Great Russell Street, and the christening taking place at St. George's Church in Hart Street.

Bloomsbury Square, which we pass on the left of Hart Street, is dealt with on page 56. Opposite is Southampton Street, whither came Mr. Grewgious to look for a lodging for Rosa Bud.

"At length he bethought himself of a widowed cousin, divers times removed, of Mr. Bazzard's, who had once solicited his influence in the lodger world, and who lived in Southampton Street, Bloomsbury Square. This lady's name, stated in uncompromising capitals of considerable size on a brass door-plate, and yet not lucidly as to sex or condition, was Billickin."

"It is not Bond Street nor yet St. James's Palace ; but it is not pretended that it is," said the Billickin in stating her terms. "Neither is it attempted to be denied —for why should it ?—that the Arching leads to a Mews. Mewses must exist."

The house was probably No. 20, next to the "Arching" leading to what was once a mews. ·

The School of Arts and Crafts at the corner of Southampton Row and Theobald's Road covers the site of Kingsgate Street, where Mrs. Gamp lived over Poll Sweedlepipe's shaving establishment.

"This lady lodged at a bird-fancier's, next door but one to the celebrated mutton-pie shop, and directly opposite to the original cat's meat warehouse ; the renown of which establishments was duly heralded on their respective fronts. It was a little house, and this was the more convenient ; for Mrs. Gamp being, in her highest walk of art, a monthly nurse, or, as her sign-board boldly had it, "Midwife," and lodging in the first-floor front, was easily assailable at night by pebbles, walking sticks, and fragments of tobacco pipe ; all much more efficacious than the street-door knocker, which was so constructed as to wake the street with ease, and even spread alarms of fire in Holborn, without making the smallest impression on the premises to which it was addressed."

Behind the School of Arts and Crafts is Red Lion Square, mentioned in *Gone Astray*.

Entering High Holborn from Southampton Row, we turn to the left, and in a short distance notice a narrow turning on the right called Great Turnstile, and another named Little Turnstile farther along. Both lead into Lincoln's Inn Fields (see page 10) and remind us, as Mr. Snagsby in *Bleak House* used to tell his two apprentices, that " a brook once ran down Holborn, when Turnstile really was a turnstile leading slap away into the meadows." Farther along on the right we reach Chancery Lane and nearly opposite is the archway leading to Gray's Inn. Both these places are visited the first day. Just beyond Gray's Inn Road is " the ancient part of Holborn " behind which is Staple Inn (page 7). Next to it is Furnival Street, formerly Castle Street, where Traddles lodged " up behind the parapet of a house."

Next we reach—on the same side—Mercers' School in the old Barnard's Inn, brought very much up to date. Here Pip had chambers on first coming to London in preparation for his great expectations. Not knowing what sort of a place Barnard's Inn was, he was not a little surprised. He had supposed that establishment to be an hotel kept by Mr. Barnard, to which the Blue Boar in his own town was a mere public-house. " Whereas I now found Barnard to be a disembodied spirit or a fiction, and his Inn the dingiest collection of shabby buildings ever squeezed together in a rank corner as a club for tom-cats."

He was content, he says, to take " a foggy view of the Inn through the windows' encrusting dirt, and to stand dolefully looking out," saying to himself that London was decidedly overrated.

Adjoining Barnard's Inn were the premises of Thomas Langdale, a distiller, the destruction of whose premises by the rioters is graphically described in Chapter 68 of *Barnaby Rudge*. The side entrance by which the distiller and Mr. Haredale entered and left the premises was in Fetter Lane.

On the opposite side of Holborn is a pile of red brick buildings occupied by the Prudential Assurance Company. This covers the site of Furnival's Inn (demolished 1897), where Dickens had chambers from 1834 until 1837, when he went to live at No. 48 Doughty Street.

A tablet in the court-yard marks the site of the chambers he occupied, and a bust of Dickens by Percy Fitzgerald adorns the wall on the left as we enter.

John Westlock, in *Martin Chuzzlewit*, also lived in Furnival's Inn, and we are told :

" There are snug chambers in those Inns where the bachelors live, and, for the desolate fellows they pretend to be, it is quite surprising how well they get on. . . . There is little enough to see in Furnival's Inn. It is a shady, quiet place, echoing to the footsteps of the stragglers who have business there ; and rather monotonous and gloomy on summer evenings."

The hotel that stood within the Inn (Wood's Hotel) was patronised by Mr. Grewgious for his meals, and from here to Staple Inn came that most amusing creation, the " flying waiter."

Here too, did Mr. Grewgious find accommodation for Rosa. " Mr. Grewgious . . . led her by the hand . . . across Holborn, and into Furnival's Inn. At the hotel door he confided her to the Unlimited head chambermaid. . . . Rosa's room was airy, clean, comfortable, almost gay . . . and Rosa tripped down the great many stairs again, to thank her guardian for his thoughtful and affectionate care of her. . . . ' You may be sure that the stairs are fireproof,' said Mr. Grewgious, ' and that any outbreak of the devouring element would be perceived and suppressed by the watchmen.' "

Beyond the Prudential buildings is Gamage's, the lower end of whose premises covers the site of the Black Bull in Holborn, where Mrs. Gamp and Betsey Prig nursed Mr. Lewsome, as described in *Martin Chuzzlewit.*

A little farther on and we are in Holborn Circus, where five important roads converge.

Ahead is Holborn Viaduct, completed in 1869, across the hills which made this road so notorious in the coaching days.

We can, in our imagination, see Job Trotter, "abating nothing of his speed," running up Holborn Hill to Mr. Perker's at Gray's Inn ; we can see Wemmick, with "such a post-office of a mouth," walking here with Pip, who had got to the top of Holborn Hill before he " knew that it was merely a mechanical appearance, and that he was not smiling at all." We can see Oliver Twist trudging along here in company with Sikes *en route* for " the Chertsey crib," looking up at the clock of St. Andrew's Church, now half-hidden by the Viaduct, and being told that it was " hard upon seven ! You must step out." This same church and clock are referred to in *David Copperfield,* when the hero of that story was a full quarter of an hour late by that clock in mustering up sufficient courage " to pull the private bell handle let into the left-hand door-post of Mr. Waterbrook's house " to see Agnes, after his night of dissipation. Mr. Waterbrook's house was in Ely Place, Holborn, a turning on the left of Charterhouse Street which branches half-left from the Circus.

St. Andrew's Street is on the right of Holborn Circus and the first turning on the right is Thavies'

Inn, renowned for its association with Mrs. Jellyby. It was " no distance " from Kenge & Carboy's, said Mr. Guppy, " round in Thavies' Inn, you know." Esther did not know, so Guppy explained it was " only round the corner. We just twist up Chancery Lane, and cut along Holborn, and there we are in four minutes' time as near as a toucher."

So they went out into the " London particular " of a fog and soon " turned up under an archway to our destination, a narrow street of high houses, like an oblong cistern to hold the fog. There was a confused little crowd of people, principally children, gathered about the house at which we stopped, which had a tarnished brass plate on the door, with the inscription, Jellyby. ' Don't be frightened ! ' said Mr. Guppy looking in at the coach window. ' One of the young Jellyby's been and got his head through the area railings ! ' "

There sure enough we can see the houses with the area railings—an uncommon sight in this part of London. Esther went to the rescue of the poor child, who was one of the dirtiest little unfortunates she ever saw. " I . . . found him very hot and frightened, and crying loudly, fixed by the neck between two iron railings, while a milkman and a beadle, with the kindest intentions possible, were endeavouring to drag him back by the legs, under a general impression that his skull was compressible by those means."

Returning again to Holborn Circus we cross it and proceed along Hatton Garden. At the far end is Clerkenwell (see page 4).

Turning into Charles Street on the right, we find on the right all that is left of the Bleeding Heart Yard of *Little Dorrit*, where the Plornish family lived. " As if the aspiring city had become puffed up in the very ground on which it stood, the ground had so risen about Bleeding Heart Yard that you got into it

down a flight of steps . . . and got out of it by a low
gate-way into a maze of shabby streets. . . . At this
end of the yard and over the gate-way was the factory
of Daniel Doyce."

The position of the yard is certainly changed to-day,
but the above description is interesting.

The next turning on the left is Little Saffron Hill.
This continues on the right of Charles Street as Great
Saffron Hill, along which our way lies into Charterhouse
Street.

Along Saffron Hill from Clerkenwell came Oliver
Twist with the Artful Dodger, on his first visit to
London. " From the Angel into St. John's Road . . .
through Exmouth Street . . . thence into Little Saffron
Hill and so into Saffron Hill the great. . . . When they
reached the bottom of the hill his conductor . . .
pushed open the door of a house near Field Lane."

Field Lane, and with it Fagin's house, was swept
away when Holborn Viaduct was built. Charterhouse
Street at the end of Saffron Hill cut through it, and
it extended right into Holborn. The block of buildings
to the left of Shoe Lane marks the site.

In Little Saffron Hill was " the Three Cripples,"
the house of call of Bill Sikes and Fagin, " a low
public-house situate in the filthiest part of Little
Saffron Hill ; a dark and gloomy den, where a flaring
gas-light burnt all day."

Phil Squod in *Bleak House* tells us how he took on
a travelling tinker's beat in this district :

" It wasn't much of a beat," he explained, " round
Saffron Hill, Hatton Garden, Clerkenwell, Smiffield
and there—poor neighbourhood, where they uses up
the kettles till they're past mending."

Reaching Charterhouse Street we turn left into
.Smithfield, crossing Farringdon Road. The old
market, with its open pens, was discontinued in 1855,
and the new building covering the site opened in

1868. It was quite a different place when Oliver Twist crossed it with Bill Sikes after he had been captured for the second time. "It was Smithfield they were crossing," we read, "although it might have been Grosvenor Square for anything Oliver knew to the contrary," and when he again crossed it *en route* for the Chertsey burglary it was the market morning, and "the ground was covered nearly ankle deep with filth and mire." They crossed the market and went "through Hosier Lane into Holborn."

Later, in *Great Expectations*, it still kept its old traditions, for Pip discovered it as a "shameful place being all asmear with filth and fat and blood and foam."

Smithfield Market is also referred to in *Barnaby Rudge* when the elder Rudge made his escape from the burning Newgate Prison. "Barnaby and his father having passed among the crowd from hand to hand, stood in Smithfield, on the outskirts of the mob, gazing at the flames like men who had been suddenly aroused from sleep. . . .

"In a corner of the market, among the pens for cattle, Barnaby knelt down, and, pausing every now and then to pass his hand over his father's face, or look up to him with a smile, knocked off his irons."

In *Little Dorrit* we read of Clennam and Doyce crossing Smithfield together—but there is no description of the market. They parted at Barbican and Clennam walked on alone down Aldersgate to St. Paul's, when he met John Baptist, who had been knocked down by a mail-coach, being conveyed to St. Bartholomew's Hospital.

Regaining Farringdon Street, we turn to the left ; the first on the left is Snow Hill, which leads to Holborn, on reaching which we turn to the left.

The Saracen's Head Inn, where Squeers had his head-quarters, was three doors from St. Sepulchre's Church, and was demolished in 1868. A police station

now occupies the site, which is recorded by a tablet.
A new inn was erected at the foot of the hill and is
now occupied by a warehouse and factory. A bust of
Dickens adorns the door-way with plaques of scenes
from *Nicholas Nickleby* connected with the older
building, on either side. The following is a description
of the old inn from *Nicholas Nickleby* :

"Near to the jail, and by consequence near to
Smithfield also, and the Compter, and the bustle and
noise of the city ; and just on that particular part of
Snow Hill where omnibus horses going eastward
seriously think of falling down on purpose ; and where
horses in hackney cabriolets going westward not
unfrequently fall by accident, is the coach-yard of the
Saracen's Head Inn; its portals guarded by two
Saracens' heads and shoulders, which it was once the
pride and glory of the choice spirits of this metropolis
to pull down at night. . . . The inn itself, garnished
with another Saracen's head, frowns upon you from
the top of the yard."

Close by are Cock Lane and Hosier Lane, both
mentioned in the novels more than once.

Between Snow Hill and Giltspur Street is St.
Sepulchre's Church, the clock of which heralded the
death of many a prisoner awaiting his end at Newgate
opposite. In *Barnaby Rudge* we read : "The concourse
waited with an impatience which increased with every
chime of St. Sepulchre's Church."

The site of Newgate Prison is now occupied by
the Sessions House. Writing of it in *Barnaby Rudge*,
Dickens refers to it as "then a new building, recently
completed at a vast expense, and considered to be of
enormous strength." To him it had a peculiar
fascination, and several times he wrote of it in the
Sketches by Boz, in one chapter of which we read :

"We shall never forget the mingled feelings of awe
and respect with which we used to gaze at the exterior

3

of Newgate in our schoolboy days. How dreadful its rough, heavy walls, and low massive doors, appeared to us . . . then the fetters over the debtors' doors, which we used to think were a *bona-fide* set of irons, just hung up there, for convenience' sake, ready to be taken down at a moment's notice. . . . Often have we strayed here, in sessions time, to catch a glimpse of the whipping place, and that dark building on one side of the yard in which is kept the gibbet with all its dreadful apparatus."

Although Newgate has its principal associations in *Barnaby Rudge, Oliver Twist,* and *Great Expectations,* one of the best descriptions of it is given in *Nicholas Nickleby* :

" There, at the very core of London, in the heart of its business and animation, in the midst of a whirl of noise and motion, stemming as it were the giant currents of life that flow unceasingly on from different quarters and meet beneath its walls, stands Newgate ; and, in that crowded street on which it frowns so darkly, scores of human beings, amidst a roar of sounds to which even the tumult of a great city is as nothing four, six, or eight strong men at a time have been hurried violently and swiftly from the world, when the scene has been rendered frightful with excess of human life ; when curious eyes have glared from casement and house-top, and wall and pillar ; and when, in the mass of white and upturned faces, the dying wretch, in his all-comprehensive look of agony, has met not one—not one—that bore the impress of pity or compassion."

The account of the burning of Newgate by the Gordon Rioters in *Barnaby Rudge* is a remarkable piece of writing. Lord George Gordon died in a cell in Newgate Prison some years after the famous riots—but not on account of them.

The Criminal Court in the Old Bailey—adjoining Newgate Prison—was the scene of some stirring events in the novels of Dickens : Fagin's trial in *Oliver Twist*, the trial of the returned convict, Magwitch, in *Great Expectations*, and the very memorable trial in *A Tale of Two Cities*, when Sydney Carton rendered such yeoman service to Charles Darnay. Of the street which gave the Court its name, Dickens writes in this book that it " was famous as a kind of deadly inn-yard, from which pale travellers set out continually, in carts and coaches, on a violent passage into the other world."

Kit, too, " honest Kit," in *The Old Curiosity Shop*, suffered trial at the Old Bailey, and was confined in the cells there until released by the assistance of Dick Swiveller.

Newgate Street itself is often mentioned by Dickens, the most memorable occasion being in *Pickwick*, when in walking along this thoroughfare Sam Weller remarked to Mr. Pickwick on the date fixed for the trial being the 14th of February, " Remarkable coincidence. . . . Walentine's day, sir, reg'lar good day for a breach o' promise trial that." He then drew Mr. Pickwick's attention to a " wery nice pork-pie shop . . . celebrated sassage factory," he explained, and told the diverting history of the man owning the shop, who was made into sausages in his own " patent never leavin' off sassage steam-ingin."

Our way now lies along Giltspur Street, in which the Compter—mentioned on page 33—used to stand, close to St. Sepulchre's Church. It was a debtor's prison and was demolished in 1855.

This leads to St. Bartholomew's Hospital, already referred to, where Jack Hopkins (in *Pickwick*) was a student and Slasher the wonderful surgeon ; and where the boy who swallowed the necklace was " wrapped in a watchman's jacket for fear of waking the patients."

Mrs. Betsey Prig was described as " of Barthemy's ; or as some said Barklemy's, or as some said Bardlemy's ;

for by all these endearing and familiar appellations had the hospital become a household word."

Keeping the hospital on our right we presently find St. Bartholomew's Church facing us, when we turn to the right, passing Bartholomew Close on our left, and so into Little Britain, which bears round to the left into Aldersgate Street.

Mr. Jaggers had written on his card that his address was Little Britain, "just out of Smithfield, and close by the coach office," and, while waiting for the lawyer, Pip had been advised to go round the corner and take a turn in the air at Smithfield, but, finding it a shameful place and seeing " the great black dome of Saint Paul's bulging " at him from " behind a grim stone building, which a bystander said was Newgate Prison," went into the prison yard and saw the gallows and whipping post and the " Debtors' Door, out of which culprits came to be hanged."

Returning, he " made the tour of Little Britain and turned into Bartholomew Close," and at length as he was " looking out at the iron gate of Bartholomew Close," he saw Mr. Jaggers coming towards him. Little Britain was described by Pip as " a gloomy street," and Mr. Jaggers' room as " lighted by a skylight only and a most dismal place ; the skylight eccentrically patched like a broken head, and the distorted adjoining houses looking as if they had twisted themselves to peep down at me through it."

On reaching Aldersgate Street we find across the road to the right the site of the Albion Hotel, where Dickens entertained his friends in 1839 to celebrate the completion of *Nicholas Nickleby*.

In " a hybrid hotel in a little square behind Aldersgate Street, near the General Post Office," John Jasper stayed when in London. It is said to have been the Falcon Hotel, formerly in Falcon Square, on the right.

Hereabouts, too, the firm of Chuzzlewit was

situated : " The old-established firm of Anthony
Chuzzlewit & Son, Manchester Warehousemen, and
so forth, had its place of business in a very narrow
street somewhere behind the Post Office ; where
every house was in the brightest summer morning
very gloomy ; and where light porters watered the
pavement, each before his own employer's premises,
in fantastic patterns, in the dog-days ; and where
spruce gentlemen, with their hands in the pockets of
symmetrical trousers, were always to be seen in warm
weather, contemplating their undeniable boots in
dusty warehouse door-ways ; which appeared to be
the hardest work they did, except now and then
carrying pens behind their ears. A dim, dirty, smoky,
tumble-down, rotten old house it was as anybody
would desire to see ; but there the firm of Anthony
Chuzzlewit & Son transacted all their business, and
their pleasure too, such as it was ; for neither the
young man nor the old had any other residence, or
any care or thought beyond its narrow limits."

No. 5 Foster Lane is pointed out as very likely
premises, having a side entrance which was found so
useful by Jonas when planning the alibi for his murder
of Montague Tigg.

Turning towards St. Paul's Cathedral (see
page 22) we have the site of the old Post Office
buildings on the left, and the new buildings on the
right occupying the site of the Bull and Mouth Inn
(demolished 1888), which must have been the halting
place of the " North country mail-coach . . . hard
by the Post Office," which brought John Browdie to
London with his bride. " A Poast Office ! " he
exclaimed. " Wa'at dost thee think o' that ? Ecod,
if that's on'y a Poast Office, I'd loike to see where
the Lord Mayor o' Lunnon lives ! "

This portion of the street being called St. Martin's-
le-Grand recalls that from the coach-stand here Mr.

Pickwick took the "bob's vorth" to the Golden Cross at Charing Cross.

From the General Post Office we turn to the left into Cheapside, along which rode Lord George Gordon, and later, Mr. Carker on his bay horse.

Mr. Mould, the undertaker, in *Martin Chuzzlewit*, lived hereabouts : " Deep in the city and within the ward of Cheap stood Mr. Mould's establishment . . . abutting on a churchyard small and shady."

His premises were in a quiet corner, " where the city strife became a drowsy hum . . . suggesting to the thoughtful mind a stoppage in Cheapside."

In Wood Street, at No. 128, formerly stood the Cross Keys Inn, at which Dickens himself arrived as a boy from Chatham on the family coming to London. " Through all the years that have passed since," he wrote in *The Uncommercial Traveller*, " have I ever lost the smell of the damp straw in which I was packed— like game—and forwarded carriage paid to the Cross Keys, Wood Street, Cheapside, London ? "

Here, naturally, coming also from Rochester, Pip arrived, and here also he later met Estella, when the waiter on being asked for a private sitting-room led them " to the black hole of the establishment."

On the left of Wood Street, we find Huggin Lane ; there is another Huggin Lane off Queen Victoria Street, and either one might have stood for what was probably the birthplace of The Pickwick Club ; for in the advertisement, undoubtedly drawn up by Dickens himself, we are referred to " The Pickwick Club, so renowned in the annals of Huggin Lane."

The continuation of Cheapside to the Bank, past King Street, is called Poultry ; a description of the firing on the rioters at this point, is given in *Barnaby Rudge*.

Grocers' Hall Court on the left is said to be the

place to which Sam Weller, whose "knowledge of London was extensive and peculiar," directed Mr. Pickwick for " a glass of brandy and water warm." Mr. Pickwick had crossed opposite the Mansion House and was proceeding up Cheapside when Sam replied, " Second court on the right-hand side—last house but vun on the same side the vay—take the box as stands in the first fire-place, 'cos there ain't no leg in the middle o' the table, vich all the others has, and it's wery inconwenient."

Authorities differ as to the exact court ; some say Honey Court, others Freeman's Court, both in Cheapside. It all depends, of course, where Mr. Pickwick was when Sam gave the direction ! Mr. F. R. Jelley, A.R.I.B.A., in *The Dickensian*, June 1931, makes a claim for Blossom's Inn in Lawrence Lane. On the new building erected on the site in 1931 there is a sculpture of Tony Weller over the archway.

We now arrive at the famous centre named the Bank. On the left is the Bank of England, on the right the Mansion House, and opposite us the Royal Exchange.

" If you please, is this the city ? " enquired little Florence Dombey.

" We . . . men of business. We (who) belong to the city," to quote old Sol Gills in the same book, say " yes " most emphatically, as anything west of St. Paul's is not quite of the city from a real business point of view, the city proper having its centre in the Bank, and being bounded on the west by St. Paul's and on the east by Aldgate Pump.

Appropriately enough, Dickens, in the guise of an Uncommercial Traveller, paid frequent visits to the one square mile centring in the Bank and known as the City. " When I think I deserve particularly well of myself," he writes, " I stroll from Covent Garden into the City of London, after business hours there, on a Saturday, or—better yet—on a Sunday, and roam about its deserted nooks and corners. It is necessary to the full enjoyment of these journeys that they should be made in summer time, for then the retired spots that I love to haunt are at their idlest and dullest. A gentle fall of rain is not objectionable, and a warm mist sets off my favourite retreats to decided advantage."

"Something in the city" undoubtedly had a peculiar fascination for Dickens, seeing the continual reference he made to city life. It was Bob Sawyer who explained to Mrs. Raddle how it was he was unable to pay her little bill. "I'm very sorry . . . but the fact is that I have been disappointed in the city to-day"—"Extraordinary place that city. An astonishing number of men always *are* getting disappointed there."

"Every morning, with an air ever new," Herbert Pocket, in *Great Expectations*, "went into the city to look about him. . . . I asked him in the course of conversation what he was. He replied, 'A capitalist—an insurer of ships . . . in the city.'"

Mr. Tibbs—whose wife kept the boarding-house described in *Sketches by Boz*—"always went out at ten o'clock in the morning and returned at five in the afternoon, with an exceedingly dirty face, and smelling mouldy. Nobody knew what he was or where he went, but Mrs. Tibbs used to say, with an air of great importance, that he was engaged in the city."

Nadgett, in *Martin Chuzzlewit*, "was always keeping appointments in the city, and the other man never seemed to come."

On the right is the Mansion House, where, to quote from *A Christmas Carol*, "the Lord Mayor, in the stronghold of the mighty Mansion House, gave orders to his fifty cooks and butlers to keep Christmas as a

Lord Mayor's household should." In *Gone Astray* we read, "there was dinner preparing at the Mansion House, and when I peeped in at the grated kitchen window . . . my heart began to beat with hope that the Lord Mayor . . . would look out of an upper apartment and direct me to be taken in."

The Bank of England recalls the visit of the elder Weller with Sam to cash the money the former received under Mrs. Weller's will, when some amusing references were made to " reduced counsels."

In *The Uncommercial Traveller* is this reference :

" To walk on to the Bank, lamenting the good old times and bemoaning the present evil period, would be an easy next step, so I would take it, and would make my houseless circuit of the Bank, and give a thought to the treasure within ; likewise to the guard of soldiers passing the night there, and nodding over the fire."

Bella Wilfer, too, " thought, as she glanced at the mighty Bank, how agreeable it would be to have an hour's gardening there, with a bright copper shovel."

The Royal Exchange finds frequent reference in Dickens. In *Sketches by Boz* we read, " We never went on 'Change, by any chance, without seeing some shabby-genteel men, and we have wondered what earthly business they can have there." A similar experience was that of Pip, in *Great Expectations*, who said " I went on 'Change and I saw fluey men sitting there . . . whom I took to be great merchants, though I couldn't understand why they should all be out of spirits." Herbert, too, in the same book, " when he felt his case unusually serious . . . would go on 'Change at a busy time and walk in and out, in a kind of gloomy country dance figure, among the assembled magnates."

Quilp " made appointments on 'Change with men in glazed hats and round jackets pretty well every day " and Scrooge, Flintwinch and Mr. Dombey were regular frequenters there.

In *Gone Astray* Dickens describes finding himself when a child on 'Change and seeing " the shabby people sitting under the placards about ships " and coming to the conclusion that " they were misers, who had embarked all their wealth to go and buy gold dust or something of that sort and were waiting for their respective captains to come and tell them that they were ready to set sail."

Mr. Toots when he could no longer bear to contemplate the bliss of Walter Gay and Florence Dombey, used to explain to Captain Cuttle that he was under the necessity of leaving the company assembled at the Little Wooden Midshipman, " to see what o'clock it is by the Royal Exchange."

The present Royal Exchange, which was not built in the Pickwick era, swallowed up, in its front, the yard formerly known as Freeman's Court. Dodson & Fogg had their offices " in the ground-floor front of a dingy house, at the very farthest end of Freeman's Court, Cornhill . . . the clerks catching as favourable glimpses of Heaven's light and Heaven's sun, in the course of their daily labours, as a man might hope to do were he placed at the bottom of a reasonably deep well ; and without the opportunity of perceiving the stars in the day-time, which the latter secluded situation affords."

Prior to 1838 when the Royal Exchange was burned down Freeman's Court was the first Court in Cornhill past the Royal Exchange just before reaching Finch Lane. It must not be confused (as is sometimes the case) with the present Newman's Court in Cornhill, or Freeman's Court in Cheapside.

By the side of the Royal Exchange runs Cornhill, where Bob Cratchit " went down a slide . . . in honour of its being Christmas Eve." Another visitor to Cornhill was Nadgett the mysterious, in *Martin Chuzzlewit*, who was " first seen every morning coming down Cornhill, so exactly like the Nadgett of the day before as to occasion a popular belief that he never went to bed or took his clothes off." The same character we are told, used to sit at Garraway's, where " he would be occasionally seen drying a very damp pocket-handkerchief before the fire." Garraway's, a famous City coffee-house, stood until 1874 in Change Alley, the third turning to the right in Cornhill. It was from Garraway's that Mr. Pickwick indited his famous " Chops and Tomata Sauce " epistle to Mrs. Bardell.

The Poor Relation used to tell the assembled family that he went into the City every day—he didn't know why—and sat in Garraway's Coffee House. Mr. Flintwinch was also a regular visitor there, as well as to the Jerusalem Coffee House in Cowper Court, the next turning to Change Alley.

In *The City of the Absent* (*Uncommercial Traveller*) Dickens refers to " Garraway's, bolted and shuttered hard and fast ! " and asks : " Where are all the people who on busy working-days pervade these scenes ? "

" It is possible to imagine the man who cuts the sandwiches, on his back in a hay-field ; it is possible to imagine his desk, like the desk of a clerk at church, without him ; but imagination is unable to pursue the men who wait at Garraway's all the week for the men who never come. When they are forcibly put out of Garraway's on Saturday night—which they must be for they never would go out of their own accord— where do they vanish until Monday morning ? . . . The man who sells the dog's collars and the little toy coal-scuttles feels under as great an obligation to go afar off as Glyn & Co., or Smith, Payne & Smith. There is an old monastery-crypt under Garraway's (I have been in it among the port wine), and perhaps Garraway's, taking pity on the mouldy men who wait in its public room all their lives gives them cool house-room down there over Sundays."

At No. 68 Cornhill is Sun Court. In *Pickwick* we read that Dodson & Fogg's clerk " bent his steps direct to Sun Court, and, walking straight into the George and Vulture, demanded to know whether one Mr. Pickwick was within."

This is a curious topographical error of Dickens, as the " George and Vulture " is in George Yard, Lombard Street (see page 54) which could be approached by St. Michael's Alley at No. 42 Cornhill, but not by Sun Court, which is on the opposite side of the road.

At the end of Cornhill we reach the junction of Leadenhall Street, Gracechurch Street and Bishopsgate Street. Here used to stand a conduit known as the Standard and referred to in *Barnaby Rudge*.

To the left is Bishopsgate, where Brogley, the broker, of *Dombey and Son*, " kept a shop where every description of second-hand furniture was exhibited in the most uncomfortable aspect." The Flower Pot Inn, Bishopsgate Street, stood until 1863 at the corner of Threadneedle Street. From here Mr. Minns took coach to his cousin at Poplar Walk.

The London Tavern was at No. 5 Bishopsgate Street. Here the first annual dinner of the General Theatrical Fund took place in 1846, with Dickens in the chair. Five years later Dickens was again in the chair here for the same Fund. Here too, in *Nicholas Nickleby*, we hear of the Public Meeting of the United Metropolitan Improved Hot Muffin and Crumpet Baking and Punctual Delivery Company.

Somewhere near Threadneedle Street stood the City Square, in which was the office of Cheeryble Brothers.

" When Nicholas and the old gentleman reached the Bank, they hurried along Threadneedle Street, and through some lanes and passages on the right, until they, at length, emerged in a quiet shady little square.

Into the oldest and cleanest looking house of business in the square he led the way."

The City Square was described as " a sufficiently desirable nook in the heart of a busy town like London . . . has no enclosure, save the lamp-post in the middle ; and has no grass but the weeds which spring up round its base. It is a quiet, little-frequented, retired spot, favourable to melancholy and contemplation, and appointments of long waiting. . . . It is so quiet that you can almost hear the ticking of your own watch when you stop to cool in its refreshing atmosphere. There is a distant hum—of coaches, not of insects—but no other sound disturbs the stillness of the square."

Returning to Cornhill, on the right almost at the corner of Gracechurch Street is St. Peter's Church, figuring in *Our Mutual Friend*, where Bradley Headstone had his fateful interview with Lizzie Hexam. " The schoolmaster and the pupil emerged upon the Leadenhall Street region, spying eastward for Lizzie. . . . ' Don't let us take the great leading streets where everyone walks and we can't hear ourselves speak. Here's a large paved court by this church, and quiet too. Let us go up here.' . . . The court brought them to a churchyard ; a paved square court with a raised bank of earth about breast high in the middle, enclosed by iron rails."

It was a coping stone in this enclosure that Headstone dislodged in his passionate appeal to Lizzie for her hand.

There is a court beside the church, as described above, and following this round we find ourselves in Gracechurch Street. Crossing the road and bearing to the right we find on the left Bull's Head Passage where the Green Dragon is supposed to have been the original of the Blue Boar, Leadenhall Market. Here Sam Weller wrote the famous valentine. " Sam Weller walked on direct towards Leadenhall Market

at a good round pace. Looking round him, he there
beheld a sign-board, on which the painter's art had
delineated something remotely resembling a cerulean
elephant with an aquiline nose in lieu of trunk. Rightly
conjecturing that this was the Blue Boar himself, he
stepped into the house."

It was to Leadenhall Market that Captain Cuttle
came, on taking charge of Sol Gills' premises in
Leadenhall Street, to make arrangements with a
private watchman there "to come and put up and
take down the shutters of the Wooden Midshipman
every night and morning," and the household duties
of the little establishment were in the hands of " the
daughter of the elderly lady who usually sat under
the blue umbrella in Leadenhall Market."

Tim Linkinwater boasted that he could buy " new-
laid eggs in Leadenhall Market any morning before
breakfast " and accordingly " pooh-poohed " the idea
of life in the country having any advantages over
the City.

We always imagine that Mr. Dombey's offices were
in Leadenhall Street. Curiously enough Dickens is
very vague in his description of the exact locality,
simply stating :

" The offices of Dombey & Son were within the
liberties of the City of London and within the hearing
of Bow Bells . . . Gog and Magog held their state
within ten minutes' walk ; the Royal Exchange was
close at hand ; the Bank of England with its vaults
of gold and silver ' down among the dead men '
underground, was their magnificent neighbour. Just
around the corner stood the rich East India House,
teeming with suggestions of precious stuffs and stones,
tigers, elephants, howdahs, hookahs, umbrellas, palm
trees, palanquins, and gorgeous princes of a brown
complexion sitting on carpets, with their slippers very
much turned up at the toes."

India House, to which Dickens often makes reference, stood in Leadenhall Street, at the corner of Lime Street on the site now occupied by the Royal Mail Steam Packet Co.

At No. 157 Leadenhall Street was the original shop of Sol Gills, then occupied by Messrs. Norie & Wilson, who have since removed to Minories, where the effigy of the " Little Wooden Midshipman " may still be seen carefully preserved inside the shop (see page 130).

" Anywhere in the immediate vicinity " of the offices of Dombey & Son, " there might be seen . . . little timber midshipmen in obsolete naval uniforms, eternally employed outside the shop doors of nautical instrument makers in taking observation of the hackney coaches. . . . One of these effigies—of that which might be called, familiarly, the woodenest . . . thrust itself out above the pavement, right leg foremost, with a suavity the least endurable, and had the shoe buckles and flapped waistcoat the least reconcilable to human reason, and bore at its right eye the most offensively disproportionate piece of machinery."

In *The Uncommercial Traveller* Dickens tells us how he walked from Covent Garden past the India House, and past " my little wooden midshipman, after affectionately patting him on one leg of his knee-shorts for old acquaintance' sake."

Almost opposite Lime Street is St. Mary Axe, but it would be quite impossible to-day to identify the " yellow, overhanging, plaster-fronted house " which was the office of Pubsey & Co., in *Our Mutual Friend*, presided over by Riah, the Jew. In the pretty roof garden on this house Lizzie Hexam and Jenny Wren loved to sit and talk.

A turning on the right leads to Bevis Marks where Dick Swiveller was clerk to Sampson Brass.

" The atmosphere of Mr. Brass's office was of a

close and earthy kind and besides being frequently impregnated with strong whiffs of the second-hand wearing apparel exposed for sale in Duke's Place and Houndsditch, had a decided flavour of rats and mice and a taint of mouldiness."

In a letter to Forster in 1840 Dickens wrote, " I intended calling on you this morning on my way back from Bevis Marks, whither I went to look at a house for Sampson Brass. But I got mingled up in a kind of social paste with the Jews of Houndsditch, and roamed about among them till I came out in Moorfields quite unexpectedly."

The Red Lion in Bevis Marks is generally considered to be the hostelry referred to by Dick Swiveller when he stated, " There is a mild porter in the immediate vicinity."

The street continues as Duke Street and leads into Aldgate (see page 130), where we turn to the right into Fenchurch Street.

A few turnings down on the left—after noting Mark Lane to which we refer later—is Mincing Lane, and like Bella Wilfer we arrive in " the drug-flavoured region of Mincing Lane, with the sensation of having just opened a drawer in a chemist's shop." The counting-house of Chicksey Veneering & Stobbles was " a wall-eyed ground-floor by a dark gateway, and Bella was considering as she approached it, could there be any precedent in the City for her going in and asking for R. Wilfer, when whom should she see, sitting at one of the windows with the plate-glass sash raised, but R. Wilfer himself, preparing to take a slight refection. On approaching nearer, Bella discerned that the refection had the appearance of a small cottage-loaf and a pennyworth of milk. Simultaneously with this discovery on her part, her father discovered her, and invoked the echoes of Mincing Lane to exclaim ' My gracious me ! ' "

The fourth house on the left—next to Dunster Court—has been identified as being a likely original of the office in question.

At the end of Mincing Lane is Great Tower Street. Here we turn to the left. The narrow streets on the right lead into Lower Thames Street and the river-side. Hereabouts was the Cripple Corner of *No Thoroughfare*. " In the court-yard in the City of London, which was No Thoroughfare either for vehicles or foot-passengers, a court-yard diverging from a steep, a slippery and a winding street connecting Tower Street with the Middlesex shore of the Thames, stood the place of business of Wilding & Co., Wine Merchants. Probably as a jocose acknowledgment of the obstructive character of this main approach, the point nearest to its base, at which one could take the river (if so inodorously minded) bore the appella-tion Break Neck Stairs. The court-yard itself had likewise been descriptively entitled in old time Cripple Corner."

There was a Breakneck Stairs in Blackfriars in 1831, but we can find no trace of a place of that name in Tower Street.

Mark Lane is on the left. The district is referred to in *The Uncommercial Traveller*, as follows :

" Rot and mildew and dead citizens formed the uppermost scent, while, infused into it in a dreamy way not at all displeasing, was the staple character of the neighbourhood. In the churches about Mark Lane, for example, there was a dry whiff of wheat ; and I accidentally struck an airy sample of barley out of an aged hassock in one of them. From Rood Lane to Tower Street, and thereabouts, there was often a subtle flavour of wine, sometimes of tea. One church near Mincing Lane smelt like a druggist's drawer. Behind the Monument the service had a flavour of damaged oranges, which, a little farther

4

down towards the river, tempered into herrings, and gradually toned into a cosmopolitan blast of fish. In one church, the exact counterpart of the church in the ' Rake's Progress ' where the hero is being married to the horrible old lady, there was no speciality of atmosphere, until the organ shook a perfume of hides all over us from some adjacent warehouse."

Passing Mark Lane and Seething Lane we reach Hart Street. On the left of Hart Street is the Church of Saint Olave, which Dickens describes as " One of my best beloved churchyards I call the churchyard of Saint Ghastly Grim ; touching what men in general call it, I have no information. It lies at the heart of the City. It is a small, small churchyard, with a ferocious strong spiked iron gate, like a gaol. This gate is ornamented with skulls and cross-bones, larger than the life, wrought in stone ; but it likewise came into the mind of Saint Ghastly Grim that to stick iron spikes a-top of the stone skills, as though they were impaled, would be a pleasant device. Therefore the skills grin aloft horribly, thrust through and through with iron spears. Hence, there is attraction of repulsion for me in Saint Ghastly Grim, and, having often contemplated it in the daylight and the dark, I once felt drawn towards it in a thunder-storm at midnight."

Crutched Friars and Coopers' Row lead us by Trinity House on to Tower Hill. It was at " the garden up by the Trinity House on Tower Hill " that the chariot of Bella Wilfer halted, while Pa bought himself " the most beautiful suit of clothes, the most beautiful hat, and the most beautiful pair of bright boots " for the purpose of their " innocent elopement " to Greenwich.

On Tower Hill, Quilp resided, " and, in her bower on Tower Hill, Mrs. Quilp was left to pine the absence of her lord when he quitted her on business." No. 2

Tower Hill, recently demolished, is said to have been the house in question. At the corner of Minories, No. 1 Tower Hill, formerly stood " The Crooked Billet " mentioned in *Barnaby Rudge* as the head-quarters of the recruiting sergeant from whom Joe Willet took the King's Shilling. A recruiting office used to stand in King Street opposite.

In the Tower of London " in a dreary room whose thick stone walls shut out the hum of life and made a stillness which the records left by former prisoners with those silent witnesses seemed to deepen and intensify, remorseful for every act that had been done by every man among the cruel crowd," Lord George Gordon was imprisoned, as described in *Barnaby Rudge*.

David Copperfield tells as that as a boy he used to meet " the orfling " on London Bridge, there to tell her " some astonishing fictions respecting the wharves and the Tower, of which I can say no more than that I hope I believed them myself." And in the same book, when up in London with his aunt, we hear of him varying " the legal character of these proceedings by going to see . . . the Tower of London."

Leaving Tower Hill and bearing to the left by the Tower Moat we turn to the right by the docks and wharves along Lower Thames Street, known in Dickens's day simply as Thames Street. The vintner, whose account Joe Willet had to settle on his visit to London had his place of business " down some deep cellars hard by Thames Street." And it may have been to the same vintner's that Simon Tappertit was going with the " complicated piece of ironmon-gery " which was " going to be fitted on a ware-us door in Thames Street " when he stopped in the Temple to speak with Sir John Chester, who requested him to remove the offending oily smelling lock outside the door. Along Thames Street " down by the Monument and by the Tower" came Mortimer Lightwood and Eugene Wrayburn in *Our Mutual Friend* in search of news of the vanished John Harmon.

On our left is the Custom House—where the late Mr. Bardell was employed ; in the concluding chapter of *Bleak House*, we read that Peepy had a position here " and doing extremely well."

David Copperfield on his return to London from his long tour abroad, after the death of Dora " landed in London on a wintry autumn evening " and " walked from the Custom House to the Monument " before he could find a coach to take him to Gray's Inn. In *Great Expectations* we read that Pip always left his boat " at a wharf near the Custom House, to be brought up afterwards to the Temple Stairs." This was part of the scheme for getting Magwitch out of the country, and as he explains " it served to make me and my boat a commoner incident among the water-side people there."

Somewhere in this neighbourhood, between the Custom House and London Bridge, Dickens placed Spigwiffin's Wharf, where Ralph Nickleby found house-room for Mrs. Nickleby and Kate. Mrs. Nickleby explained that the way to the house was " all down Newgate Street, all down Cheapside, all up Lombard Street, down Gracechurch Street, and along Thames Street, as far as Spigwiffin's Wharf. Oh ! it's a mile."

When Newman Noggs first introduced them to it " they went into the City, turning down by the river side ; and, after a long and very slow drive . . . stopped in front of a large old dingy house in Thames Street, the door and windows of which were so bespattered with mud that it would have appeared to have been uninhabited for years. . . . Old, and gloomy, and black, in truth it was, and sullen and dark were the rooms, once so bustling with life and

enterprise. There was a wharf behind, opening on
the Thames. An empty dog-kennel, some bones of
animals, fragments of iron hoops and staves of old
casks, lay strewn about, but no life was stirring there.
It was a picture of cold, silent decay."

In the same district was Mrs. Clennam's house.
When Arthur Clennam visited it on his return to
England, " he crossed by Saint Paul's and went down,
at a long angle, almost to the water's edge, through
some of the crooked and descending streets which
lie (and lay more crookedly and closely then) between
the river and Cheapside." The house he sought
was " an old brick house, so dingy as to be all but
black, standing by itself within a gateway. Before it,
a square court-yard where a shrub or two and a patch
of grass were as rank (which is saying much) as the
iron railings enclosing them were rusty ; behind it, a
jumble of roofs. It was a double house, with long,
narrow heavily framed windows. Many years ago
it had had it in its mind to slide down sideways ; it
had been propped up, however, and was leaning on
some half-dozen gigantic crutches : which gymnasium
for the neighbouring cats, weather-stained, smoke-
blackened, and overgrown with weeds, appeared in
these latter days to be no very sure reliance."

It was at one of the wharves in Thames Street that
poor Florence, after having been robbed of her clothes
by " good Mrs. Brown," was discovered by Walter
Gay.

Passing Billingsgate and the Monument (page
109), we reach the foot of London Bridge, where
we turn to the right and then to the left for Cannon
Street, where, according to Mr. Jinkins, was Todgers's
rival ; but, he declared, he would stick to Todgers's
until " the Cannon Street establishment shall be able
to produce such a combination of wit and beauty
as has graced that board that day and shall be able

to serve up such a dinner as that of which they had just partaken."

The first to the left out of Gracechurch Street is Lombard Street. The office of Barbox Brothers was in a "dim den up in a corner of a court off Lombard Street," and here was the banking esablishment of Giles, Jeremie & Giles, of *No Thoroughfare*. The Poor Relation used to take little Frank to walk in Lombard Street, on account of the "great riches there."

In *Little Dorrit* we have a splendid account of a visit by Mr. Dorrit and Mr. Merdle, to "the golden Street of the Lombards."

On the right of Lombard Street is George Yard, at the bottom of which is the George and Vulture. After leaving Mrs. Bardell's in Goswell Street "Mr. Pickwick and Sam took up their abode in very good, old-fashioned, and comfortable quarters ; to wit, the George and Vulture Tavern, George Yard, Lombard Street."

Here the Pickwickians were served with subpœnas in the famous action for breach of promise, and from here they all went to the trial at the Guildhall.

At No. 1 Lombard Street, was the banking house of Smith, Payne & Smith. Their successors, the Union of London & Smiths Bank, now occupy the premises, which have been rebuilt. It is referred to in *Pickwick* when the elder Weller was handed "a cheque on Smith, Payne & Smith for five hundred and thirty pounds, that being the sum of money to which Mr. Weller, at the market price of the day, was entitled, in consideration of the balance of the second Mrs. Weller's funded savings."

At No. 2 Lombard Street was the Bank where George Beadnell resided, with whose daughter, Maria, Dickens, as a youth, fell madly in love.

"He, too," writes Forster, "had his Dora, at

apparently the same hopeless elevation; striven
for as the one only thing to be attained, and even
more unattainable, for neither did he succeed nor
happily did she die; but the one idol, like the other,
supplying a motive to exertion for the time, and
otherwise opening out to the idolater, both in fact
and fiction, a highly unsubstantial, happy, foolish
time."

In a letter written to Forster, twenty-five years
after this time, Dickens laid bare this secret of his
early infatuation:

" It excluded every other idea from my mind for
four years, at a time of life when four years are equal
to four times four; and that I went at it with a determination to overcome all the difficulties, which fairly
lifted me up into that newspaper life, and floated
me away over a hundred men's heads. . . . I have
positively stood amazed at myself ever since! And
so I suffered, and so worked, and so beat and hammered
away at the maddest romances that ever got into any
boy's head and stayed there, that to see the mere
cause of it all, now, loosens my hold upon myself.
Without for a moment sincerely believing that it
would have been better if we had never got separated,
I cannot see the occasion of so much emotion as I
should see anyone else. No one can imagine in the
most distant degree what pain the recollection gave
me in *Copperfield*. And, just as I can never open that
book as I open any other book, I cannot see the face
(even at four-and-forty) or hear the voice, without
going wandering away over the ashes of all that
youth and hope in the wildest manner."

ROUND THE SQUARES OF THE WEST END

THE squares of London had not quite the same fascination for Dickens as the ordinary streets possessed ; the people who dwelt in them were for the most part not those who interested him, although, when he came to deal with the meaner square of the type of Golden Square or Soho Square, we find him quite in his usual element.

Between Holborn and Hyde Park, to the north and south of Oxford Street, are two lines of squares, and it is the purpose of this day's ramble to traverse the streets leading to them.

Making Dickens's house in Doughty Street our starting point once again, we are reminded that the correct postal address included the mention of Mecklenburg Square, though Dickens himself seldom used it. We turn right from the house and left into Guilford Street, past the site of the Foundling Hospital (see page 119) on the right, and then skirt Queen Square on the left. It was Richard Carstone in *Bleak House* whc had " a neat little furnished lodging house in a quiet old house near Queen Square."

A little farther on we reach Russell Square, across which young Dickens used to walk from Somers Town in the morning on the way to the Blacking Warehouse " with some cold hotch-potch in a small basin tied up in a handkerchief." Russell Square is also referred to twice in *Nicholas Nickleby*.

Turning to the left along Southampton Row, and to the right where it joins Theobald's Road, we reach Bloomsbury Square, which figures largely in *Barnaby Rudge* in the account of the sacking of Lord Mansfield's

house on the site of No. 29, and finally as the scene
of the execution of several of the leading rioters,
Barnaby himself, being happily rescued at the
eleventh hour. In *Master Humphrey's Clock* we hear
of the recommendation of " a charming fellow who
had performed the feat six times of carrying away
every bell handle in Bloomsbury Square."

On the far side of the Square is Great Russell
Street, and by turning to the left and passing the
front of the British Museum, and then to the right
along Bloomsbury Street, we reach Bedford Square,
mentioned in two delightful stories in the *Sketches*
(*Horatio Sparkins* and *The Bloomsbury Christening*) a
once aristocratic neighbourhood, for Mr. Kitterbell
who lived at No. 14 Great Russell Street delighted
to have Bedford Square added to his address : his
Uncle Dumps, however, would insist in his replies
" in lieu thereof the dreadful words, Tottenham Court
Road."

Montague Place is to the right ; here Mr. Perker
lived and here came Lowten with the news of the
arrest of Mrs. Bardell for the costs which Mr. Pickwick
would not pay. " Mr. Perker had had a dinner-party
that day, as was testified by the appearance of lights
in the drawing-room windows, the sound of an improved
grand piano, and an improvable cabinet voice issuing
therefrom, and a rather overpowering smell of meat
which pervaded the steps and entry."

Turning to the left along the north side of Bedford
Square we reach the Tottenham Court Road, where
at the cheap linen drapers, Messrs. Jones, Spruggins
& Smith, the true identity of Horatio Sparkins was
revealed. Turning to the right we remember that it
was at the broker's shop " up at the top of Tottenham
Court Road " that " the little round table with the
marble top " and " the precious flower pot," belonging
to Traddles and seized by the brokers when the

Micawber household in Camden Town was sold up, were recovered by the aid of Clara Peggotty.

In *Nicholas Nickleby* we are introduced to Miss Knag's brother, " an ornamental stationer and small circulating library keeper," who lived " in a by-street off Tottenham Court Road ; and who let out by the day, week, month or year the newest old novels, whereof the titles were displayed in pen-and-ink characters on a sheet of pasteboard, swinging at his door-post."

Dickens himself used to come this way as a boy from his home in Gower Street, to the blacking factory near Charing Cross (see page 92).

" In going to Hungerford Stairs of a morning," he says, " I could not resist the stale pastry put out at half-price on trays at the confectioners' doors in Tottenham Court Road ; and I often spent in that the money I should have kept for my dinner. Then I went without my dinner, or bought a roll, or a slice of pudding."

Grafton Street on the left leads into Fitzroy Square, whereof in *Nicholas Nickleby* we are informed of its " dowager barrenness and frigidity."

At No. 13 Fitzroy Street Dickens lodged as a youth in 1830.

Keeping straight on, with the Square to the right, we reach Cleveland Street, formerly Norfolk Street. Here Dickens lived as a child in 1816. The house is said to be No. 10.

We again find him lodging in Norfolk Street as a young man in 1831, probably in the same house as that in which as a baby boy he made his first acquaintance with London.

Cleveland Street was formerly Green Lanes, where the rioters in *Barnaby Rudge* had a meeting-place.

Turning to the right on reaching Cleveland Street, we soon arrive in Euston Road. Almost opposite, a little to the left, is Osnaburgh Terrace, where, at No. 9, Dickens lived temporarily in 1844.

We now proceed along the Marylebone Road, with Regent's Park to the right, we reach High Street on the left. Here at the corner is No. 1 Devonshire Terrace, where Dickens lived from 1839 to 1851. The house has been considerably altered since that time. It saw the output of many of the most important novels, *The Old Curiosity Shop, Barnaby Rudge, Martin Chuzzlewit, Dombey and Son,* and *David Copperfield ;* also three of the famous *Christmas Books*.

A little beyond Devonshire Terrace, on the same side is Marylebone Church which may possibly have witnessed the christening of little Paul Dombey and the second marriage of Mr. Dombey, but no direct reference is made to it in the novel.

The next turning past the church leads into Paddington Street, where we turn right for Baker Street, on reaching which we turn left. Dorset Street, on the right, leads us into Montague Place.

Montague Square is on the left. " Mr. Jorkins . . . lived by himself in a house near Montague Square, which was fearfully in want of painting."

The next square is Bryanston Square, which we cross into Upper George Street, where we turn left. We now traverse the district between Bryanston Square and Portland Place, in which Mr. Dombey's house was situated. It was " a large one on the shady side of a tall, dark, dreadfully genteel street in the region between Portland Place and Bryanston Square. It was a corner house, with great wide areas containing cellars frowned upon by barred windows, and leered at by crooked-eyed doors leading to dust-bins. It was a house of dismal state, with a circular back to it, containing a whole suite of drawing-rooms looking upon a gravelled yard, where two gaunt trees, with blackened trunks and branches, rattled rather than rustled, their leaves were so smoke-dried."

It is probable that Dickens had in mind his own

house in Devonshire Terrace when writing this description.

Gloucester Place, on the right, leads into Portman Square. " The Podsnaps lived in a shady angle adjoining Portman Square. They were a kind of people certain to dwell in the shade, wherever they dwelt."

Turning to the left along the top of the square we reach Baker Street, crossing which into Berkeley Street we are in Manchester Square, and by crossing same and continuing straight on along Hinde Street reach Bentinck Street. At No. 18 (now rebuilt) the Dickens family lived in 1833. Bentinck Street leads into Welbeck Street, whither rode Lord Geo. Gordon " along the Strand, up Swallow Street into the Oxford Road, and thence to his house in Welbeck Street, near Cavendish Square, whither he was attended by a few dozen idlers." Lord George Gordon's house was No. 64 (since rebuilt), close to Wigmore Street.

Turning right along Welbeck Street and then left into Wigmore Street we soon reach Harley Street, where at " the handsomest house " the Merdles lived.

" Upon that establishment of state, the Merdle establishment in Harley Street, Cavendish Square, there was the shadow of no more common wall than the fronts of other establishments of state on the opposite side of the street. Like unexceptionable Society the opposing rows of houses in Harley Street were very grim with one another. Indeed, the mansions and their inhabitants were so much alike in that respect that the people were often to be found drawn up on opposite sides of dinner-tables, in the shade of their own loftiness, staring at the other side of the way with the dullness of the houses."

At the junction of Harley Street with Wigmore Street is Cavendish Square.

" ' The lady's name,' said Ralph, ' is Mantalini,

Madame Mantalini. I know her. She lives near Cavendish Square. If your daughter is disposed to try after the situation, I'll take her there, directly.' . . . They arrived without any further conversation at the dressmaker's door, which displayed a very large plate, with Madame Mantalini's name and occupation and was approached by a handsome flight of steps. There was a shop to the house, but it was let off to an importer of otto of roses. Madame Mantalini's showrooms were on the first floor ; a fact which was notified to the nobility and gentry by the casual exhibition, near the handsomely curtained windows, of two or three elegant bonnets of the newest fashion, and some costly garments in the most approved taste."

Near here was the Boffin mansion, outside which the evil genius Silas Wegg presided. " Over against a London house, a corner house not far from Cavendish Square, a man with a wooden leg had sat for some years, with his remaining foot in a basket in cold weather."

Cavendish Place leads into Regent Street, where to the left we see All Souls' Church, referred to in the description of Sam Weller's valentine, on which " a representation of the spire of the church in Langham Place, London, appeared in the distance."

Turning to the right, we reach Oxford Circus, where we turn right to Marble Arch.

Close to Oxford Circus and near Great Portland Street is Oxford Market, where Towlinson, Dombey's butler, " had visions of leading an altered and blameless existence as a serious greengrocer."

It was in the neighbourhood of Oxford Street that Nicholas Nickleby first saw Madeline Bray at the General Agency Office, and here later on he made his first acquaintance with Mr. Charles Cheeryble, who " dragged him back into Oxford Street, and, hailing an omnibus on its way to the City, pushed Nicholas in before him, and followed himself."

In the search for Miss Wade, Mr. Meagles and Arthur Clennam " rode to the top of Oxford Street and, there alighting, dived in among the great streets of melancholy stateliness."

Esther Summerson and her guardian had " a cheerful lodging near Oxford Street, over an upholsterer's shop. London was a great wonder to us, and we were out for hours and hours at a time, seeing the sights, which appeared to be less capable of exhaustion than we were. We made the round of the principal theatres, too, with great delight and saw all the plays that were worth seeing."

On the railings of Hyde Park, opposite Edgware Road, is a tablet to show where Tyburn once stood. We read in *A Tale of Two Cities* : " They hanged at Tyburn in those days, so the streets outside Newgate had not obtained the infamous notoriety that has since attached to it."

It was in the region of Edgware Road that Nicholas, accompanied by Newman Noggs, came to see his lady love—but only found " Bobster " !

The Regal Cinema occupies the site of 5 Hyde Park Place, the last London home of Dickens. This he rented in January, 1870, for his readings. " We live here —opposite the Marble Arch "—he wrote to J. T. Fields, " in a charming house, until the 1st of June, and then return to Gad's. . . . I have a large room here, with three fine windows overlooking the Park."

Other houses in the neighbourhood in which Dickens lived for a time were 16 Somers Place, Hyde Park, in 1865, 6 Southwick Place, Hyde Park Square, in 1866.

It may have been the house in Hyde Park Place that Dickens had in view when Mr. Micawber mentioned " a terrace at the western end of Oxford Street, fronting Hyde Park, on which he had always had his eye, but which he did not expect to attain immediately as it would require a large establishment."

When Magwitch announced himself to Pip as his benefactor he advised him " to look out at once for a ' fashionable crib ' near Hyde Park in which he could have ' a shakedown.' "

Rose Maylie was staying at " a family hotel in a quiet but handsome street near Hyde Park " when Nancy visited her and informed her of Monks's plot against Oliver Twist.

Our way now lies along Park Lane. It was in this region—to one of the streets at the back of Park Lane, between Grosvenor Square and Piccadilly—that Mr. Meagles and Arthur Clennam came in search of Miss Wade and Tattycoram " among the great streets of melancholy stateliness, and the little streets that try to be as stately and succeed in being more melancholy, of which there is a labyrinth near Park Lane. Wildernesses of corner-houses, with barbarous old porticoes and appurtenances ; horrors that came into existence under some wrong-headed person in some wrong-headed time, still demanding the blind admiration of all ensuing generations and determined to do so until they tumbled down, frowned upon the twilight. Parasite little tenements with the cramp on their whole frame, from the dwarf hall-door on the giant model of His Grace's in the Square to the squeezed window of the boudoir commanding the dunghills in the Mews, made the evening doleful."

Upper Brook Street, on our left, takes us into Grosvenor Square.

" The aristocratic gravity of Grosvenor Square," as it is called in *Nicholas Nickleby*, was exemplified in a later book, *Little Dorrit*, when it was made the place of residence of Mr. Tite Barnacle—" or very near it," as Dickens adds to emphasise the difference ; for the house was on the verge of " aristocratic gravity," being at No. 24 Mews Street, Grosvenor Square, " A hideous little street of dead wall, stables and dunghills, with lofts over coach-houses inhabitated by coachmen's families, who had a passion for drying clothes and decorating their window sills with miniature turnpike gates."

The two or three airless houses at the entrance of Mews Street (one of which was occupied by the Barnacles) were let " at enormous rents on account of their being abject hangers-on to a fashionable situation."

When Arthur Clennam visited No. 24 he found it " a squeezed house, with a ramshackle bowed front, little dingy windows and a little dark area like a damp waistcoat pocket."

Brook Street runs from the far side of the square, across New Bond Street and into Hanover Square. Mrs. Skewton in *Dombey and Son*, " borrowed a house in Brook Street, Grosvenor Square, from a stately relative (Lord Feenix), who was out of town " and who did not mind letting her have the house for Edith's wedding to Mr. Dombey, " as the loan implied his final release and acquittance from all further loans and gifts to Mrs. Skewton and her daughter."

In an hotel in Brook Street Mr. Dorrit resided in the days of his affluence, and here the advent of the great Merdle to visit Mr. Dorrit caused great commotion in the office.

It was in " one of the thoroughfares which lie between Park Lane and Bond Street " that Nicholas Nickleby stopped at a handsome hotel for " a pint of wine and a biscuit," and in the coffee-room heard the disparaging conversation between Sir Mulberry Hawk and Lord Frederick Verisopht concerning " little Kate Nickleby " which resulted in the fight between Nicholas and Mulberry Hawk.

The centre of what Dickens called " the aristocratic gravity of Hanover Square " is St. George's Church, the place for fashionable marriages, and thoughts of Sir Mulberry Hawk caused Mrs. Nickleby to dream of Kate's marriage " with great splendour at St. George's, Hanover Square."

It was at the Hanover Square Rooms (on the site of No. 4) that Dickens and his friends gave several representations of *Not so Bad as We Seem*, and where he gave some of his public readings later on.

In Tenterden Street formerly stood the Royal Academy of Music, which had a personal association with Dickens. As a boy of 12 he was living in Camden Town, parted from his parents, who were in the Marshalsea Prison for debt. His sister Fanny was a student at the Academy, and he tells us that " Sundays, Fanny and I passed in the prison. I was at the academy in Tenterden Street, Hanover Square, at nine o'clock in the morning, to fetch her ; and we walked back there together, at night."

We leave the Square by Hanover Street at the side of the church, and crossing Regent Street pass along Argyll Place into Great Marlborough Street ; the famous police court here is said to be the one to which Inspector Bucket conducted Esther before commencing his search for Lady Dedlock.

In *The Steam Excursion* (*Sketches by Boz*) we are referred to " Mrs. Taunton's domicile in Great Marlborough Street."

Returning to Regent Street, and turning left, we continue until we reach Vigo Street, on the right. The first turning on the left of Vigo Street is Sackville Street. It was here that Mr. and Mrs. Lammle, in *Our Mutual Friend*, had a temporary residence.

" It had done well enough, they informed their friends, for Mr. Lammle when a bachelor, but it would not do now. So they were always looking at palatial residences in the best situations, and always very nearly taking or buying one, but never quite concluding the bargain."

5

A little farther along Vigo Street, opposite Savile Row, is Albany. It is also in *Our Mutual Friend* that we read, " He lived in chambers in the Albany, did Fledgeby, and maintained a spruce appearance." Of the district between Savile Row, Burlington Gardens and Old Bond Street, Dickens wrote a charming paper in *The Uncommercial Traveller* entitled *Arcadian London*. It is too full of references to these streets to quote here ; suffice it to say he writes of the West End of London as it is in the autumn when most of the people are absent.

" I have taken a lodging for six weeks in the most unfrequented part of England—in a word, in London," he writes. " The retreat into which I have withdrawn myself is Bond Street. From this lonely spot I make pilgrimages into the surrounding wilderness, and traverse extensive tracts of the Great Desert."

Long's Hotel in Bond Street, at which Cousin Feenix, in *Dombey and Son*, used to stay, was at No. 15 New Bond Street.

Returning to Regent Street, we turn left. It was in " a handsome suite of private apartments," in Regent Street, that Lord Frederick Verisopht lived in *Nicholas Nickleby*.

We now cross the road and turn to the right into Beak Street. On the right is Warwick Street, where at No. 12 is a Roman Catholic Church, no doubt the one referred to in *Barnaby Rudge*. " The men who are loitering in the streets to-night are half-disposed to pull down a Romish Chapel or two . . . they only want leaders." Later in the same book Sim Tappertit denies to the Vardens that he was " at Warwick Street," but he proudly asserts that " he was at Westminster " !

Beak Street was formerly called Silver Street. At No. 38, at the corner of Upper James Street, stood until a few years ago a little public-house called the Crown. This was the house of call of Newman Noggs, himself " a gentleman once."

" If ever you want a shelter in London (don't be angry at this, *I* once thought I never should)," he wrote, " they know where I live, at the sign of the Crown, in Silver Street, Golden Square. It is at the corner of Silver Street and James Street, with a bar-door both ways. You can come at night."

Upper James Street will take us into Golden Square.

Ralph Nickleby " lived in a spacious house in Golden Square, which, in addition to a brass plate upon the street door, had another brass plate two sizes and a half smaller upon the left-hand door-post, surmounting a brass model of an infant's fist grasping a fragment of a skewer, and displaying the word ' Office ' ; it was clear that Mr. Ralph Nickleby did, or pretended to do, business of some kind."

There are just a few of the old houses remaining to give us an idea of what Ralph Nickleby's house was like. No. 7, now rebuilt, is pointed out as the most likely house. It was once the house of William à Beckett, with whom Dickens was acquainted.

Of the square itself the following is an extract from the long and interesting description in *Nicholas Nickleby* :

" Although a few members of the graver professions live about Golden Square, it is not exactly in anybody's way to or from anywhere. It is one of the squares that have been ; a quarter of the town that has gone down in the world, and taken to letting lodgings. . . . Its boarding-houses are musical, and the notes of pianos and harps float in the evening time round the head of the mournful statue, the guardian genius of a little wilderness of shrubs, in the centre of the square."

The home of the Kenwigs family where Noggs lodged, and Nickleby too, later on, was either in

Beak Street, Brewer Street, Carnaby Street, or in Broad Street ; at any rate, it was close at hand :

"In that quarter of London in which Golden Square is situated there is a bygone, faded, tumble-down street, with two irregular rows of tall meagre houses, which seem to have stared each other out of countenance years ago. The very chimneys appear to have grown dismal and melancholy from having had nothing better to look at than the chimneys over the way. Their tops are battered, and broken, and blackened with smoke ; and, here and there, some taller stack than the rest, inclining heavily to one side and toppling over the roof, seems to meditate taking revenge for half a century's neglect by crushing the inhabitants of the garrets beneath."

It is quite easy to imagine that in a house in one of these streets David Copperfield, assisted by Martha, found Little Em'ly and restored her to her uncle. They alighted at one of the entrances to Golden Square and hurried to "one of the sombre streets, of which there are several in that part where the houses were once fair dwellings in the occupation of single families, but have, and had, long degenerated into poor lodgings let off in rooms. Entering at the open door of one of these, and releasing my arm, she beckoned me to follow her up the common staircase, which was like a tributary channel to the street."

Passing along Lower James Street, we cross Brewer Street, where some of the old houses still remain, and then with the Regent Palace Hotel on our right, we proceed through Denman Street, across Shaftes-bury Avenue, and along Great Windmill Street into Coventry Street, where we turn to the left, and in a few minutes reach Leicester Square.

Leicester Square was known as Leicester Fields in the days of *Barnaby Rudge* when the rioters plotted to burn down Sir George Saville's house there.

DOCTOR MANETTE'S HOUSE, NEAR SOHO SQUARE

It was " in that curious region lying about the Haymarket and Leicester Square, which is a centre of attraction to indifferent foreign hotels and indifferent foreigners, racket-courts, fighting-men, swordsmen, foot-guards, old china, gaming-houses, exhibitions, and a large medley of shabbiness and shrinking out of sight," that Mr. George in *Bleak House* had his shooting gallery.

At the south-east corner of the Square is Green Street, where No. 10, since rebuilt, was said to be the original Old Curiosity Shop.

By the side of the Empire runs Leicester Place, where formerly stood the Prince of Wales Hotel. Here Dickens gave a dinner in 1837 to celebrate the completion of *The Pickwick Papers*.

The second turning on the right of Wardour Street is Gerrard Street, where, at No. 10, Dickens's uncle, Thomas Barrow, lived in the upper part of the house of a bookseller named Manson. Here Dickens had access to an array of books, and was, for some time, supremely happy.

In the same street—possibly the same house— lived Mr. Jaggers, the lawyer in *Great Expectations*. It was " rather a stately house of its kind, but dolefully in want of painting and with dirty windows."

Gerrard Street leads round by the Theatre into Shaftesbury Avenue, and by turning to the right we reach Cambridge Circus. We here reach the St. Giles district dealt with on pages 117–18. Keeping to the left along Charing Cross Road we find on the left Manette Street, named after the Doctor in *A Tale of Two Cities*, who lived close by.

Manette Street leads into Greek Street, where by turning to the right we find ourselves in Soho Square. Directing our " steps towards the north side " as did Vendale in *No Thoroughfare*, we find ourselves at Soho Street. In this part of Soho Square, among what Dickens described as " a curious colony of mountaineers " who had " long been enclosed within that small flat London district of Soho," lived Obenreizer in a house that was a bit of " domestic Switzerland " shielding the beautiful Miss Marguerite and the mysterious Madame Dor.

In *Bleak House*, Soho Square is referred to as " a quiet place in the neighbourhood of Newman Street," where Caddy Jellyby met Esther and walked round the garden in the centre.

Carlisle Street, a little farther on, reminds us that near here stood Carlisle House. In *Barnaby Rudge* we read of Emma Haredale and her uncle attending one of the masquerades here.

" The quiet lodgings of Doctor Manette " were in " a quiet street corner not far from Soho Square," and No. 10 Carlisle Street is generally supposed to be the house.

" A quainter corner than the corner where the Doctor lived was not to be found in London. There was no way through it, and the front windows of the Doctor's lodgings commanded a pleasant little vista of street that had a congenial air of retirement on it. . . . It was a cool spot, staid but cheerful, a wonderful place for echoes, and a very harbour from the raging streets. . . . The Doctor occupied two floors of a large, still house, where several callings purported to be pursued by day, but whereof little was audible any day, and which was shunned by all of them at night. In a building at the back, attainable by a court-yard where a plane tree rustled its green leaves, church-organs claimed to be made, and silver to be chased, and likewise gold to be beaten by some mysterious giant who had a golden arm starting out of the wall of the front hall—as if he had beaten himself precious, and menaced a similar conversion of all visitors."

TURVEYDROP'S ACADEMY, NEWMAN STREET

Around these silent streets we can picture in our fancy Sydney Carton wandering at night time.

" And yet he did care something for the streets that environed that house, and for the senseless stones that made their pavements. Many a night he vaguely and unhappily wandered there, when wine had brought no transitory gladness to him ; many a dreary daybreak revealed his solitary figure lingering there, and still lingering there when the first beams of the sun brought into strong relief, removed beauties of architecture in spires of churches and lofty buildings, as perhaps the quiet time brought some sense of better things else forgotten and unattainable, into his mind."

Dean Street takes us into Oxford Street. Crossing that thoroughfare we find, almost opposite, Newman Street, where at No. 26 is the house of Mr. Turveydrop, " a sufficiently dingy house at the corner of an archway, with busts in all the staircase windows. In the same house there were also established as I gathered from the plates on the door, a drawing-master, a coal-merchant (there was certainly, no room for his coals), and a lithographic artist. On the plate which, in size and situation, took precedence of all the rest, I read MR. TURVEYDROP. . . . Mr. Turveydrop's great room . . . was built out into a mews at the back, was lighted by a skylight. It was a bare resounding room smelling of stables."

THE BANK TO ISLINGTON, HAMPSTEAD, AND HIGHGATE

TRUE to the popular song of his time, Dickens takes us in his books " up and down the City Road " in company with Mr. Micawber and young David Copperfield, with Polly Toodles, the Charitable Grinder and little Florence Dombey ; also " in and out the Eagle " with Miss Jemima Evans and her friends. We will go in company with this glorious assemblage.

The road from the Bank to Islington is a straight one ; or as straight a one as we can expect to meet in London, and, although we shall make an occasional diversion off the main road, we shall not complete the journey by such a roundabout route as that made by Tom Pinch when he first came to London and was living in Islington :

" Now Tom, in his guileless distrust of London, thought himself very knowing in coming to the determination that he would not ask to be directed to Furnival's Inn if he could help it ; unless, indeed, he should happen to find himself near the Mint, or the Bank of England ; in which case he would step in, and ask a civil question or two, confiding in the perfect respectability of the concern. So on he went, looking up all the streets he came near, and going up half of them ; and thus, by dint of not being true to Goswell Street, and filing off into Aldermanbury and bewildering himself in Barbican, and being constant to the wrong point of the compass in London Wall, and then getting himself crosswise into Thames Street, by an instinct that would have been marvellous if he had the least desire or reason to go there, he found himself at last hard by the Monument."

With the Bank of England on our right, we proceed along Princes Street. Lothbury, mentioned below, is on the right ; on the left is the end of Gresham Street which was formerly known as Cateaton Street, and thus referred to in the original advertisement of *Pickwick*, undoubtedly drawn up by Dickens himself :

" The Pickwick Club, so renowned in the annals of Huggin Lane, so closely entwined with a thousand interesting associations connected with Lothbury and Cateaton Street, was founded in the year one thousand eight hundred and twenty-two by Mr. Samuel Pickwick."

The third turning on the right of Gresham Street leads to the Guildhall, whither the four Pickwickians drove for the famous trail of Bardell *v.* Pickwick. The Guildhall Court has been rebuilt since those days.

Of the Guildhall itself we read in that delightful essay of personal juvenile adventure, *Gone Astray* :

" I made up my little mind to seek my fortune. . . . My plans . . . were first to go and see the Giants in Guildhall. . . . I found it a long journey to the giants and a slow one. . . . Being very tired I got into the corner under Magog, to be out of the way of his eye, and fell asleep."

The following description of the City Giants, as seen by Jo Toddyhigh, is taken from *Master Humphrey's Clock* :

" The statues of the two giants, Gog and Magog, each above fourteen feet in height, those which succeeded to still older and more barbarous figures after the Great Fire of London, and which stand in the Guildhall to this day, were endowed with life and motion. These guardian genii of the City had quitted their pedestals, and reclined in easy attitudes, in the great stained glass window. Between them was an ancient cask, which seemed to be full of wine ; for the younger Giant, clapping his huge hand upon it, and throwing up his mighty leg, burts into an exulting laugh, which reverberated through the hall like thunder."

Lothbury leads into Throgmorton Street, on the left of which is Austin Friars, which Tom Pinch said sounded ghostly. Here was the office of Mr. Fips, " in a very dark passage on the first floor, oddly situated at the back of a house, across some leads, they found a little blear-eyed glass door up in one corner, with ' Mr. Fips ' painted on it in characters which were meant to be transparent."

On the opposite side of Throgmorton Street is the Stock Exchange, where, according to *Dombey and Son*, " a sporting taste (originating generally in bets of new hats) is much in vogue."

In *Pickwick* we read that the two Wellers " proceeded from the Bank to the gate of the Stock Exchange, to which Wilkins Flasher, Esquire, after a short absence, returned with a cheque on Smith, Payne & Smith, for five hundred and thirty pounds ; that being the sum of money to which Mr. Weller, at the market price of the day, was entitled, in consideration of the balance of the second Mrs. Weller's funded savings."

Returning to Lothbury, we turn to the right into Moorgate. The second court on the left is Great Bell Alley, formerly Bell Alley, and this leads into Coleman Street.

It has been entirely rebuilt since Dickens's day but, in its continuation the other side of Coleman Street, one can get a fair idea of what the Alley was some eighty years ago. "Namby, Bell Alley, Coleman Street," was the Sheriff's Officer, and to his house Mr. Pickwick was taken prior to being put into the Fleet Prison.

Continuing along Moorgate we pass the street

called London Wall—marking the course of the old wall of the city—and enter into the district of Finsbury. Arthur Clennam and Daniel Doyce " shared a portion of a roomy house in one of the grave old-fashioned city streets, lying not far from the Bank of England, by London Wall."

To the right, between London Wall and as far to the north as Old Street, were once Moorfields, the scene of an exploit of the rioters in *Barnaby Rudge*.

From about this point we can take a motor-bus or tram-car to the Angel at Islington, and so save what would be a rather tiring walk of nearly two miles. Finsbury Square is passed on the right. This square was built on part of Moorfields.

Oliver Twist and Bill Sikes came this way to do the burglary at Chertsey. From the Bethnal Green Road, " turning down Sun Street and Crown Street and crossing Finsbury Square, Mr. Sikes struck, by the way of Chiswell Street, into Barbican, thence into Long Lane and so into Smithfield."

Sun Street is a continuation of the south side of Finsbury Square. Chiswell Street is directly on the left and leads into Barbican, in which neighbourhood was the meeting place of the Prentice Knights of *Barnaby Rudge*, in an " ill-favoured pit . . . profoundly dark and reeking with stagnant odours."

Mr. A. W. Wickens writing in *The Dickensian* for September, 1931, points out that there are still very spacious cellars under Barbican very much like those described by Dickens. Entrance is at No. 51.

Long Acre is a continuation of Barbican, the farther side of Aldersgate Street.

For Smithfield, see page 32.

Continuing past Finsbury Square, we arrive in City Road. When writing *The Old Curiosity Shop*, Dickens got lost in this district judging from what he wrote to Forster : " I intended calling on you this morning on my way back from Bevis Marks, whither I went to look at a house for Sampson Brass. But I got mingled up in a kind of social paste with the Jews of Houndsditch, and roamed about among them till I came out in Moorfields quite unexpectedly. So I got into a cab, and came home again, very tired, by way of the City Road."

Little Paul Dombey, in charge of Polly Toodles and Susan Nipper, wandered here from Camden Town to meet the newly made " Charitable Grinder " —little Biler—in his full charity dress ; and somewhere about here Florence was stolen by " good Mrs. Brown."

The portion of Old Street on the right running eastward was formerly known as Old Street Road. Here Mrs. Guppy lived at No. 302 " in an independent though unassuming manner," said Mr. Guppy to Esther in *Bleak House*. " She is eminently calculated for a mother-in-law," he added.

Further along City Road on the right, after passing No. 221, is Shepherdess Walk, on the right of which, almost at the corner, stands a modern public-house, the Eagle, on the site of the famous gardens of that name. In *Sketches by Boz* is a story dealing with the Eagle, entitled " Miss Evans and the Eagle."

On the opposite side of Shepherdess Walk formerly stood St. Luke's Workhouse.

When David came to live with the Micawbers in Windsor Terrace, he tells us that the servant there was " a dark-complexioned young woman, with a habit of snorting ; and informed me, before half an hour had expired, that she was ' a Orfling,' and came from St. Luke's Workhouse, in the neighbourhood."

The next street but one on the right is Windsor Terrace. " My address," said Mr. Micawber, " is Windsor Terrace, City Road. I—in short," said Mr. Micawber, with the same genteel air, and in another burst of confidence—" I live there."

WINDSOR TERRACE, CITY ROAD

And sure enough here are houses, any one of which might have been the house of Mr. Micawber, " shabby like himself, but also, like himself, making all the show it could."

Here David had a room " at the top of the house, at the back . . . and very scantily furnished." Here poor Mrs. Micawber, like Mrs. Dickens in real life, had tried to exert herself, and had covered the centre of the street door with " a great brass-plate, on which was engraved, ' Mrs. Micawber's Boarding Establishment for Young Ladies ' : but," as David Copperfield continues to inform us, " I never found that any young lady had ever been to school there ; or that any young lady ever came, or proposed to come ; or that the least preparation was ever made to receive any young lady. The only visitors I ever saw or heard of were creditors." This was a sad household for the young boy of fiction, a replica of the household Dickens had known at Camden Town when a boy himself. " Mr. Micawber had a few books on a little chiffonier, which he called the library ; and those went first. I carried them, one after another, to a bookstall in the City Road—one part of which, near our house, was almost all book-stalls and bird-shops then—and sold them for whatever they would bring."

A row of shops similar to Dickens's description stood in the City Road, opposite Windsor Terrace, until about twenty years ago, when the present warehouses were erected.

City Road now leads us straight to the Angel at Islington. Those who are walking can turn to the left into Sidney Street and then to the right into Mr. Pickwick's portion of Goswell Road (Goswell Street it was then called), and so to the Angel, where it joins City Road.

" Mr. Samuel Pickwick . . . threw open his chamber window, and looked out upon the world beneath. Goswell Street was at his feet, Goswell Street was on his right hand—as far as the eye could reach, Goswell Street extended on his left ; and the opposite side of Goswell Street was over the way. ' Such,' thought Mr. Pickwick, ' are the narrow views of those philosophers who, content with examining the things that lie before them, look not to the truths which are hidden beyond. As well might I be content to gaze on Goswell Street for ever, without one effort to penetrate to the hidden countries which on every side surround it.' "

At the end of Goswell Road, just after its junction with City Road, we arrive in Islington. The High Street runs to the right, and St. John Street to the left. Before we proceed on our way into Pentonville Road, we must make a short stay in Islington.

In Dickens's day, Islington was a pleasant suburb for we read in *Sketches by Boz* that " the early clerk population of . . . Islington and Pentonville are fast directing their steps towards Chancery Lane and the Inns of Court." It was the gate of London for all the coaches coming from the north. The coach conveying John Browdie and his bride in their honeymoon trip to London is described as traversing " with cheerful noise the yet silent streets of Islington." And in *Bleak House* we read of Inspector Bucket and Esther on their return from their search for Lady Dedlock coming " at between three and four o'clock in the morning into Islington. . . . We stopped in a High Street where there was a coach-stand."

When Joe Willet left London, " he went out by Islington," and, in the same book, Barnaby and his father, after escaping from Newgate, " made towards Clerkenwell, and, passing thence to Islington as the nearest point of egress, were quickly in the fields." Bill Sikes, in his flight to Hatfield, also " went through Islington."

Mr. Morfin, " a great amateur in his way—after business "—lived in Islington, and the first lodgings let by Mrs. Lirriper were also in this district ; which brings us to that delightful couple, Tom Pinch and his sister Ruth, who were on the look-out for lodgings. " It ought to be a cheap neighbourhood," said Tom, " and not too far from London. Let me see. Should you think Islington a good place? . . . It used to be called Merry Islington once upon a time. Perhaps it's merry now ; if so, it's all the better. . . . At length, however, in a singular little old-fashioned house, up a blind street, they discovered two small bedrooms and a triangular parlour, which promised to suit them well enough."

A house in Terrett's Place, off Upper Street, is pointed out as the possible original of the lodgings of Tom Pinch and his sister, as it possesses the requisite " triangular parlour."

The Peacock at Islington (a modern public-house of that name is to be seen a few doors past the Angel) was the first stopping place of the coach that bore Nicholas away to the Yorkshire school, and again we find it mentioned in *The Holly Tree* as the inn from which the teller of the story started off on his Christmas coach ride to the north. It was a bitterly cold night, and, when he got to the Peacock, he tells us, " I found everybody drinking hot purl in self-preservation."

The modern building at the corner of Pentonville Road and High Street replaces the older Angel Tavern ; but the entrance of Oliver Twist into London at this point loses nothing of its interest.

On the seventh morning after his flight from the workhouse where he was born, Oliver met the Artful Dodger at Barnet, and the next we hear of the pair .is in Islington. " They crossed from the Angel into St. John's Road, struck down the small street which terminates at Sadler's Wells Theatre ; through Exmouth

Street and Coppice Row ; down the little court by the side of the workhouse ; across the classic ground which once bore the name of Hockley-in-the-Hole; thence into Little Saffron Hill, and so into Saffron Hill the great."

As this is a link with the Saffron Hill district referred to in our first day's walk, it is interesting to trace out here the above route, which, with the construction of Rosebery Avenue (running from St. John Street to the corner of Gray's Inn Road and Clerkenwell Road— see page 4), has been greatly altered. St. John Street was formerly St. John's Street Road. The first turning on the right is Arlington Street, " the small street which terminates at Sadler's Wells Theatre." This leads us to the back of Sadler's Wells Theatre, rebuilt, and by turning round to the left we get into Rosebery Avenue, by the side of the reservoirs known as the New River Head, which has an association with Uriah Heep. " The 'ouse that I am stopping at—a sort of private hotel and boarding-house, Master Copperfield, near the New River 'Ed—will have gone to bed these two hours."

From Sadler's Wells, the Artful Dodger's route would lie across the road, down Garnault Place by the side of the Town Hall, and then to the right along Exmouth Street to Farringdon Road, formerly Coppice Row. When Oliver was taken home to Mr. Brownlow's at Pentonville, " the coach rattled away, down Mount Pleasant and up Exmouth Street."

On the left of Exmouth Street is Spa Fields, of which we read in *The Old Curiosity Shop* : " I remember the time when old Maunders had in his cottage in Spa Fields . . . eight male and female dwarfs setting down to dinner every day, who was waited on by eight old giants in green coats, red smalls, blue cotton stockings and high-lows."

Reaching Farringdon Road, the Parcels Post Office, on the right, at the corner of King's Cross Road, is

on the site of the old Clerkenwell Gaol. Here is
Mount Pleasant, mentioned above, and also in *Bleak
House*, as the district in which the Smallweed family
resided.

" In a rather ill-favoured and ill-savoured neighbourhood, though one of its rising grounds bears the
name of Mount Pleasant . . . in a little narrow
street, always solitary, shady, and sad, closely bricked
in on all sides like a tomb, but where there yet lingers
the stump of an old forest tree, whose flavour is about
as fresh and natural as the Smallweed smack of youth."

Coppice Row was cleared away in 1860 by the
making of Farringdon Road. "The little court by the
side of the workhouse " is Crawford Passage in Farringdon Road on the right, opposite Bowling Green Lane.
Hockley-in-the-Hole has disappeared, but Back Hill
and Ray Street mark the site of this once muddy
bull-baiting ground.

Thence we could get straight into Little Saffron
Hill (page 31), but there is little of the Dickens period
left in these streets to-day.

Another set of *Oliver Twist* characters arrived at
the Angel at a still later date. Noah Claypole and
Charlotte, and their advent is described as follows :

" Mr. Claypole went on, without halting, until he
arrived at the Angel, Islington, where he wisely judged,
from the crowd of passengers and numbers of vehicles,
that London began in earnest. . . . He crossed into
St. John's Road, and was soon deep in the obscurity
of the intricate and dirty ways which, lying between
Gray's Inn Lane and Smithfield, render that part of
the town one of the lowest and worst that improvement
has left in the midst of London."

Returning along Rosebery Avenue, and passing the
New River Head, and the front of Sadler's Wells
Theatre, we bear to the left and again reach the Angel
at Islington, when we turn left into Pentonville Road.

6

Pentonville was quite a fashionable suburb when Dickens wrote of it. Mr. Brownlow lived in "a neat house in a quite shady street near Pentonville," at the time he rescued Oliver from the clutches of Fagin, and of Mr. Fang, the Hatton Garden Magistrate ; and so did Mr. Pancks, "the fairy" of *Little Dorrit*. Mr. Micawber indited at least two of his epistles from his "residence, Pentonville, London," and Mr. Nicodemus Dumps, in *The Bloomsbury Christening*, "rented a first-floor furnished at Pentonville," which "commanded a dismal prospect of an adjacent churchyard." Perhaps this was the churchyard on the right in which Grimaldi the clown (whose memoirs Dickens edited) lies buried. He lived at No. 37 Penton Street, a turning on the right. In Penton Street formerly stood White Conduit House, to which Dickens makes one or two references.

In Penton Place, on the left of Pentonville Road, lived Mr. Guppy. "It is lowly," he explained, in declaring his love to Esther, in *Bleak House*, "but airy ; open at the back, and considered one of the 'ealthiest outlets."

Unfortunately there never was a No. 57 in this little street ; but we may nevertheless enjoy the privilege of selecting for ourselves a suitable residence for the "young man by the name of Guppy."

In Amwell Street George Cruikshank lived at the time he illustrated *Sketches by Boz* and *Oliver Twist*.

Returning to the Angel, a tram or bus should be taken to Highgate. To the east of our road lies Ball's Pond, the home of Mr. Perch in *Dombey and Son*. In his youth, Dickens had some friends who lived in this direction, which probably accounts for Ball's Pond being mentioned also in the *Sketches*, whilst Poplar Walk at Stamford Hill has the distinction of being the very first example of Dickensian topography.

In Holloway the Wilfers lived ; it must have been

to the left between the Holloway Road and the dust mounds at Battle Bridge (King's Cross) ; see page 124.

We alight at the Archway Tavern, Highgate. To the right Archway Road leads to Barnet. This was the road by which Oliver Twist, accompanied by the Dodger, arrived in London ; this was the road Mr. Jarndyce used to and from Bleak House, which was near St. Albans. Through Highgate Archway, the one that was replaced by the present bridge, Noah Claypole and Charlotte came, and in *The Holly Tree Inn* we are told of the coach " rattling for Highgate Archway over the hardest ground I have ever heard the ring of iron shoes on." And it was " at the Archway toll over at Highgate " Bucket first picked up the trail of Lady Dedlock.

The road to Highgate runs to the left of the Archway Tavern, and leads up Highgate Hill ; Bill Sikes went " through Islington " when endeavouring to escape after the murder of Nancy, and " strode up the hill at Highgate, on which stands the stone in honour of Whittington." The stone referred to is to be seen on the left, incorporated in a lamp-post. When Swiveller was taunted by Quilp, he threatened to run away " towards Highgate, I suppose." He said to himself, " Perhaps the bells might strike up ' Turn again, Swiveller.' " Joe Willet came this way when he ran away from home and Dolly : " He went out by Islington and so on to Highgate, and sat on many stones, and gates, but there were no voices in the bells to bid him turn," says Dickens.

Highgate is mentioned in *Pickwick* as the scene of some of " the unwearied researches " of the founder of the famous Club.

Dickens knew Highgate fairly well ; in 1832 he was lodging there at " Mrs. Goodman's, next door to the Red Lion." The Red Lion was in North Road, and was demolished in 1900, but the post on which the sign used to swing is still to be seen in the roadway opposite the modern house on its site.

In South Grove, Highgate, is Church House, said to be the house of Mrs. Steerforth ; "an old brick house . . . on the summit of the hill. . . . A genteel, old-fashioned house, very quiet and orderly. From the windows of my room I saw all London lying in the distance like a great vapour with here and there some lights twinkling through it."

The Steerforths were not alone of the *David Copperfield* party at Highgate. Doctor Strong, after leaving Canterbury, took a cottage here. " It was not in that part of Highgate where Mrs. Steerforth lived, but quite on the opposite side of the little town."

On his way to visit his old schoolmaster, David went into a cottage that was to let, and examined it narrowly : " It would do for me and Dora admirably," he writes, " with a little front garden for Jip to run about in and bark at the tradespeople through the railings, and a capital room upstairs for my aunt." And here he brought his child-wife, and here she died.

Of St. Michael's Church, in South Grove, Dickens writes in the same book : " The church with the slender spire, that stands on the top of a hill now, was not there then to tell me the time. An old red-brick mansion, used as a school, was in its place ; and a fine old house it must have been to go to school at, as I recollect it."

Dickens's father and mother are both buried in Highgate Cemetery, where also lies his little daughter, Dora Annie ; two names very reminiscent of two characters in *David Copperfield*.

Hampstead Lane leads past Caen Wood into Spaniards Road and Hampstead. Caen Wood—or Ken Wood—now preserved as an open space—was

Lord Mansfield's country house, which the Gordon Rioters endeavoured to destroy.

The Spaniards Inn, which we pass on the right, is introduced into *Pickwick*, when Mrs. Bardell, Mrs. Raddle and other friends spent an afternoon here. " They all arrived safely in the Spaniards tea gardens, where the luckless Mr. Raddle's very first act nearly occasioned his good lady a relapse ; it being neither more nor less than to order tea for seven, whereas (as the ladies one and all remarked) what could have been easier than for Tommy to have drunk out of any-body's cup—or everybody's, if that was all—when the waiter wasn't looking ; which would have saved one head of tea, and the tea just as good ! "

To the Spaniards she was traced by Mr. Jackson, clerk to Dodson & Fogg, and conveyed to the Fleet Prison for the costs in the action which Mr. Pickwick had so steadfastly refused to pay.

Hampstead Heath opens out just beyond the Spaniards. Walter Gay " knew of no better fields than those near Hampstead " for reflecting on the unknown life before him when he was ordered by the house of Dombey to sail for the Barbadoes. Bill Sikes, in his flight from London, " skirted Caen Wood, and so came out on Hampstead Heath. Traversing the hollow by the Vale of Health, he mounted the opposite bank, and, crossing the road which joins the villages of Hampstead and Highgate, made along the remaining portion of the heath to the fields at North End, in one of which he laid himself down under a hedge, and slept."

A walk to Hampstead and Highgate, after a dip in the Roman Bath in the Strand, was often indulged in by David Copperfield.

Dick Swiveller, in *The Old Curiosity Shop*, when he married, lived in " a little cottage at Hampstead, . . . which had in its garden a smoking-box, the envy of

the civilised world," and here he was visited regularly
every Sunday by Mr. Chuckster, who became "the great
purveyor of general news and fashionable intelligence."

On the left may be seen the Hampstead Ponds—the
speculations on the source of which formed one of the
papers communicated to the Club by Mr. Pickwick,
" the man who had traced to their source the mighty
ponds of Hampstead." Whether or not the tittlebats
on which Mr. Pickwick had agitated the scientific
world with his theory were found in these self-same
ponds, history is silent.

Jack Straw's Castle was a very popular rendezvous
with Dickens. Forster quotes the following typical
letter from Dickens suggestive of a walk and dinner
at this hostelry : " You don't feel disposed, do you, to
muffle yourself up and start off with me for a good brisk
walk over Hampstead Heath ? . . . I knows a good
'ouse there where we can have a red-hot chop for
dinner, and a glass of good wine." This, Forster adds,
" led to our first experience of Jack Straw's Castle,
memorable for many happy meetings in coming years."

During the writing of *Pickwick*, after the death of
his sister-in-law Mary, Dickens went for a few months
to live at Hampstead ; in later years, whilst writing
Bleak House, he spent a summer at Wylde's Farm, near
North End.

At Finchley, Barnaby Rudge and his father, after
escaping from Newgate, " found in a pasture . . . a
poor shed with walls of mud, and a roof of grass and
brambles, built for some cowherd, but now deserted.
Here they lay down for the rest of the night."

Abel Cottage, the home of Mr. Garland, where Kit
and Barbara were employed, was at Finchley. " It
was a beautiful little cottage with a thatched roof, and
little spires at the gable ends, and pieces of stained
glass in some of the windows, almost as large as
pocket-books."

In *Dombey and Son*, Mr. Toots refers to going " as far as Finchley to get some uncommonly fine chickweed that grows there," for Miss Dombey : and it was no doubt at Finchley that Mr. Carker, the junior, lived with his sister, " near to where the busy great north road of bygone days is silent and almost deserted, except by wayfarers, who toil along on foot. . . . It is neither of the town nor country."

At Cobley's Farm, Finchley, Dickens took longings in 1843, whilst writing a part of *Martin Chuzzlewit*.

Forster, in his Life of Dickens, tells us that 'while walking here " in the green lanes as the midsummer months were coming on, his introduction of Mrs. Gamp, and the uses to which he should apply that remarkable personage, first occurred to him."

No 70 Queens Avenue, Finchley, marks the site of Cobley's Farm, and a tablet on the house connects the spot with Dickens and Mrs. Gamp.

In Hornsey Churchyard, Betsy Trotwood's husband was laid to rest.

Hornsey, to, is noted as one of the places in which Mr. Samuel Pickwick, G.C.M.P.C., had made " unwearied researches."

TRAFALGAR SQUARE TO THE MONUMENT, VIA THE BOROUGH

THERE are many associations connected with the boyhood of Dickens to be encountered on this day's journey, which makes it a most popular one with most visitors to Dickens's London.

We start from the steps of St. Martin's Church in Trafalgar Square, where David Copperfield had that memorable meeting with Mr. Peggotty on the latter's return from his search for little Em'ly.

The district was not unknown to young David, for, in a court at the back of the church, was a famous pudding shop, where the pudding " was made of currants, and was rather a special pudding, but was dear, twopenny-worth not being larger than a penny-worth of more ordinary pudding," and in St. Martin's Lane adjacent stood the coffee shop, also visited alike by young C.D. and young D.C., with the glass inscription on the door, to read which backward on the wrong side, " ꟽoo⁊-ɘɘⱯoꟲ " always gave a shock through his blood.

Near by stood the Golden Cross Hotel. Until 1831 it occupied a site where Nelson's monument now stands and it was to the old hotel that Dickens referred in *Sketches by Boz*, *Pickwick* and *David Copperfield*.

From the older hostelry the Pickwickians started off for Rochester, the archway through which the coach passed causing Jingle to cry " Heads, heads, take care of your heads ! ", as a prelude to one of his amusing stories.

It was to the back entrance of the hotel that David took Peggotty after the meeting on the Church steps.

David was already acquainted with this hostelry, for on his first visit to London as a young man he described it as " a mouldy sort of establishment in a close neighbourhood." His small bedroom " smelt like a hackney coach and was shut up like a family vault." Steerforth coming to his rescue, he secured a better room in the front, where " the early morning coaches rumbling out of the archway underneath " made him " dream of thunder and the gods."

He describes himself next morning "peeping out of window at King Charles on horseback, surrounded by a maze of hackney coaches and looking anything but regal in the drizzling rain and a dark brown fog."

Another account of the Golden Cross is given in the chapter on *Early Coaches* in *Sketches by Boz.*

Mr. Haredale, during the Gordon Riots, was refused refreshment at " an hotel near Charing Cross," but no name is given to it ; and, at Charing Cross also, Eugene Wrayburn witnessed the " ridiculous and feeble spectacle " of Jenny Wren's bad boy trying to cross the road.

Nowhere in the streets of London is the ebb and flow of the tide of Dickens's life better mirrored than in the illustrious highway called the Strand ; it reflects the novelist as " a very small boy indeed, both in years and stature," going to view the lion over the gateway of Northumberland House (*Gone Astray*) ; it reflects him, but a few years later, walking disconsolately to Warren's Blacking Factory, near Hungerford Bridge, and to the shop at the corner of Chandos Street and Bedford Street, to tie up the pots of blacking in company with Bob Fagin, " near the second window as you come from Bedford Street " ; it reflects him, still in those days, making his dinner off " a stout hale pudding, heavy and flabby, with great raisins in it, stuck in whole at great distances apart," which " came up hot at about noon every day," at " a cookshop . . . in the Strand, somewhere near where the Lowther Arcade is now . . . and many and many a day did I dine off it " ; it reflects him as the young reporter, at the age of twenty-two, going to the office of *The Morning Chronicle* at No. 332 (now demolished) ; it reflects him as a parliamentary reporter, having lodgings, like Mr. Watkins Tottle, in Cecil Street, Strand, and giving warning because they " put too much water in the hashes, lost the nutmeg grater and attended on me most miserably." Cecil Street was swallowed up by Hotel Cecil and its successor, Shell-Mex House. It reflects him walking into Fleet Street with his first literary contribution to the old *Monthly Magazine,* which, " when it appeared in all the glory of print," he purchased from a shop in the Strand, and walked with it to Westminster Hall, his eyes dimmed with joy and pride ; it reflects many of the night-walks of an " Uncommercial Traveller " in the hey-day of his fame, from the offices of *Household Words* and *All the Year Round,* in Wellington Street ; and, finally and imperishably, it reflects a whole host of the children of his fancy who traversed the ancient highway in the pages of his books.

" We walked down the Strand a Sunday or two ago," he writes in *Sketches by Boz,* " behind a little group, and they furnished food for our amusement the whole way."

David Copperfield walked the Strand at many stages of his history, notably on the day of his party, when, " observing a hard mottled substance in the window of a ham and beef shop, which resembled marble, but was labelled Mock Turtle, I went in and bought a slab of it," and towards the close of the story, when he walked along the Strand, through Temple Bar, following the clue of Martha, to be picked up at Blackfriars, and to end so happily at Millbank.

Ralph Nickleby " made the best of his way to the
Strand " to visit Miss La Creevy, " and stopped at a
private door about half-way down the crowded
thoroughfare. A miniature painter lived there, for
there was a large gilt frame screwed upon the street
door." Her house was opposite Exeter Hall (the
Strand Palace Hotel stands on the site), from which
she could watch the clerics coming and departing.

In far different frame of mind, Mr. Haredale
" walked along the Strand " after the burning of the
Warren by the rioters, " too proud to expose himself
to another refusal, and of too generous a spirit to
involve in distress or ruin any honest tradesman who
might be weak enough to give him shelter."

Bradley Headstone, with Rogue Riderhood at his
side, also " walked along the Strand " on an eventful
occasion, the former meditating, the latter muttering.
And in *Little Dorrit* we read of Arthur Clennam
" passing at nightfall along the Strand, and the lamplighter going on before him."

Young Martin Chuzzlewit, after finding a lodging
for Mark and himself, " in a court in the Strand not
far from Temple Bar . . . passed more Golden Balls
than all the jugglers in Europe have juggled with, in
the course of their united performances, before he
could determine in favour of any particular shop
where those symbols were displayed." That this was
in the Strand there is but little doubt.

Then, too, we must not forget that graphic scene in
A Tale of Two Cities after the crowd at Temple Bar
had mobbed the hearse of the spy :

" The remodelled procession started, with a chimney
sweep driving the hearse . . . and with a pieman . . .
driving the mourning coach. A bear leader . . . was
impressed as an additional ornament, before the
cavalcade had gone far down the Strand."

Finally, we remember Dick Swiveller's ambition to

join the tide of life that swept along the Strand once
received a serious check. " There's only one avenue
to the Strand left open now," he declared. " And I
shall have to stop up that to-night with a pair of
gloves. . . . In about a month's time, unless my
aunt sends me a remittance, I shall have to go three
or four miles out of town to get over the way."

So much for those who were more or less merely
passers-by along the Strand ; other interests are
attached to the highway and its vicinity.

Grand Buildings occupies the site of Northumberland House (referred to on page 89) to which
Dickens also humorously alludes in *Horatio Sparkens*,
when he says " Miss Malderton was as well known
as the lion on the top of Northumberland House,
and had equal chance of going off."

Proceeding eastward, Craven Street on the right
reminds us that in his lodgings here Mr. Brownlow
had the interview with Rose Maylie that resulted in
the recovery of Oliver Twist, and that, at the bottom,
on the site now occupied by the Railway Station,
formerly stood Hungerford Market, and the Blacking
Warehouse, where Dickens worked as a boy.

" The blacking warehouse was the last on the left-
hand side of the way at old Hungerford Stairs " says
Dickens in his autobiographical fragment. " It was a
crazy, tumble-down old house, abutting of course on
the river, and literally overrun with rats. . . . The
counting-house was on the first floor looking over the
coal barges and the river. There was a recess in it,
in which I was to sit and work. My work was to
cover the pots of paste blacking first with a piece of
oil paper, and then with a piece of blue paper, to tie
them round with a string, and then to clip the paper
close and neat all round until it looked as smart as a
pot of ointment from an apothecary's shop."

It was in this neighbourhood that Mr. Peggotty

lodged in the intervals of his travels abroad to find his niece " over a chandler's shop only two streets away from Buckingham Street," where the meals were flavoured by " a miscellaneous taste of tea, coffee, butter, bacon, cheese, new loaves, firewood, candles and walnut ketchup continually ascending from the shop."

Mr. Dick occupied Mr. Peggotty's lodging on the occasion when Mrs. Crupp had informed him " that there wasn't room to swing a cat there " ; but as Mr. Dick justly observed ". . . you know, Trotwood, I don't want to swing a cat. I never do swing a cat. Therefore what does that signify to me ? "

" There was a low wooden colonnade before the door (not very unlike that before the house where the little man and woman used to live in the old weather-glass) which pleased Mr. Dick mightily."

From Hungerford Stairs the Micawbers set off by boat to Gravesend, *en route* for Australia. They had lodgings meanwhile in " a little dirty tumble-down public house which in those days was close to the stairs and whose protruding wooden rooms overhung the river." Their room we are told was " one of the wooden chambers upstairs, with the tide flowing underneath." This was no doubt the White Swan that stood near to the Blacking Warehouse and figures in *David Copperfield* :

" When I dined regularly and handsomely, I had a saveloy and a penny loaf, or a fourpenny plate of red beef from a cook's shop ; or a plate of bread and cheese and a glass of beer from a miserable old public-house opposite our place of business, called the Lion, or the Lion and something else, that I have forgotten."

In Buckingham Street—at the last house on the left (demolished a few years ago)—lived young David with Mrs. Crupp ; here, too, Dickens himself had lodgings in about 1834.

Farther along, on the left, is Bedford Street, where the Civil Service Stores occupy the site of the shop already mentioned in which the young Dickens so dexterously covered the tops of the blacking pots. We cross the road to Durham House Street, leading to the Adelphi Arches referred to below. The next turning takes us to the Adelphi Hotel, where Mrs. Edson stayed prior to her taking lodgings at Mrs. Lirriper's ; but its greate^ claim to fame is that as Osborne's Hotel, Adelphi, it figures in the closing scenes of *The Pickwick Papers*.

Farther on is Adelphi Terrace where the same Mrs. Edson " went straight down to the terrace and along it, and looked over the iron rail. . . . The desertion of the wharf below, and the flowing of the high water there, seemed to settle her purpose . . . and among the dark and dismal arches she went in a wild way. . . . We were on the wharf and she stopped " ; fortunately to be saved by good Mrs. Lirriper, who exclaimed innocently, " Well I never thought nobody ever got here except me to order my coal, and the Major to smoke his cigar."

The view from the terrace overhanging the river, whither Arthur Clenman in *Little Dorrit* followed Tattycoram and Rigaud, and where they were met by Miss Wade, is a very interesting one, as below here was the coal wharf and the old Fox-under-the-Hill public-house referred to in *David Copperfield*.

" I was fond of wandering about the Adelphi," he says, " because it was a mysterious place with those dark arches. I see myself emerging one evening from some of these arches, on a little public-house close to the river, with an open space before it, where some coal-heavers were dancing ; to look at whom I sat down on a bench."

We too can explore a portion of these arches to-day, entering from the Strand by Durham House Street, at the side of the Tivoli Cinema. The way is quite safe, though somewhat dark and lonesome. It has its exit on the Embankment, and the waste land marks the site of the little public-house to which Dickens refers.

Our way now lies along the Embankment, with the river on our right. Passing under Waterloo Bridge, we are reminded that in the dry arches below Sam Weller once had " unfurnished lodgings for a fortnight." Somerset House is passed on our left. This is dealt with in our next day's journey. A little later we pass Temple Gardens (see page 16) and soon arrive at the next bridge, which is Blackfriars.

In the autobiographical fragment which Forster has preserved for us in the second chapter of his Life of Dickens we read : " My usual way home was over Blackfriars Bridge, and down that turning in the Blackfriars Road which has Rowland Hill's Chapel on one side and the likeness of a golden dog licking a golden pot over a shop-door on the other. . . .

" My old way home by the Borough made me cry, after my eldest child could speak. In my walks at night I have walked there often since then."

At the time of which Dickens writes, he described himself as " such a little fellow with my poor white hat, little jacket and corduroy trousers," working at Warren's Blacking Factory, by Hungerford Bridge ; his father was in the Marshalsea Prison for debt, and a back attic was found for the boy Charles " at the house of an Insolvent Court agent, who lived in Lant Street in the Borough, where Bob Sawyer lodged many years afterwards."

We have already come most of the way Dickens would have traversed on his way home from the blacking warehouse ; it now remains for us to complete the journey.

Although Murdstone & Grinby's warehouse, where David Copperfield washed the bottles in company with the same lads who had been young Charles's companions, is one and the same as Warren's Blacking Factory, yet Dickens made one great alteration—he described it as being "down in Blackfriars," and in so doing uses almost the same words as in the autobiographical fragment (see page 92).

Arthur Clennam drove with Daniel Doyce over Blackfriars Bridge to the Marshalsea. Hugh broke open the Toll House here during the Gordon Riots ; but the greatest of all the memories of Blackfriars Bridge is that of Poor Jo at Long Vacation time finding there " a baking stony corner wherein to settle to his repast. And there he sits munching and gnawing, and looking up to the great cross on the summit of St. Paul's Cathedral until . . . he is stirred up and told to ' move on.' "

Unfortunately, the railway bridge across the river now blocks out the view of St. Paul's.

Crossing Blackfriars Bridge we find Union Street on our left ; the shop on the right-hand corner was formerly graced with the sign of a " golden dog licking a golden pot." This was unfortunately removed in 1931 and is now exhibited in the Cuming Museum, Southwark. On the opposite corner of the road is Rowland Hill's Chapel, sadly fallen from its former high position ; in turns it has been a metal warehouse, cinema, and boxing ring !

" There are a great many little low-browed old shops in that street and some are unchanged now." Dickens tells us of Union Street. Even after a farther lapse of close on seventy years, some—a few—are still " unchanged now."

Dickens goes on to say, " I looked into one a few weeks ago, where I used to buy boot-laces on Saturday nights, and saw the corner where I once sat down on a stool to have a pair of ready-made half-boots fitted on."

What an interesting mean street it is—although the show van at the corner is no longer a visitor ; but we can conjure up a vision of young Dickens going in " with a very motley assemblage to see the Fat Pig, the Wild Indian, and the Little Lady."

The far end of Union Street leads into Southwark Bridge Road, and we bear to the right. To the left takes us to the bridge itself, but gone is the old iron bridge upon which Little Dorrit loved to walk in solitude, because, as she explained, " if you go by the Iron Bridge . . . there is an escape from the noise of the street " ; gone is the toll gate, but not the memories of Young John Chivery laying down " his penny on the toll plate of the Iron Bridge and . . . looking about him for the well-known and well-beloved figure " . . . of Little Dorrit. He met her here " towards the Middlesex side . . . standing still and looking at the water," and here declared his hopeless passion.

It was on the river here that *Our Mutual Friend* opens, with Gaffer Hexam plying his nefarious trade " between Southwark Bridge, which is of iron, and London Bridge, which is of stone."

This portion of the road reminds us of another personal touch. One day young Charles was taken ill at the Blacking Factory, so ill indeed that it was decided he must go home. Thus he records the incident :

" Bob (who was much bigger and older than I) did not like the idea of my going home alone, and took me under his protection. I was too proud to let him know about the prison ; and after making several efforts to get rid of him, to all of which Bob Fagin in his goodness was deaf, shook hands with him on the steps of a house near Southwark Bridge, on the Surrey side, making believe that I lived there. As a finishing piece of reality in case of him looking back, I knocked at the door, I recollect, and asked, when the woman opened it, if that was Mr. Robert Fagin's house."

A short way farther on we turn left into Marshalsea Road. Here, streets on the right and left are named Quilp Street, Dorrit Street, and Clenham (*sic*) Street. In Harrow Street, on the left, is all that remains of the Farm House—a notorious lodging-house visited by Dickens and Inspector Field, and close by is a children's playground named Little Dorrit's Playground, after the heroine of the book. Harrow Street on the right of Marshalsea Road leads into Lant Street.

"There's my lodgings," said Mr. Bob Sawyer, "Lant Street, Borough ! It's near Guy's—and handy for me, you know. Little distance after you've passed Saint George's Church—turns out of the High Street on the right-hand side of the way."

"There is a repose about Lant Street, in the Borough, which sheds a gentle melancholy upon the soul. There are always a good many houses to let in the street : it is a by-street, too, and its dulness is soothing. . . . If a man wished to abstract himself from the world—to remove himself from within the reach of temptation— to place himself beyond the possibility of any inducement to look out of the window—he should by all means go to Lant Street. . . .

"The majority of the inhabitants either direct their energies to the letting of furnished apartments, or devote themselves to the healthful and invigorating pursuit of mangling. The chief features in the still life of the street are green shutters, lodging-bills, brass door-plates, and bell-handles ; the principal specimens of animated nature, the pot-boy, the muffin youth, and the baked-potato man. The population is migratory, usually disappearing on the verge of quarter day, and generally by night. His Majesty's revenues are seldom collected in this happy valley ; the rents are dubious ; and the water communication is very frequently cut off."

To Dickens's personal connection with Lant Street
we have already referred. He further tells us that
" A bed and bedding were sent over for me, and made
up on the floor. The little window had a pleasant
prospect of a timber yard, and, when I took possession
of my new abode, I thought it was a Paradise."

Almost the same description is given of David
Copperfield's lodging when the Micawbers were in
the King's Bench, so there is no doubt about its also
being in Lant Street.

It was doubtless in Lant Street that Frederick
Dorrit lodged at Mr. Cripples's Academy, a house not
far from the Marshalsea, where there were so many
lodgers " that the door-post seemed to be as full of
bell-handles as a cathedral organ is of stops."

On reaching the main road we see St. George's
Church on the left. We shall return to the church
presently ; meanwhile our way lies to the right. At
the corner of the Borough Road, its site now occupied
by dwellings called Queen's Buildings, stood the
King's Bench Prison, where Micawber was incarcerated.
" The outside of the south wall of that place of incar-
ceration on civil process," at which Mr. Micawber
fixed an appointment with David and Traddles on a
later occasion, is now only a memory. All the incidents
Dickens records in his autobiographical fragment as
occurring to his own father in the Marshalsea are
transferred by him to Mr. Micawber and the King's
Bench Prison.

" The Rules " of King's Bench Prison, referred to
in *Nicholas Nickleby*, was a district about three miles in
circumference, which came as far south as the Borough
High Street. Here some of the more favoured debtors
lived. Here came Nicholas in search of Madeleine
Bray's father in " a row of mean and not over-cleanly
houses . . . not many hundred yards from the Obelisk
in Saint George's Fields." The obelisk—now outside

the Bethlem Hospital site—was replaced by an ornate clock tower some years ago ; here, it will be remembered, little David Copperfield lost his luggage and his half-guinea in starting out for his walk to Dover in search of his aunt (see page 159).

Opposite Borough Road is Union Road, where young John Chivery " assisted his mother in the conduct of a snug tobacco business, round the corner of Horsemonger Lane." Since the notorious gaol has given place to a recreation ground the name of the lane has been altered to Union Road. The little shop, the " rural establishment, one storey high, which had the benefit of the air from the yards of Horsemonger Lane Gaol and the advantage of a retired walk under the wall of that pleasant establishment," with a life-size Highlander " on a bracket on the door-post," looking " like a fallen cherub that had found it necessary to take a kilt," remained until 1930.

Dickens witnessed the last public hanging from the terrace opposite the prison, and wrote that impressive letter to *The Times* on the 13th November, 1849, concluding : " I do not believe that any community can prosper where such a scene of horror and demoralization, as was enacted this morning outside Horsemonger Lane Gaol, is presented at the very doors of good citizens, and is passed by unknown and forgotten."

" The Church of Saint George in the Borough of Southwark " is a well-known Dickens landmark ; chiefly is it endeared to us through its connection with Little Dorrit, who was born in the adjacent Marshalsea Prison, and " christened one Sunday afternoon, when the turnkey being relieved was off the lock . . . at the font of Saint George's Church," the said turnkey acting as sponsor. On the night of " Little Dorrit's Party " she and Maggie were locked out of the Marshalsea, and the sexton made up a bed for her in the vestry, where there was a fire " on account of the painters."

ST. GEORGE'S CHURCH, BOROUGH, SOUTHWARK
SHOWING SITE OF MARSHALSEA PRISON

Here, too, she was married ; and walking out of the church with her husband, Arthur Clennam, " they paused for a moment on the steps of the portico looking at the fresh perspective of the street in the autumn morning sun's bright rays, and then went down. Went down into a modest life of usefulness and happiness . . . into the roaring streets, inseparable and blessed."

There is another memory associated with St. George's Church ; it is also with Little Dorrit, for we read that her lover, John Chivery, after drawing tears from his eyes in silent thoughts of a lifelong union with Little Dorrit, was accustomed to " finish the picture with a tombstone in the adjoining churchyard, close against the prison wall," on which, following his own name, would be inscribed, " Also of his truly beloved and truly loving wife Amy . . . who breathed her last in the Marshalsea. . . . There she was born, there she lived, there she died."

After his momentous interview and declaration on Southwark Bridge, when he was delicately turned aside and asked never to refer to the matter again, we read of him creeping along by the worst back-streets and composing as he went a new inscription for a tombstone in St. George's Churchyard, declaring how he died " of a broken heart, requesting with his last breath that the word Amy might be inscribed over his ashes."

On the wall of the churchyard are two interesting tablets connecting Dickens with the spot, inscribed :

This Site was originally the
Marshalsea Prison,
made famous by the late
Charles Dickens,
in his well-known work,
" Little Dorrit "

Appropriately enough, these tablets are on the outer wall of the old Debtors' Prison, and the old buildings to the left are a portion of the quarters of the debtors, and associated in our minds with the room in which " The Child of the Marshalsea " was born. Thus does Dickens write of it in *Little Dorrit* :

" Thirty years ago there stood, a few doors short of the church of Saint George, in the borough of Southwark, on the left-hand side of the way going southward, the Marshalsea Prison. It had stood there many years before, and it remained there some years afterwards ; but it is gone now, and the world is none the worse without it.

" It was an oblong pile of barrack building, partitioned into squalid houses standing back to back so that there were no back rooms ; environed by a narrow paved yard, hemmed in by high walls duly spiked on top."

Turning into Borough High Street, we can find the other side of the wall by passing through Angel Court, to which Dickens refers in the preface to *Little Dorrit* :

" Wandering . . . down . . . Angel Court . . . I came to Marshalsea Place, the houses in which I recognised, not only as the great block of the former prison, but as preserving the rooms that arose in my mind's eye when I became Little Dorrit's bio-grapher. . . .

" Whosoever goes into Marshalsea Place, turning out of Angel Court leading to Bermondsey, will find his feet on the very paving stones of the extinct Marshalsea Gaol ; will see its narrow yard to the right, and to the left, very little altered, if at all, except that the walls were lowered when the place got free ; will look upon the rooms in which the debtors lived ; will stand among the crowding ghosts of many miserable years."

MARSHALSEA PRISON

RIGHT, MAIN PRISON BUILDINGS ; TABLET TO DICKENS ON WALL IN
FOREGROUND ; LEFT, THE TURNKEY'S HOUSE

So it was in 1857 ; there is very little change in
the place to-day : the printing works on the right
are actually in the rooms occupied by the debtors
of old ; except that the partitions have been removed,
to make the place more suitable for business purposes.

The Marshalsea also formed the subject of one
of the stories told in *Pickwick*, " The Old Man's
Tale about the Queer Client."

Here we find what is really a personal note,
one of the first uttered by Dickens on his connection
with the place : " It may be my fancy, or it may be
that I cannot separate the place from the old recollections associated with it, but this part of London I
cannot bear."

Forster tells us that, when Charles had his " little
paradise " in Lant Street, " he used to breakfast
' at home,' in other words, in the Marshalsea, going
to it as early as the gates were open, and for the most
part much earlier." The family were waited on by
the same little waiting-maid as they had had at
Camden Town ; she was the original of the Marchioness.
" She, too, had a lodging in the neighbourhood,"
continues Forster, " that she might be early on the
scene of her duties ; and when Charles met her, as he
would do occasionally, in his lodging-place by London
Bridge, he would occupy the time before the gates
opened by telling her quite astonishing fictions about
the wharves and the Tower. ' But I hope I believed
them myself,' he would say. Besides breakfast, he
had supper also in the Prison ; and got to his lodging
generally by nine o'clock. The gates closed always at
ten."

Returning to the Borough and walking towards
London Bridge, we are reminded how that " Mr.
'F.'s aunt, publicly seated on the steps of the Marshal's
official residence, had been for two or three hours a
great boon to the younger inhabitants of the Borough,

whose sallies of humour she had considerably flushed herself by resenting, at the point of her umbrella, from time to time."

We can picture, too, the pie-shop to which Flora took Little Dorrit and Mr. F.'s aunt, as an excuse for conversation, as being one of these old shops on the left-hand side. Flora proposed to Little Dorrit " an adjournment to any place . . . even if not a pie-shop . . . and a back parlour, though a civil man . . . your good nature might excuse under pretence of three kidney ones, the humble place of conversation . . .

" Flora accordingly led the way across the road to the pie-shop in question . . . when the three kidney ones were set before them on three little tin platters, each kidney one ornamented with a hole at the top into which the civil man poured hot gravy out of a spouted can."

In the account of Bob Sawyer's party at his lodgings in Lant Street, we are informed that the ham " was from the German-sausage shop round the corner." (May it not have been the very same pie-shop associated with Little Dorrit ?) And that " Mr. Bob Sawyer had himself purchased the spirits at a wine vaults in High Street, and had returned home preceding the bearer thereof to preclude the possibility of their delivery to the wrong house."

We can picture, too, Mr. Ben Allen, returning from seeing Mr. Pickwick on his way home after the party at Lant Street, " knocking double knocks at the door of the Borough Market Office," and taking " short naps on the steps alternately until daybreak, under the firm impression that he lived there and had forgotten the key."

Another link with the Borough is in the last chapter of *Barnaby Rudge*, where we are told that Gashford was found dead in his bed at an obscure inn in the Borough, where he was quite unknown.

But the glory of the Borough to-day is the quaint old George Inn, mentioned only once in Dickens (in *Little Dorrit*), but bringing back to us most vividly all the romance that is woven around the coaching inns of old ; the gallery, the court-yard, the tap-room, the bar, the coffee-room, all so delightfully reminiscent of so many descriptions Dickens has left us of a phase of life that is no more—and consequently invested with a halo.

The introduction of Sam Weller in *Pickwick* is thus heralded :

" In the Borough especially, there still remain some half-dozen old inns, which have preserved their external features unchanged. . . . Great rambling queer, old places they are, with galleries, and passages, and staircases, wide enough and antiquated enough to furnish material for a hundred ghost stories, supposing we should ever be reduced to the lamentable necessity of inventing any, and that the world should exist long enough to exhaust the innumerable veracious legends connected with old London Bridge, and its adjacent neighbourhood on the Surrey side.

" It was in the yard of one of these inns—of no less celebrated a one than the White Hart—that a man was busily employed in brushing the dirt off a pair of boots."

The " White Hart " exists in name only, a few doors beyond the George, whilst remains of the other old inns Dickens referred to in the above quotation are still to be seen in the Borough High Street, mostly in the shape of the inn yard and the old name.

St. Thomas's Street close by leads to Guy's Hospital, where Bob Sawyer was a medical student, " a carver and cutter of live people's bodies," as Mrs. Raddle called him.

Passing under the railway arch, we arrive on London Bridge.

The River Thames about London Bridge is often described by Dickens. *Our Mutual Friend* opens on it " as an autumn evening was closing in." In *Barnaby Rudge* we read that Mr. Haredale, when in hiding at his lodging in Vauxhall, " usually came to London Bridge from Westminster by water, in order that he might avoid the busy streets."

Betsey Trotwood " was quite gracious on the subject of the Thames," which, we are told, " really did look very well with the sun upon it, though not like the sea before the cottage." And in *Great Expectations* it figures in the exploit of Pip to get his benefactor safely aboard the Continental-bound steamer in the reaches below Gravesend.

In *Martin Chuzzlewit* Nadgett discloses that Jonas Chuzzlewit, after the murder, changed his clothes and came out of his house " with a bundle . . . and went down the steps at London Bridge and sank it in the river."

This no doubt occurred on the opposite side (the Middlesex side) to the well-remembered steps where Nancy made her disclosures to Rose Maylie and Mr. Brownlow. They were " those which, on the Surrey bank, and on the same side of the bridge as Saint Saviour's Church, form a landing-stairs from the river. . . . These stairs are a part of the bridge ; they consist of three flights. Just below the end of the second, going down, the stone wall on the left terminates in an ornamental pilaster facing towards the Thames. At this point the lower steps widen so that a person turning that angle of the wall is necessarily unseen by any others on the stairs who chance to be above him, if only a step."

Here it was that Noah Claypole hid, heard Nancy's story, and disclosed it to Fagin, resulting in Nancy's murder at the brutal hands of Sikes.

London Bridge itself, a favourite haunt of young

THE GEORGE INN, SOUTHWARK

Charles Dickens, as we have shown, often figures in the adventures of his later heroes ; and a crowd of characters cross this historic thoroughfare.

The elder Rudge crossed London Bridge for the City and Smithfield, after leaving the widow's house, which was " in a by-street in Southwark, not far from London Bridge."

Riah, the kind Jew, in *Our Mutual Friend*, " passed over London Bridge, and returned to the Middlesex shore by that of Westminster," recrossing it later the same evening with Jenny Wren. Pip crossed London Bridge in an agony after hearing that Estella was to be married to Bentley Drummle, to receive at Whitefriars Gate in the Temple Wemmick's laconic message, " Don't go home."

It was while accompanying the Pickwickians to London Bridge on their way home from Bob Sawyer's party that Mr. Ben Allen confided to Mr. Winkle that " he was resolved to cut the throat of any gentlemen, except Mr. Bob Sawyer, who should aspire to the affections of his sister Arabella."

David Copperfield made his first acquaintance with London Bridge in the company of Mr. Mell, who met him at the inn in Whitechapel where the Yarmouth coach stopped, and conveyed him to Salem House on Blackheath.

The almshouses they visited, when Mr. Mell played his flute to his old mother and Mrs. Fibbitson, were probably in the neighbourhood of the Borough, where several almshouses once existed. We are told that " by an inscription on a stone over the gate . . . they were established for twenty-five poor women."

A year or two later, when Mr. Micawber was in the Marshalsea, and David was working at the Bottle Factory, he tells us :

" My favourite lounging place was old London Bridge, where I was wont to sit in one of the stone recesses, watching the people going by, or to look over the balustrades at the sun shining in the water and lighting up the golden flame on the top of the Monument . . .

" As I walked to and fro daily between Southwark and Blackfriars, and lounged about at meal-times in obscure streets, the stones of which may, for anything I know, be worn at this moment by my childish feet. I wonder how many of these people were wanting in the crowd that used to come filing before me in review again. . . . When my thoughts go back now . . . I wonder how much of the histories I invented for such people hangs like a mist of fancy over well-remembered facts. When I tread the old ground, I do not wonder that I seem to see and pity going on before me an innocent, romantic boy, making his imaginative world out of such strange experience and sordid things."

Looking down the river, one of the many wharves beyond Tower Bridge may well be associated with Quilp's Wharf, which, we are told, was opposite his house on Tower Hill, " on the Surrey side of the river . . . a small, rat-infested, dreary yard . . . in which were a little wooden counting-house burrowing all awry in the dust."

This must have been quite near to Jacob's Island, where Bill Sikes met his terrible end. Here is Dickens's description from *Oliver Twist* :

" Near to that part of the Thames on which the church at Rotherhithe abuts . . . beyond Dockhead, in the Borough of Southwark, stands Jacob's Island, surrounded by a muddy ditch, six or eight feet deep and fifteen or twenty wide when the tide is in, once called Mill Pond, but known in these days as Folly Ditch. It is a creek or inlet from the Thames, and can always be filled at high water by opening the sluices at the lead mills, from which it took its name.

At such times, a stranger, looking from one of the wooden bridges thrown across it at Mill Lane, will see the inhabitants of the houses on either side lowering from their back doors and windows buckets, pails, domestic utensils of all kinds, in which to haul the water up."

The Dickens Estate now occupies the site of Eckell Street, where the reputed home of Sikes was situated.

On the City side of London Bridge we find, on the right, Fresh Wharf, undoubtedly the place where Mrs. Gamp was enquiring for "The Ankworks package," wishing it "was in Jonadge's belly."

The first turning on the right after the end of the bridge leads to Fish Street Hill, where David Copperfield on his return from abroad noticed an old house had been pulled down ; he had "walked from the Custom House to the Monument before finding a coach."

Here is the Monument, which, as Mr. F.'s aunt sagely remarks, "was put up arter the Great Fire of London . . . not the fire in which your Uncle George's workshops was burned down ! " This was the place of "no temptation" recommended by the elder Willet to his son, when he gave him "sixpence . . . to spend in the diversions of London"—the diversions he recommended being "to go to the top of the Monument and sitting there."

Tom Pinch came up from Salisbury, it will be remembered, lost his way and "found himself at last hard by the Monument," and discovered "the man in the Monument quite as mysterious a being as the man in the moon." That he was a cynic was evidenced by his remark after a customer had paid his humble "tanner" for admission :

"They don't know what a many steps there is. . . . It's worth twice the money to stop here. Oh my eye ! "

It has always been a regret that the "kind of

paved yard near the Monument," which sheltered
the commercial boarding-house of Mrs. Todgers
in *Martin Chuzzlewit*, has never been satisfactorily
identified, so that its site could be pointed out to
the pilgrim ! However Mrs. Gwen Major in *The
Dickensian* for September, 1932, made out a very good
case for the yard in Love Lane leading to what was
once known as Wren's House as the place Dickens
had in mind when he found a commercial boarding-
house for Mrs. Todgers.

" Surely there never was, in any other borough,
city or hamlet in the world, such a singular sort
of a place as Todgers's. And surely London, to
judge from that part of it which hemmed Todgers's
round, and hustled it, and crushed it, and stuck its
brick-and-water elbows into it, and kept the air
from it, and stood perpetually between it and the
light, was worthy of Todgers's, and qualified to be on
terms of close relationship and alliance with hundreds
and thousands of the odd family to which Todgers's
belonged. You couldn't walk about Todgers's neighbourhood as you could in any other neighbourhood.
You groped your way for an hour through lanes,
and by-ways, and court-yards, and passages ; and
you never once emerged upon anything that might
be reasonably called a street."

In Monument Yard, Mark Tapley met his old
neighbours from Eden in America and embraced
them affectionately and here Mr. Dorrit's solicitors
Peddle & Pool, are described as having their office.

SOMERSET HOUSE TO CAMDEN TOWN

IN our journey yesterday we dealt with the Strand generally; but there are one or two places we did not visit, so we will start to-day from Somerset House on our way northwards.

Dickens's father was a clerk at Somerset House at the same time as Thomas Barrow, whose sister he married in 1809 at St. Mary-le-Strand Church, almost opposite. Soon after this event he was transferred to Portsmouth, where his second child and first son, Charles, was born.

Mr. Minns, of Dickens's first story, *Mr. Minns and His Cousin*, was also a clerk at Somerset House.

A little beyond Somerset House is Strand Lane, where the Roman Bath, in which David Copperfield had many a cold plunge, is to be found.

Norfolk Street—entirely rebuilt—once sheltered Major Jackman at *Mrs. Lirriper's Lodgings*.

The Major it was who said, when taking the parlours, that there was " no smell of coal sacks," which drew forth from Mrs. Lirriper the scathing remark that she thought he was " referring to Arundel, or Surrey, or Howard, but not to Norfolk," indicating by that the streets adjacent.

Mrs. Lirriper was married at St. Clement Danes Church in the Strand close by.

At the corner of Arundel Street is Kelly's, on the site of the shop of Chapman & Hall, where Dickens purchased the magazine containing his first effort at fiction " in all the glory of print."

In Essex Street, Pip found for his uncle, Mr. Provis, *alias* Magwitch, " a respectable lodging-house, the back of which looked into the Temple " and was almost within hail of his own chamber in Garden Court (see page 16).

We now retrace our steps and cross to the Lyceum Theatre on the opposite side of the road.

The office of *Household Words* stood in Wellington Street, opposite the Lyceum Theatre, but the building was pulled down when Aldwych was constructed. At No. 26 (formerly 11) Wellington Street, was the office of *All the Year Round*. The building still stands. Here Dickens furnished bachelor chambers in his later years, for use during his London reading season.

As an *Uncommercial Traveller* in the fancy goods line, as he described himself, he always wrote as starting out from his rooms in Covent Garden.

Covent Garden had a great fascination for Dickens.

" To be taken out for a walk . . . especially if it were anywhere about Covent Garden or the Strand, perfectly entranced him with pleasure," says Forster.

Of his earliest researches into its deep mysteries Forster also tells us that when Dickens was living at Bayham Street he borrowed a copy of George Colman's " Broad Grins," which " seized his fancy very much ; and he was so impressed by its description of Covent Garden in the piece called the ' Elder Brother ' that he stole down to the market by himself to compare it with the book. He remembered, as he said in telling me this, snuffing up the flavour of the faded cabbage leaves, as if it were the very breath of comic fiction. Nor was he far wrong, as comic fiction then and for some time after was. It was reserved for himself to give sweeter and fresher breath to it."

" Mr. Minns occupied a first floor in Tavistock Street, Covent Garden, where he had resided for twenty years, having been in the habit of quarrelling with his landlord the whole time : regularly giving notice of his intention to quit on the first day of every quarter, and as regularly countermanding it on the second."

The Tavistock Hotel was formerly the Piazza Hotel (known as Cuttris's), where Dickens stayed in 1844 on coming to London from Italy specially to read *The Chimes* to a select circle of his friends. That he was familiar with the place is shown from a letter he wrote to Forster at the time saying, " I shall look for you at the further table by the fire, where we generally go." In *David Copperfield*, Steerforth anounced to David that he was going " to breakfast with one of those fellows who is at the Piazza Hotel in Covent Garden."

The other hotel in the Market was the Hummums Hotel at the corner of Russell Street. The present building dates from 1892 and occupies the site of the older hotel of that name. This or the Piazza was probably the hotel in Covent Garden where " the Finches of the Grove " used to meet in *Great Expectations*. When Pip received at the Temple Gate Wemmick's warning, " Don't go home," he " got a late hackney chariot and drove to the Hummums in Covent Garden, . . . in those times a bed was always to be got there at any hour of the night. . . . It was a sort of vault on the ground floor at the back, with a despotic monster of a four-post bedstead in it, straddling over the whole place, putting one of his arbitrary legs into the fire-place, and another into the doorway, and squeezing the wretched little washing-stand in quite a Divinely Righteous manner."

Being so much to the fore in Dickens's mind, it is hardly to be wondered at that Covent Garden Market should appear, one way or another, in nearly all his books. In *Sketches by Boz* there is an account of it at early morning in the article entitled *The Streets* ; in *Pickwick* we read of Job Trotter sleeping here " in a vegetable basket." In *Oliver Twist*, Sikes refers to it

8

as " Common Garden," where fifty boys could be found any night to pick from, so why " take so much pains about one chalk-faced kid ! "

In *The Old Curiosity Shop* there is a description of Covent Garden at sunrise " in the spring or summer, when the fragrance of sweet flowers is in the air." When David Copperfield had no money he used to stroll as far as Covent Garden Market and stare at the pineapples ; and, when he had money and gave his party, he bought his dessert there. When in love, he tells us, " at six in the morning I was in Covent Garden Market buying a bouquet for Dora." Still later he and his aunt had a temporary lodging in Covent Garden after vacating the two cottages at Highgate. Like David, Herbert Pocket, in *Great Expectations*, also went to Covent Garden Market for " a little fruit for after dinner, so as to get it good," as he thought Pip, having only just come up from the country, might thereby be pleased.

In *Our Mutual Friend*, we read how the drunken father of Jenny Wren " staggered into Covent Garden Market and there bivouacked to have an attack of the trembles, succeeded by an attack of the horrors, in the doorway."

Passing through Russell Street we reach Bow Street on the left. The Police Court of Dickens's day was on the left side, between Russell Street and Covent Garden Theatre.

The Artful Dodger was brought up at Bow Street Police Station, and hither Noah Claypole was conducted by Charley Bates, in order to hear the result of the court proceedings.

Opposite the present Police Court is Covent Garden Theatre, at which, in the days before *Pickwick*, Dickens aspired for an engagement ; he actually had an appointment with the stage manager which—perhaps fortunately for us—was never kept.

A further reference to this is made on page 23.

On two occasions in *David Copperfield* did the hero go to the theatre ; on the first, it was Covent Garden Theatre that he chose, " and there from the back of the centre box " he tells us he " saw Julius Caesar and the new pantomime." The second occasion was after his bachelors' party ; he does not name the theatre, not being in a condition to know, we suppose, but we can give a guess at its being Covent Garden.

The present building dates from 1858 ; the previous building was destroyed by fire two years previously.

Opposite the Theatre and by the side of the Police Court is Broad Court. Said Mr. Snevellici, in *Nicholas Nickleby*, " I am not ashamed of myself. Snevellicci is my name. I'm to be found in Broad Court, Bow Street, when I'm in town. If I'm not at home, let any man ask for me at the stage door."

At the end of Bow Street, Long Acre runs right and left. Dick Swiveller was accustomed to get his meals and articles of attire on credit. " I enter in this little book," he explained, " the names of the streets than I can't go down while the shops are open. This dinner to-day closes Long Acre. I bought a pair of boots in Great Queen Street last week, and made that no thoroughfare too. There's only one avenue to the Strand left open now, and I shall have to stop up that to-night with a pair of gloves. The roads are closing so fast in every direction that, in about a month's time, unless my aunt sends me a remittance, I shall have to go three or four miles out of town to get over the way."

On the site now occupied by No. 92 Long Acre formerly stood St. Martin's Hall, where Dickens gave his first series of paid readings in 1858. It was burnt down in 1860, rebuilt, and later reconstructed as the Queen's Theatre. It was converted into a warehouse in about 1880.

Returning along Bow Street to Russell Street, we turn to the left and find Drury Lane Theatre on the right at the corner of Catherine Street and Russell Street.

Miss Petowker, of the Vincent Crummles Company, was described as " of the Theatre Royal, Drury Lane," and in *Pickwick* we read Smangle's description of Mr. Mivens as a man with " comic powers that would do honour to Drury Lane Theatre."

Dickens himself tells us that the father of Poll Green, one of his companions at the Blacking Warehouse " had the additional distinction of being a fireman, and was employed at Drury Lane Theatre, where another relation of Poll's, I think his little sister, did imps in the pantomimes."

Crown Court on the left leads to a playing ground called Drury Lane Gardens, the original of Poor Jo's churchyard where Captain Hawdon was buried. It was described as " a hemmed-in churchyard, pestiferous and obscene, whence malignant diseases are communicated to the bodies of our dear brothers and sisters who have not departed ; while our dear brothers and sisters who hang about official backstairs —would to Heaven they *had* departed !—are very complacent and agreeable."

To the gate with the lamp over it came Lady Dedlock to be shown by poor Jo the last resting-place of " Nemo," and here, later, Esther found her mother dead upon the step.

It is thought probable that Dickens had in mind the neighbourhood of Drury Lane when he described Tom-all-alone's in *Bleak House*, although Field Lane, off Holborn (see page 31), may have stood for it, as Phiz's drawing shows a church like St. Andrew's, Holborn, in the background.

" It is a black, dilapidated street," says Dickens, " avoided by all decent people ; where the crazy

houses were seized upon, when their decay was far
advanced, by some bold vagrants, who, after estab-
lishing their own possession, took to letting them out
in lodgings."

To Drury Lane itself there are several references
in *Sketches by Boz*, " and in the neighbourhood of
Drury Lane," we read in the *Old Curiosity Shop*, were
the apartments of Dick Swiveller, which, " in addition
to this conveniency of situation, had the advantage
of being over a tobacconist's shop, so that he was
enabled to procure a refreshing sneeze at any time
by merely stepping out on the staircase, and was saved
the trouble and expense of maintaining a snuff-box."

Both David Copperfield and the young Dickens
knew this district intimately. In *David Copperfield* we
read : " Once, I remember, carrying my own bread
(which I had brought from home in the morning)
under my arm, wrapped in a piece of paper, like
a book, and going to a famous alamode beef house
near Drury Lane, and ordering a ' small plate ' of
that delicacy to eat with it. What the waiter thought
of such a strange little apparition coming in all alone,
I don't know ; but I can see him now, staring at me
as I ate my dinner, and bringing up the other waiter
to look. I gave him a halfpenny for himself, and I
wish he hadn't taken it."

In the fragment of autobiography published in
Forster's Life of Dickens, which Dickens used almost
word for word in the early chapters of *David Copperfield*, the exact site of the " alamode beef house "
is given as Clare Court. Clare Court was cleared away
in 1905 for the Aldwych improvement ; Kean Street,
Drury Lane, marks its site.

Russell Street leads into Drury Lane itself and
. here we turn to the left, passing the end of Long
Acre, and then reach Great Queen Street on the
right. On the right of Great Queen Street is the

Freemason's Tavern, referred to in *Sketches by Boz*
and later the scene of the farewell dinner given to
Dickens in 1867, on the eve of his departure to America,
when Lord Lytton was in the chair.

A little farther along Drury Lane, Short's Gardens
on the left takes us across Endell Street and Neal
Street to the spot known as Seven Dials, where seven
roads converge. The place is entirely altered since
the days of Dickens, when even as a boy he was so
much attracted to it. Forster tells us " he had a
profound attraction of repulsion to St. Giles's. If
he could only induce whosoever took him out to take
him through Seven Dials, he was supremely happy.
' Good Heaven ! ' he would exclaim, ' what wild
visions of prodigies of wickedness, want and beggary,
arose in my mind out of that place ! ' "

A whole chapter in *Sketches by Boz* is devoted to
this district ; " Where is there such another maze
of streets, courts, lanes and alleys ? " he asks ; and,
although Shaftesbury Avenue demolished many of
these courts and lanes, the district is still an unsavoury
one. In *Nicholas Nickleby*, too, we are introduced to
" that labyrinth of streets which lies between Seven
Dials and Soho," and to the cellar of a house where
Nicholas and Kate discovered Mr. Mantalini goaded
by his nagging companion to turn the mangle. " I
am perpetually turning like a demn'd old horse in a
demnition mill. My life is one demn'd horrid grind ! "

Through St. Andrew's Street on the right we
reach the top end of Shaftesbury Avenue, which
demolished Monmouth Street, " the only true and
real emporium of second-hand wearing apparel,"
which formed the subject of another chapter in
Sketches by Boz. High Street goes off to the left and
takes us past St. Giles's Church and into New Oxford
Street, where we turn to the right ; and at the fork
we leave the main road running to Holborn and keep

to the left along Hart Street, passing St. George's Church, where *The Bloomsbury Christening* took place (*Sketches by Boz*). Bury Street to the left leads into Great Russell Street and the British Museum, where Dickens as a young man was an assiduous attendant at its reading-room. At No. 14 Great Russell Street, Mr. Charles Kitterbell lived, as described in the above-mentioned story.

We turn to the right along Great Russell Street, and then left into Southampton Row. The first on the right leads into Great Ormond Street ; here is situated the Hospital for Sick Children, where Little Johnny died with a kiss for the " boofer Lady."

Before writing *Our Mutual Friend*, Dickens had taken a personal interest in this hospital, and in 1858 took the chair at a dinner held on its behalf, at which he made an eloquent appeal for funds. Forster in his Life of Dickens has recorded the incident in full.

As a result the sum of three thousand pounds was raised that night, and a short time afterwards Dickens gave a reading of the *Carol* on its behalf, the great success of which led him to commence the series of Public Readings he continued so successfully both in this country and in America until his death.

The next turning on the right in Southampton Row is Guilford Street, where until 1929 stood the Foundling Hospital to which Dickens often referred.

Tattycoram in *Little Dorrit* came from the Foundling Hospital, and the story of *No Thoroughfare* opens there with a very dramatic scene in which the mother prevails upon one of the servants to point out her son.

Returning to Southampton Row, we turn to the right at the Hotel Russell to Woburn Place, referred to in *Sketches of Young Gentlemen* : " We were to make for Chigwell . . . and to start from the residence of the projectors, Woburn Place, Russell Square."

Keeping along Woburn Place we reach on the right Coram Street, down which we shall turn, but on the left, a little farther on, it may be noted, is Tavistock Square, in which was once situated Tavistock House, where Dickens lived for nearly ten years, from 1851, leaving it for Gad's Hill Place. The offices of the British Medical Association now occupy the site.

Coram Street was formerly Great Coram Street, and is described in *The Boarding House* as " somewhere in that partially explored tract of country which lies between the British Museum and a remote village called Somers Town. . . . The house of Mrs. Tibbs was, decidedly, the neatest in all Great Coram Street. The area and the area-steps, and the street-door and the street-door steps, and the brass handle, and the door-plate and the knocker, and the fan-light, were all as clean and bright as indefatigable white-washing, and hearth-stoning, and scrubbing and rubbing, could make them. The wonder was, that the brass door-plate, with the interesting inscription ' Mrs. TIBBS,' had never caught fire from constant friction, so perseveringly was it polished. There were meat-safe-looking blinds, in the parlour-windows, blue and gold curtains in the drawing-room, and spring-roller blinds, as Mrs. Tibbs was wont in the pride of her heart to boast, ' all the way up.' "

From Coram Street we turn left along Hunter Street, which continues into Judd Street, and at No. 78 on the right is Cromer Street, where at No. 116 we find the Boot Tavern—on the site of the old " Boot " of *Barnaby Rudge*, described as " a lone house of public entertainment, situated in the fields at the back of the Foundling Hospital ; a very solitary spot at that period, and quite deserted after dark. The tavern stood at some distance from any high road, and was approachable only by a dark and narrow lane."

Returning to Judd Street we keep to the right

and emerge in the Euston Road, where we turn left. Euston Station is almost opposite.

Although Dickens was of the railway era, and wrote of the iron horse, yet he never did so with the same charm as when writing of the horse of flesh and blood. Euston, King's Cross and Camden Town were the great termini that Dickens saw under construction, and we shall give a brief glance at some of his remarks on railways from *Dombey and Son* (in which Carker is killed on the railway) and *Miscellaneous Papers*, whilst traversing a district that was also very intimately associated with his boyhood.

Passing in front of Euston Station in a westerly direction we soon reach, on the left, Gower Street, where on the site of Maple's premises formerly stood No. 4 Gower Street North, where the Dickens family lived for a short time in 1824. They had been in the Bayham Street house just a year, and no school had been found for Charles ; the family were in difficulties and removed to Gower Street, where the mother tried to start a young ladies' school, just as Mrs. Micawber did years after. Forster describes the position for us very clearly :

" A house was soon found at No. 4, Gower Street North ; a large brass plate on the door announced Mrs. Dickens's establishment and the result I can give in the exact words of the then small actor in the comedy whose hopes it had raised so high : ' I left, at a great many other doors, a great many circulars calling attention to the merits of the establishment. Yet nobody ever came to the school, nor do I recollect that anybody ever proposed to come, or that the least preparation was made to receive anybody. But I know that we got on very badly with the butcher and baker ; that very often we had not too much for dinner ; and that at last my father was arrested.' "

On the right of Euston Road, opposite Gower

Street, is George Street, on the right of which and leading to Euston Station is Drummond Street, where, at No. 47, "the mistaken milliner," Miss Marton, lived. Keeping straight ahead along George Street we arrive in Hampstead Road ; opposite is the Sol's Arms, reminiscent of a house of that name in Chancery Lane, mentioned in *Bleak House* (see, page 10). As this is the only Sol's Arms in London Dickens, no doubt, transferred the name from the Hampstead Road to Chancery Lane.

Turning to the right in Hampstead Road we pass on the left at the corner of Granby Street the house at which Dickens went to school after his father had come out of the Marshalsea Prison and brighter days shone on the family. It was called Wellington House Academy, and, except that the railway has cut off a portion of the building, it is the same as it was a century ago. Dickens himself has left the record that he "went as day scholar to Mr. Jones's establishment, which was in Mornington Place, and had its schoolroom sliced away by the Birmingham Railway, when that change came about. The schoolroom, however, was not threatened by directors or civil engineers then, and there was a board over the door graced with the words, Wellington House Academy."

Writing later in *Reprinted Pieces*, he further tells us : " We went to look at the place only this last midsummer, and found that the railway had cut it up, root and branch. A great trunk line had swallowed the playground, sliced away the schoolroom, and pared off the corner of the house, which, thus curtailed of its proportions, presented itself in a green stage of stucco, profile-wise towards the road, like a forlorn flat-iron without a handle, standing on end."

A little past Granby Street we take the turning on the right, into Harrington Square and keeping straight on reach Seymour Street on the right. Turning along her find on the left Johnson Street. At No. 29 now 13, and marked with a tablet of the London County Council, Dickens lived in 1825, while at Wellington House Academy.

Johnson Street is in the district of Somers Town, where Snawley, the accomplice of Squeers, lived in " a little house one storey high, with green shutters." Mr. Squeers took lodgings here because the Saracen's Head at Snow Hill, where he usually stopped, " having experience of Master Wackford's appetite," had declined to receive him on any other terms than as a full-grown customer. At Seymour Street Chapel Dickens used to attend service, and in connection with Drummond Street, a turning out of Seymour Street, we have the following personal recollection of Dr. Dawson, one of his schoolfellows :

" I quite remember Dickens on one occasion heading us in Drummond Street in pretending to be poor boys, and asking the passers-by for charity— especially old ladies ; one of whom told us ' she had no money for beggar boys.' On these adventures, when the old ladies were quite staggered by the impudence of the demand, Dickens would explode with laughter and take to his heels."

Before reaching Drummond Street, we turn left along Charles Street to Clarendon Square, where formerly stood a little group of houses called the Polygon. Here the Dickens family lived in 1827–8, probably as lodgers. In *Bleak House* we read that Harold Skimpole " lived in a place called the Polygon, in Somers Town, where there were at that time a number of poor Spanish refugees, walking about in cloaks, smoking little paper cigars . . . It was in a state of dilapidation quite equal to our expectation. Two or three of the area railings were gone ; the water-butt was broken ; the knocker was loose ; the

bell-handle had been pulled off a long time, to judge
from the rusty state of the wire ; and dirty footprints
on the steps were the only signs of its being inhabited."

If we continue along the side of the Square to
Phœnix Street we reach Pancras Road, cross into
Battle Bridge Road, and so come into York Road.

The railway cut up this district in Dickens's day,
and even lately further changes have been made.

What we now know as King's Cross was prior
to 1830 called Battle Bridge, and it is indelibly associated in our minds with the Harmon mounds, which
are so prominent a feature of *Our Mutual Friend.*
" I live over Maiden Lane way," Mr. Boffin explained
to Silas Wegg, " out Holloway direction. Where I
live is called the Bower. Boffin's Bower is the name
Mrs. Boffin christened it when we came into it as a
property. If you should meet with anybody that
don't know it by that name (which hardly anybody
does), when you've got nigh upon about a odd mile,
or say and a quarter, if you like, up Maiden Lane,
Battle Bridge, ask for Harmony Jail, and you'll be
put right."

Maiden Lane is now known as York Road. The
dust-heaps were a reality and many such did exist
to the south of King's Cross Station, where the Gray's
Inn Road begins.

R. Wilfer, in the same book, also lived in this
neighbourhood. " His home was in the Holloway
region north of London, and then divided from it
by fields and trees. Between Battle Bridge and that
part of the Holloway district in which he dwelt was
a tract of suburban Sahara, where tiles and bricks
were burnt, bones were boiled, carpets were beat,
rubbish was shot, dogs were fought, and dust was
heaped by contractors. . . ."

Mrs. Wilfer, like Mrs. Dickens and Mrs. Micawber,
had essayed fortune in a Ladies' School, and Mrs.

Wilfer's was no more successful ; and the man who had supplied the brass plate, seeing he had no expectation of ever being paid for it, " came himself with a pair of pincers, took it off and took it away."

The Cattle Market partly covers the tea gardens of Copenhagen House, mentioned in the *Sketches*.

Turning to the right at the end of York Road we pass in front of King's Cross Station and bear round along Pancras Road. On the right is old St. Pancras Church, where Roger Cly was buried, as described in *A Tale of Two Cities*. Here Jerry Cruncher and his son came later " fishing," as Jerry called it—but with a spade : in other words " body snatching."

Farther along Pancras Road is Great College Street, where we find the Veterinary Hospital. This corner is a *Pickwick* landmark, being referred to in the " Tale of the Queer Client." " They met on the appointed night, and, hiring a hackney coach, directed the driver to stop at that corner of the Old Pancras Road at which stands the parish workhouse. By the time they alighted there it was quite dark ; and, proceeding by the dead wall in front of the Veterinary Hospital, they entered a small by-street, which is, or was at that time, called Little College Street, and which, whatever it may be now, was in those days a desolate place enough, surrounded by little else than fields and ditches."

Little College Street, mentioned above, is now College Place. To reach it we take the second turning on the left in Great College Street, Pratt Street, and College Place is the first on the left.

Here Dickens lodged for a while after the family left the Gower Street house and the father and mother were in the Marshalsea for debt. In his own words Dickens tells the story :

" I was handed over as a lodger to a reduced old lady, long known to our family, in Little College

Street, Camden Town, who took children in to board, and had once done so at Brighton ; and who, with a few alterations and embellishments, unconsciously began to sit for Mrs. Pipchin in *Dombey* when she took in me.

" She had a little brother and sister under her care then ; somebody's natural children, who were very irregularly paid for ; and a widow's little son. The two boys and I slept in the same room. My own exclusive breakfast, of a penny cottage loaf and a pennyworth of milk, I provided for myself. I kept another small loaf, and a quarter of a pound of cheese on a particular shelf of a particular cupboard, to make my supper on when I came back at night. They made a hole in the six or seven shillings, I know well ; and I was out at the blacking-warehouse all day, and had to support myself upon that money all the week. I suppose my lodging was paid for by my father. I certainly did not pay it myself ; and I certainly had no other assistance whatever (the making of my clothes, I think, excepted) from Monday morning until Saturday night. No advice, no counsel, no encouragement, no consolation, no support, from anyone that I can call to mind, so help me God."

Continuing along Pratt Street we reach Bayham Street and turn to the right, passing the almshouses mentioned below. The Dickens family lived for a year (1823) in Bayham Street on first coming to London, at No. 16 (renumbered 141) and demolished in 1910. The Bayham Street days had sad memories for Dickens, for he had left a kindly schoolmaster at Chatham ; and so far no school had been found for him in London.

Bob Cratchit lived in Camden Town, and it is thought probable that Dickens had in his mind his Bayham Street home when he wrote of the Cratchits' home in the *Carol*. It was doubtless in Bayham

Street that Traddles lodged with Micawber, at a house that was " only a storey high above the ground floor." It was " in a little street near the Veterinary College at Camden Town, which was principally tenanted, as one of our clerks who lived in that direction informed me, by gentlemen students, who bought live donkeys, and made experiments on those quadrupeds in their private apartments. . . . I found that the street was not as desirable a one as I could have wished it to be for the sake of Traddles. The inhabitants appeared to have a propensity to throw any little trifles they were not in want of into the road ; which not only made it rank and sloppy, but untidy, too, on account of the cabbage-leaves. The refuse was not wholly vegetable either, for I myself saw a shoe, a doubled-up saucepan, a black bonnet, and an umbrella, in various stages of decomposition, as I was looking out for the number I wanted."

Here the Micawbers, like the Dickenses, had an execution put into their house for rent.

It is only natural that Camden Town should often find mention in the writings of Dickens and there are many scattered references—mostly uncomplimentary.

The building of the London and Birmingham Railway, Euston Station, and the goods yards at Camden, prompted Dickens to go into detail on the matter in *Dombey and Son*, where he introduces us to the Toodles family at Staggs's Gardens. " This euphonious locality was situated in a suburb known by the inhabitants of Staggs's Gardens by the name of Camberling Town ; a designation which the stranger's map of London . . . condenses, with some show of reason, into Camden Town. . . . The first shock of a great earthquake had, just at that period, rent the whole neighbourhood to its centre. . . . Houses were knocked down ; streets broken through and stopped ; deep pits and trenches dug in the ground . . . in short, the yet unfinished and unopened railroad was in progress. . . . But as yet the neighbourhood was shy to own the railroad."

At a later date, when Walter Gay went to find Polly Toodles in Staggs's Gardens, to bring some consolation to the dying Paul, he found a great change in the place :

" There was no such place as Staggs's Gardens. It had vanished from the earth. Where the old rotten summer-houses once had stood, palaces now reared their heads, and granite columns of gigantic girth opened a vista to the railway world beyond. The miserable waste ground, where the refuse matter had been heaped of yore, was swallowed up and gone ; and in its frowsy stead were tiers of warehouses, crammed with rich goods and costly merchandise. The old by-streets now swarmed with passengers and vehicles of every kind ; the new streets that had stopped disheartened in the mud and waggon-ruts formed towns within themselves, originating wholesome comforts and conveniences belonging to themselves, and never tried nor thought of until they sprang into existence."

A few years after the publication of *Dombey and Son*, Dickens wrote an article entitled *An Unsettled Neighbourhood* (reprinted in *Miscellaneous Papers*) showing how " the railroad has done it all," and that since the railroad came " it has ever since been unable to settle down to any one thing, and will never settle down again." His reason for all the unrest in the district—which is plainly the Euston-Camden Town district—is the one word Luggage. " I have come to the conclusion," he says, " that the moment Luggage begins to be always shooting about a neighbourhood . . . everybody wants to be off somewhere . . . everybody has the strongest ideas of its being vaguely his or her business to ' go down the line.' "

EASTWARD UNCOMMERCIALLY, WITH AN EXTENSION TO CHIGWELL

THE East End of London was by no means neglected by Dickens. Early visits to his godfather in Limehouse doubtless afforded him material for the descriptions of the Docks and the River generally in *Dombey and Son* and *Great Expectations*, and whilst writing *Edwin Drood* he paid more than one visit to the opium dens in Shadwell.

The Pickwickians set off for Ipswich from the Bull Inn in Whitechapel, and David Copperfield on his first visit to London arrived at the " Blue Boar " there. Young Joe Willet, up to pay the vintner, had his meals arranged for at the " Black Lion " ; so here at least are a variety of hostelries in the great eastern thoroughfare whose names have been handed down to immortality through their connections with Dickens.

However it is from his walks described in *The Uncommercial Traveller* papers that the personal connection of the East End with Dickens is best obtained, as our references throughout this ramble will amply illustrate. In the third paper of the series, he tells us how he wended his way eastwards. " My day's no-business," he writes, " beckoning me to the East End of London, I had turned my face to that point of the metropolitan compass on leaving Covent Garden, and had got past the India House, thinking in my idle manner of Tippoo Sahib and Charles Lamb, and had got past .my little wooden midshipman, after affectionately patting him on one leg of his knee-shorts for old acquaintance' sake, and had got past Aldgate Pump, and had got past the Saracen's Head (with an ignominous rash of posting bills disfiguring his swarthy countenance), and had strolled up the empty yard of his ancient neighbour, the Black or Blue Boar or Bull, who departed this life I don't know when, and whose coaches are all gone I don't know where."

Our starting point is Aldgate Pump, at the junction of Fenchurch Street with Leadenhall Street, already visited on our second day (see page 48).

In one of his early Boz *Sketches* Dickens refers to shabby gentility being " as purely local as . . . the pump at Aldgate."

In *Dombey and Son*, when Toots could not bear to see the happiness of Florence and Walter, we read, " Well might Mr. Toots leave the little company that evening . . . to take a little turn to Aldgate Pump and back " ; and the mad old man who lived next door to the Nicklebys at Bow referred to " the statue at Charing Cross having been lately seen on the Stock Exchange at midnight walking arm in arm with the Pump from Aldgate, in a riding habit."

Of Aldgate itself Mr. Blotton (of the Pickwick Club) was a worthy inhabitant, and in *Barnaby Rudge* is an account of the initiation to the secret society of the Prentice Knights of "Mark Gilbert—bound to Thomas Curzon, Hozier, Golden Fleece, Aldgate."

Saracen's Head Yard, at No. 92 Fenchurch Street, nearly opposite the Pump, marks the site of the inn referred to above. The " Little Wooden Midshipman " which was formerly in Leadenhall Street (see page 47) is now to be seen at No. 123 Minories, the turning opposite Houndsditch Church.

America Square, which turns out of John Street on the right of Minories, is referred to in *A Message from the Sea*, as the place of business of Dringworth Brothers.

St. Botolph Church at the corner of Houndsditch, where Cruncher " received the added appellation of

Jerry," was to Dickens the dividing line between East
and West, for we read in *The Uncommercial Traveller* :
" A single stride at Houndsditch Church . . . a single
stride, and everything is entirely changed in grain
and character. West of the stride, a table or a chest
of drawers on sale shall be of mahogany and French-
polished ; East of the stride, it shall be of deal, smeared
with a cheap counterfeit resembling lip-salve. West
of the stride, a penny loaf or bun shall be compact
and self-contained ; East of the stride it shall be of
a sprawling and splay-footed character, as seeking
to make more of itself for the money."

The Bull Inn stood until 1868 on the spot now
occupied by Aldgate Avenue. " I shall work down
to Ipswich the day after to-morrow, sir," said Mr.
Weller the elder, " from the Bull in Whitechapel ;
and, if you really mean to go, you'd better go with me."
Which advice Mr. Pickwick took, and " away went
the coach up Whitechapel, to the admiration of the
whole population of that pretty densely populated
quarter."

Near to the " Bull " was the " Blue Boar," at
which young David Copperfield arrived from Blunder-
stone *en route* for Salem House. " I forget," he says,
" whether it was the ' Blue Bull,' or the ' Blue Boar,'
but I know it was the Blue something, and that its
likeness was painted up on the back of the coach."
The effigy of the " Blue Boar " is retained by the
tobacco factory at No. 31 Aldgate High Street, on
the left-hand side.

Commercial Road, a little farther along on the
right, reminds us that, " on a dead wall in the Commercial Road," Captain Cuttle bought the " ballad
of considerable antiquity . . . which set forth the
courtship and nuptials of a promising young coal-
whipper with a certain ' lovely Peg.' "

Our way is along the road opposite Commercial

Road, called Commercial Street. The route followed will bring us out again in the Whitechapel Road, half a mile farther on.

"On a July morning of this summer, I walked towards Commercial Street (not Uncommercial Street), Whitechapel," writes Dickens. " I had been attracted by the following handbill printed on rose-coloured paper : Self-Supporting Cooking Depot for the Working Classes, Commercial Street, Whitechapel, where accommodation is provided for dining comfortably 300 persons at a time. Open from 7 a.m. till 7 p.m."

The building referred to, a house of refreshment no longer, stands at the corner of Flower and Dean Street, the third street on the right. Here it was Dickens sampled the excellent fare provided at a cost of 4½d., and, says, " I dined at my Club in Pall Mall a few days afterwards for exactly twelve times the money and not half so well."

Continuing along Commercial Street, we take the fourth on the right, Hanbury Street. This presently crosses Brick Lane. At No. 160 is a Mission Hall, generally accepted as the original of the famous one in *Pickwick*, where " the monthly meetings of the Brick Lane Branch of the United Grand Junction Ebenezer Temperance Association were held in a large room, pleasantly and airily situated at the top of a safe and commodious ladder . . . Previous to the commencement of business, the ladies sat upon forms, and drank tea, till such time as they considered it expedient to leave off ; and a large wooden money-box was conspicuously placed upon the green baize cloth of the business table, behind which the secretary stood, and acknowledged, with a gracious smile, every addition to the rich vein of copper which lay concealed within."

Continuing along Hanbury Street, we reach Vallence Road, where, turning to the left, we find on the right

Whitechapel Workhouse, the subject of a deeply sympathetic paper entitled *A Nightly Scene in London* in *Miscellaneous Papers*.

Returning, Vallence Road leads us into Whitechapel Road about half a mile farther on from the spot where we turned off into Commercial Street. We turn to the left for the Mile End Road and Bow. If, however, instead of returning into the Whitechapel Road, we proceeded to the other end of Commercial Street, we should reach Shoreditch. We read, in *Oliver Twist*, that Sikes and Oliver, *en route* for the burglary at Chertsey, "threaded the streets between Shoreditch and Smithfield."

Nearly opposite Shoreditch Church is the Olympia Cinema, formerly the Standard Theatre, to which reference is made in *Amusements of the People*, in *Miscellaneous Papers*. Behind this theatre is Hoxton Street, in which is situated the Britannia Theatre, which received the praise of Dickens for its great work, particularly for its religious services on a Sunday.

To the right of Shoreditch High Street runs Bethnal Green Road, traversed by Oliver Twist and Bill Sikes on the way to the burglary at Chertsey : "By the time they had turned into the Bethnal Green Road, the day had fairly begun to break."

At the eastern end of this is Bethnal Green, whither Eugene and Mortimer lured the schoolmaster in *Our Mutual Friend*. " ' There is a rather difficult country about Bethnal Green,' said Eugene. ' And we have not taken in that direction lately. What is your opinion of Bethnal Green ? ' Mortimer assented to Bethnal Green and they turned eastward."

Returning to Whitechapel Road by way of Vallence Road described above, we turn to the left on reaching the main road. On the right is the London Hospital, where, " in the open street just opposite the Hospital,"

Brass informed Dick Swiveller : " Sally found you a
second-hand stool, sir, yesterday evening. She's a rare
fellow at a bargain. . . ."

In *Barnaby Rudge* we find several references to
Whitechapel. Lord George Gordon, after leaving
the " Maypole," rode " the whole length of Whitechapel, Leadenhall Street, Cheapside into St. Paul's
Churchyard " ; and at the Black Lion Inn—whose
yard is still to be seen at No. 75 Whitechapel Road—
Joe Willet had his meals ordered for him and was
recommended by his father not to score up too large
a bill there, much to Joe's annoyance.

We have an amusing account of Whitechapel in
Pickwick, when Sam remarked " Not a wery nice
neighbourhood this. . . . It's a wery remarkable
circumstance, sir, that poverty and oysters always
seems to go together. . . . Look here, sir ; here's a
oyster stall to every half-dozen houses—the street's
lined vith 'em. Blessed if I don't think that ven a
man's wery poor he rushes out of his lodgings and eats
oysters in reg'lar desperation." Just beyond Whitechapel Station we reach Mile End Gate—but the gate
itself has long since disappeared ; although the Gate
House stood until a later date.

The road now becomes the Mile End Road.

In *Bleak House*, we read of Mrs. Jellyby " having
gone to Mile End directly after breakfast, on some
Borrioboolan business " ; and, during the Riots in
Barnaby Rudge, the party from Chigwell, on coming
to Mile End, " passed a house the master of which,
a Catholic gentleman of small means, having hired
a wagon to remove his furniture by midnight, had it
all brought down into the street to wait the vehicle's
arrival, and save time in packing."

On the left we find the Trinity Almshouses, and a
little farther on the Vintners' Almshouses ; these latter
no doubt the original of Titbull's Almshouses in

The Uncommercial Traveller. " Titbull's Almshouses are in the east of London, in a great highway, in a poor, busy and thronged neighbourhood Old iron and fried fish, cough drops and artificial flowers, boiled pigs' feet and household furniture that looks as if it were polished up with lip-salve, umbrellas full of vocal literature and saucers full of shell-fish in a green juice which I hope is natural to them when their health is good, garnish the paved sideways as you go to Titbull's. I take the ground to have risen in those parts since Titbull's time, and you drop into his domain by three stone steps. So did I first drop into it, very nearly striking my brows against Titbull's pump, which stands with its back to the thoroughfare just inside the gate, and has a conceited air of reviewing Titbull's pensioners."

On the right of Mile End Road is Stepney Green, to which Silas Wegg referred when he asked, " Would Stepney Fields be considered intrusive ? If not remote enough, I can go remoter."

The Mile End Road continues as Bow Road and leads to Bow, which was " quite a rustic place to Tim Linkinwater."

The " little cottage at Bow," let to the Nicklebys at a very low rental by the kind-hearted Cheeryble Brothers, was no doubt situated near the present Grove Hall Park off the Fairfield Road by Bow Station : the park is on the site of Grove Hall Asylum in which the " gentleman next door " was doubtless an inmate.

At this point we can take a 'bus to Chigwell, an account of which is given at the end of this Chapter.

If we return along the Bow Road to Mile End Station we can get a 'bus through Burdett Road into West India Dock Road and along the docks. Somewhere in the region of the West India Docks must have been Brig Place, where Captain Cuttle lodged at No. 9 with Mrs. MacStinger.

"Captain Cuttle lived on the brink of a little canal near the India Docks, where there was a swivel bridge which opened now and then to let some wandering monster of a ship come roaming up the street like a stranded leviathan. The gradual change from land to water, on the approach to Captain Cuttle's lodgings, was curious. It began with the erection of flagstaffs, as appurtenances to public-houses ; then came slopsellers' shops, with Guernsey shirts, sou'-wester hats, and canvas pantaloons, at once the tightest and loosest of their order, hanging up outside. These were succeeded by anchor and chain-cable forges, where sledge-hammers were dinging upon iron all day long. Then came rows of houses, with little vane-surmounted masts uprearing themselves from among the scarlet beans. Then ditches. Then pollard willows. Then more ditches. Then unaccountable patches of dirty water, hardly to be descried for the ships that covered them. Then the air was perfumed with chips ; and all other trades were swallowed up in mast, oar, and block-making, and boat-building. Then the ground grew marshy and unsettled. Then there was nothing to be smelt but rum and sugar. Then Captain Cuttle's lodgings— at once a first floor and a top storey, in Brig Place— were close before you."

The river beyond West India Docks leads to Greenwich (page 162). "The house with the low window being by the river-side down the pool then between Limehouse and Greenwich," at which the convict Magwitch was temporarily lodged by Pip and Herbert in *Great Expectations*, has not been identified : we should search in vain for either the Old Green Copper Rope-Walk, or Chink's Basin, or Mill Pond Bank. Mr. W. Laurence Gadd thinks that these places are to be found on the Surrey side, where there is a Mill Pond at Rotherhithe.

" It was," we read, " a fresh kind of place, all circumstances considered, where the wind from the river had room to turn itself round ; and there were two or three trees in it, and there was the stump of a ruined windmill, and there was the Old Green Copper Rope-Walk, whose long and narrow vista I could trace in the moonlight, along a series of wooden frames set in the ground, that looked like super-annuated haymaking rakes which had grown old and lost most of their teeth.

" Selecting from the few queer houses upon Mill Pond Bank a house with a wooden front and three stories of bow-window (not bay-window, which is another thing) I looked at the plate upon the door, and read there Mrs. Whimple."

We are now in the Borough of Poplar, where lived William Ravender (*Wreck of the Golden Mary*).

Returning along West India Dock Road we find, on our left, Limehouse Church, where " Miss Abbey Potterson, of the ' Six Jolly Fellowship Porters,' had been christened some sixty and odd years before."

John Harmon described this as the spot where he waited for his assailant. " I disembarked with my valise in my hand—as Potterson the steward, and Mr. Jacob Kibble, my fellow-passenger, afterwards remembered—and waited for him in the dark by that very Limehouse Church which is now behind me."

Of a visit to a lead mills " close to Limehouse, Church," Dickens devotes a chapter of *The Uncommercial Traveller*, under the title of *On an Amateur Beat*.

The next turning past the church on the left is Church Row. Here at No. 5 lived Christopher Huffam, a " rigger in His Majesty's Navy," godfather to Dickens, whose full name was Charles John Huffham

Dickens (Huffham incorrectly so spelled in the church register).

Church Row leads to Ropemakers' Fields and the river : bearing to the right we are in the riverside street called Narrow Street, where the Grapes Inn, at No. 76, is said to be the original of " The Six Jolly Fellowship Porters " of *Our Mutual Friend* : " A red-curtained tavern, that stood dropsically bulging over the causeway."

" In its whole constitution," we are told, " it had not a straight floor, and hardly a straight line ; but it had outlasted, and clearly would yet outlast, many a better-trimmed building, many a sprucer publichouse. Externally, it was a narrow lopsided wooden jumble of corpulent windows heaped one upon another as you might heap as many toppling oranges with a crazy wooden verandah impending over the water ; indeed the whole house, inclusive of the complaining flagstaff on the roof, impended over the water, but seemed to have got into the condition of a faint-hearted diver who has paused so long on the brink that he will never go in at all. . . .

" The bar of the ' Six Jolly Fellowship Porters ' was a bar to soften the human breast. The available space in it was not much larger than a hackney coach ; but no one could have wished the bar bigger, that space was so girt in by corpulent little casks, and by cordial-bottles radiant with fictitious grapes in bunches, and by lemons in nets, and by biscuits in baskets, and by the polite beer-pulls that made low bows when customers were served with beer, and by the cheese in a snug corner, and by the landlady's own small table in a snugger corner near the fire, with the cloth everlastingly laid. This haven was divided from the rough world by a glass partition and a half-door with a leaden sill upon it for the convenience of resting your liquor.

" For the rest, both the tap and parlour of the ' Six Jolly Fellowship Porters ' gave upon the river, and had red curtains matching the noses of the regular customers."

Rogue Riderhood " dwelt deep and dark in Limehouse Hole, among the riggers, and the mast, oar and block-makers, and the boat-builders, and the sail-lofts. . . . It was a wretched little shop, with a roof that any man standing in it could touch with his hand ; little better than a cellar or cave, down three steps."

The home of Lizzie Hexam was also in this neighbourhood ; a low building which " had the look of having once been a mill. There was a rotten wart of wood upon its forehead which seemed to indicate where the sails had been."

At the end of Narrow Street the road turns right, and then left into Broad Street.

In Glamis Road to the right is the fairly modern building of the East London Hospital for Children, which has grown from the tiny place at Ratcliff Cross, visited and described by Dickens in a paper entitled *The Small Star in the East.*

" I found the children's hospital established in an old sail-loft or storehouse, of the roughest nature, and on the simplest means. There were trap-doors in the floors, where goods had been hoisted up and down ; heavy feet and heavy weights had started every knot in the well-trodden planking ; inconvenient bulks and beams and awkward staircases perplexed my passage through the wards. But I found it airy, sweet, and clean."

We return to High Street, Shadwell, the region of the opium den of *Edwin Drood*, whither came John Jasper. " Eastward and still eastward through the stale streets he takes his way, until he reaches his destination, a miserable court, specially miserable among many such."

Dickens paid a visit to an opium den in Shadwell, in company with his American friend, J. T. Fields, and wrote, a month before he died : " The opium smoking I have described, I saw (exactly as I have described it, penny ink bottle and all) down in Shadwell this last autumn. A couple of the Inspectors of Lodging Houses knew the woman and took me to her as I was making a round with them to see for myself the working of Lord Shaftesbury's Bill."

The den was probably situated in New Court, Victoria Street, E., to the right of St. George's Street, close to the church, on the site of which a playground now stands.

J. T. Fields has thus put the visit on record :

" In a miserable court, at night, we found a haggard old woman blowing at a kind of pipe made of an old ink bottle ; and the words that Dickens puts into the mouth of this wretched creature in *Edwin Drood* we heard her croon as we leaned over the tattered bed in which she was lying."

St. George's Street was in Dickens's day known as Ratcliff Highway. It is described in *Sketches by Boz* ; and Ratcliff is referred to in *Oliver Twist* as a " remote but genteel suburb."

On our left we pass Old Gravel Lane and reach the bridge once called " Mr. Baker's trap " on account of the number of suicides taking place there. Dickens describes it in *The Uncommercial Traveller.*

This road now takes us through the heart of the London Docks, but we look in vain for " Number Thirty, Little Gosling Street, London Docks," where Mr. F. breathed his last, as described by Flora in *Little Dorrit.*

This way, we remember, came Mortimer Lightwood in search of news of John Harmon. " The wheels rolled on . . . by the Tower, and by the Docks ; down by Ratcliff and by Rotherhithe " : and a

particularly interesting description of the district is to
be found in chapter twenty of *The Uncommercial Traveller*.

Old Gravel Lane continued straight on leads to
Wapping, where, in *Barnaby Rudge*, we read that the
rioters " were bound for Wapping to destroy a chapel."

Dickens visited the workhouse at Wapping to make
personal enquiries on an important question, " because
an Eastern police magistrate had said, through the
morning papers, that there was no classification at the
Wapping Workhouse for women, and that it was a
disgrace and a shame, and divers other hard names,
and because I wished to see how the fact really stood " ;
and on the way he makes a reference to an ancient
landmark in this neighbourhood, Wapping Old Stairs,
which is reached by turning to the right along High
Street at the end of Gravel Lane.

" I at last began to file off to the right, towards
Wapping. Not that I intended to take boat at
Wapping Old Stairs, or that I was going to look at
the locality because I believe (for I don't) in the con-
stancy of the young woman who told her sea-going
lover, to such a beautiful old tune, that she had ever
continued the same, since she gave him the 'baccer-
box marked with his name ; I am afraid he usually
got the worst of those transactions, and was frightfully
taken in."

Farther on, on the right, Nightingale Lane takes
us back again into a continuation of St. George's
Street called Upper East Smithfield and leading by
the left to the Tower (see page 51). We turn
right, and shortly afterwards to the left along Well
Street, following the footsteps of young Dickens as
narrated in *Gone Astray* :

" I must have strayed by that time, as I recall my
course, into Goodman's Fields, or somewhere thereabouts. The picture represented a scene in a then
performing at a theatre in that neighbourhood which

is no longer in existence. It stimulated me to go to that theatre and see that play. . . . I found out the theatre. . . . Of its external appearance, I can only remember the loyal initials G.R. untidily painted in yellow ochre on the front."

The theatre in Goodman's Fields (where Garrick made his first London appearance) disappeared in 1802, so the one Dickens refers to was no doubt that in Well Street called The Royalty or East London Theatre, burnt down in April, 1826. The site is now occupied by a Sailors' Home.

To the right of Well Street is Wellclose Square, where in the same adventure he " found a watchman in his box ; . . . this venerable man took me to the nearest watch-house . . . a warm and drowsy sort of place embellished with great-coats and rattles hanging up."

The other end of Well Street brings us to Cable Street, where we turn to the left, and then right, along Leman Street. The streets to the left cover the site of Goodman's Fields, referred to above.

At the end of Leman Street we are in Whitechapel High Street once again and turn left for Aldgate and the Bank.

CHIGWELL

" Chigwell, my dear fellow, is the greatest place in the world. Name your day for going. Such a delicious old Inn, opposite the Church-yard—such a lovely ride —such beautiful forest scenery—such an out of the way, rural, place—such a sexton ! I say again name your day."

Such was the invitation given by Dickens to John Forster in a letter dated 25th March, 1841.

" The day was named at once," says Forster, " and

the whitest of stones marks it, in now sorrowful memory. Dickens's promise was exceeded by our enjoyment ; and his delight in the double recognition of himself and of Barnaby, by the Landlord of the nice old Inn, far exceeded any pride he would have taken in what the world thinks the highest sort of honour."

Although Chigwell is only a dozen miles from London, it has so far escaped the ruthless hand of the builder, and presents all the rural charms of a village in the heart of the country.

It is doubtful if Dickens has endeared us more to any inn than he has to The Maypole at Chigwell in *Barnaby Rudge* ; how alluring is his description, at the very outset of the story, of the " house of public entertainment called the Maypole " that, " in the year 1775 . . . stood upon the borders of Epping Forest, at a distance of about twelve miles from London " with its " emblem reared on the roadside over against the house " ; how attractive are the characters we first meet round the blazing fire ; old John Willet, the landlord, with his staring, stolid face ; little Soloman Daisy " the parish clerk and bell-ringer of Chigwell : a village hard by " and the teller of " the famous Maypole story " ; " short Tom Cobb, the general chandler " ; and " long Phil Parkes, the ranger."

" The Maypole was an old building," he writes, " with more gable ends than a lazy man would care to count on a sunny day ; huge zig-zag chimneys, out of which it seemed as though even smoke could not choose but come in more than naturally fantastic shapes, imparted to it in its tortuous progress : and vast stables, gloomy, ruinous, and empty. . . . The Maypole was really an old house, a very old house, perhaps as old as it claimed to be, and perhaps older, which will sometimes happen with houses of an uncertain, as with ladies of a certain age. Its windows were old diamond-pane lattices, its floors were sunken and uneven, its ceilings blackened by the hand of time, and heavy with massive beams. Over the doorway was an ancient porch, quaintly and grotesquely carved ; and here on summer evenings the more favoured customers smoked and drank—ay, and sang many a good song too, sometimes—reposing on two grim-looking high-backed settles, which, like the twin dragons of some fairy tale, guarded the entrance to the mansion. . . . With its overhanging stories, drowsy little panes of glass, and front bulging out and projecting over the pathway, the old house looked as if it were nodding in its sleep. Indeed, it needed no very great stretch of fancy to detect in it other resemblances to humanity. The bricks of which it was built had originally been a deep dark red, but had grown yellow and discoloured like an old man's skin ; the sturdy timbers had decayed like teeth ; and here and there the ivy, like a warm garment to comfort it in its age, wrapt its green leaves closely round the time-worn walls."

The exterior of the King's Head presents the very quaint appearance so very aptly described by Dickens, and the solitude of its surroundings is an enhancement to its picturesqueness.

If, from the interior, we miss the kitchen with its cosy chimney corner which was so alluring to Gabriel Varden that, rather than break his promise to his wife by looking in, he very often went out of his way to avoid the Maypole on his way home from the Warren, we have the pleasure of taking our refreshment in the Chest Room—the " best apartment, spacious enough in all conscience, occupying the whole depth of the house, and having at either end a great bay window, as large as many modern rooms . . . although the best room in the Inn, it had the melancholy aspect of grandeur in decay and was much too

THE MAYPOLE INN, CHIGWELL

vast for comfort," and of reviewing there all the coming
and goings at the Maypole described in the story.

The whole story of *Barnaby Rudge* centres round the
Maypole, and Dickens describes it fully both inside
and out, with the little exaggeration that is the writer's
license. It is somewhat remarkable therefore that
Dickens should have chosen to give it a fictitious name,
for there is no Maypole at Chigwell, the only inn there
being the King's Head, the name it has borne for over
a couple of centuries. There is, however, at Chigwell
Row, which is referred to by Solomon Daisy in his
story, as being a mile and half away, a Maypole Inn
whose name may possibly have suggested itself to
Dickens as a more suitable one for his story.

Mr. A. T. Wintersgill in an article in the Spring
Number of *The Dickensian* for 1927 points out that at
the time Dickens and Forster visited the King's Head,
the three gabled portion which is now the principal
part of the inn was a private house, and that the inn
itself was the remaining portion of the present building,
now no longer used for that purpose.

Mr. Wintersgill is also of opinion that Dickens was
actually referring to the Maypole Inn at Chigwell
Row, which still stands—as a cottage—at the rear of
the modern public-house of that name.

Mr. Haredale's house, the Warren, figures largely
in the story and was ultimately destroyed by the rioters.

It is described as "The old red brick house that
stands in its own grounds and that fifteen or twenty
years ago stood in a park five times as broad, which
with other and richer property has bit by bit changed
hands and dwindled away—more's the pity !

" It was a dreary, silent building, with echoing
courtyards, desolated turret-chambers, and whole
suites of rooms shut up and mouldering to ruin.

" The terrace-garden, dark with the shades of overhanging trees, had an air of melancholy that was quite

10

oppressive. Great iron gates, disused for many years, and red with rust, drooping on their hinges and overgrown with long rank grass, seemed as though they tried to sink into the ground, and hide their fallen state among the friendly weeds. The fantastic monsters on the walls, green with age and damp, and covered here and there with moss, looked grim and desolate. There was a sombre aspect even on that part of the mansion which was inhabited and kept in good repair, that struck the beholder with a sense of sadness ; of something forlorn and failing, whence cheerfulness was banished. It would have been difficult to imagine a bright fire blazing in the dull and darkened rooms, or to picture any gaiety of heart or revelry that the frowning walls shut in."

There is no such thing in the district to-day ; nor have we been able to trace one in Dickens's day to answer the description ; but there was a Warren House in existence in 1770, about a mile away from the church, the residence of Sir Peter Warren, M.P. for Westminster, and Dickens may have heard of it. He usually called it the Warren, but in chapter thirty-four it is referred to as Warren House.

HYDE PARK CORNER AND WESTMINSTER TO GREENWICH, AND A FEW OUTLYING LANDMARKS IN THE SOUTH AND WEST

BEFORE we commence our journey to-day, which will first take us along Piccadilly, let us give a glance at a few places in the Belgravia district which we have not already been able to touch upon.

Lady Tippins, "that charmer," in *Our Mutual Friend* dwelt "over a staymaker's in the Belgravian Borders, with a life-size model in the window on the ground floor of a distinguished beauty in a blue petticoat, stay-lace in hand, looking over her shoulder at the town in innocent surprise. As well she may, to find herself dressing under the circumstances."

In an article in *Reprinted Pieces* entitled *Out of Town*, Dickens tells how in Belgrave Square he met " the last man—an ostler—sitting on a post in a ragged red waistcoat, eating straw and mildewing away."

Cadogan Place, Sloane Street," was the address of Mrs. Wititterly in *Nicholas Nickleby*.

" Cadogan Place is the one slight bond that joins two great extremes ; it is the connecting link between the aristocratic pavements of Belgrave Square and the barbarism of Chelsea. It is in Sloane Street, but not of it. The people in Cadogan Place look down upon Sloane Street, and think Brompton low. They affect fashion too, and wonder where the New Road is. Not that they claim to be on precisely the same footing as the high folks of Belgrave Square and Grosvenor Place, but that they stand, with reference to them, rather in the light of those illegitimate children of the great who are content to boast of their connections, although their connections disavow them."

"The long rows of lamps in Piccadilly after dark are beautiful" said Henrietta in *Somebody's Luggage*; and the same remark holds good to-day. The pavement-artist in that story did not wish his loved one to go to Piccadilly so shy was he of his work which was to be found on the "fine broad eligible piece of pavement" by the railings of the Green Park.

Piccadilly was once chosen by Mr. Micawber in one of his flights of fancy as "a very suitable place of residence—a cheerful situation for Mrs. Micawber"!

Near the corner of Dover Street is the White Horse Cellar. The present building dates from 1884 only, but the old coaching inn of that name stood here before then, after it had been removed from the opposite side of the way, where it stood in Pickwick's day at the corner of Arlington Street on the site now occupied by the Ritz Hotel.

Here Mr. Pickwick and Sam Weller took the coach for Bath, at which time Sam made the discovery that the coach was owned by a Moses Pickwick, which was a fact, Moses Pickwick being a well-known coach proprietor of Bath.

When Esther Summerson arrived in London, the coach had the White Horse Cellar as its destination. Here she was met by Mr. Guppy, "a young gentleman who had inked himself by accident," and conducted to Kenge & Carboy's in Lincoln's Inn.

Farther along Devonshire House marks the site of the former home of the Duke of Devonshire, where in 1851 Dickens acted before Queen Victoria in Lytton's comedy "Not so bad as we seem"—the prelude to some "splendid strolling" by Dickens and his friends for the noble cause of charity.

The Piccadilly Hotel stands on the site of the St. James's Hall, where Dickens gave his last reading in March 1870.

We cross Piccadilly here and turn back towards Hyde Park. At St. James's Church, Alfred Lammle was married to Sophronia, as so delightfully described in *Our Mutual Friend*.

A little farther on, at No. 193, is the site of the publishing office once occupied by Chapman & Hall, which saw the issuing of all Dickens's books from 1859. The next turning but one is St. James's Street ; some chambers at the corner here were the scene of the *Two Ghost Stories* : at No. 50 St. James's Street was the famous club Crockford's, mentioned in *Nicholas Nickleby*.

Ryder Street on the left leads into Duke Street, the abode of Twemlow, in *Our Mutual Friend* the "innocent piece of dinner-furniture that went upon easy castors and was kept over a livery stable yard in Duke Street, Saint James's, when not in use."

Near Pall Mall "in a first floor over a tailor's" were the West End offices of "The Anglo-Bengalee Disinterested Loan and Life Assurance Company," and, in Pall Mall itself, Tigg Montague lived in a house the lower storey of which "was occupied by a wealthy tradesman, but Mr. Montague had all the upper portion, and a splendid lodging it was."

In Chapter 28 of *Martin Chuzzlewit* there is an interesting account of how Mr. Bailey Junior drove Tigg Montague's cab, "tempting boys, with friendly words, to get up behind, and immediately afterwards cutting them down ; and the like flashes of a cheerful humour, which he would occasionally relieve by going round St. James's Square at a hard gallop, and coming slowly into Pall Mall by another entry, as if, in the interval, his pace had been a perfect crawl."

In Pall Mall, too, Chops the dwarf, when "going into Society," had his lodgings, and "blazed away" the lottery fortune.

At the corner of Waterloo Place is the Athenæum Club, to which Dickens was elected in 1838. The lobby is memorable as the scene of the reconcilation between Dickens and Thackeray a few days before the latter's death. Meeting by accident in the lobby, after a period of strained relationship, " the unrestrained impulse of both was to hold out the hand of forgiveness and fellowship."

Down the steps at Waterloo Place leads us to St. James's Park, where Mark Tapley arranged for an interview between young Martin Chuzzlewit and Mary Graham ; the Park was also the scene of a long conversation between Clennam, Meagles and Daniel Doyce, the latter having been lately met at the Circumlocution Office in Whitehall.

In dealing with the ultimate fate of Sally Brass in *The Old Curiosity Shop*, Dickens says it was "darkly whispered that she had enlisted as a private . . . and had been seen in uniform, and on duty, to wit, leaning on her musket and looking out of a sentry box in St. James's Park."

Keeping to the left we leave the Park by the Horse Guards, viewing as we pass, like Mr. Dick and Peggotty, the soldiers there. In the conclusion of *Barnaby Rudge* we are told that Sim Tappertit, " on two wooden legs, shorn of his graceful limbs," was by the locksmith's aid " established in business as a shoeblack and opened a shop under an archway near the Horse Guards."

We now turn right along Whitehall, passing on the left the old Palace of Whitehall itself, which caused Mr. Jingle to remark, " Looking at Whitehall, sir—fine place—little window—somebody else's head off there—eh, sir ? " referring of course to the execution of King Charles.

At Whitehall, John Rokesmith stopped to read the placard posted there notifying that he himself had been " found dead and mutilated in the river under circumstances of strong suspicion." Whitehall is so full of Government Offices that we may take any one of them as being the Circumlocution Office to which

Arthur Clennam went so often to interview the various members of the Tite Barnacle family.

Scotland Yard on the left is altogether changed from the time when Dickens described it in *Sketches by Boz* as being occupied by "a race of strong and bulky men" engaged in unloading coal from the adjacent wharves.

At the corner of Derby Street is the Red Lion—rebuilt in 1899—associated with Dickens as a boy. He tells us how one evening in walking to the Borough via Westminster Bridge he "went into a public-house in Parliament Street, which is still there, though altered, at the corner of the short street leading to Cannon Row and ordered a glass of ale, ' the *very best* . . . with a good head to it. . . .' They asked me a good many questions as to what my name was, how old I was, where I lived, how I was employed, etc., etc. To all of which, that I might commit nobody, I invented appropriate answers. They served me with the ale, though I suspect it was not the strongest on the premises ; and the landlord's wife . . . bending down, gave me a kiss."

This story has its counterpart in *David Copperfield*, when he asked for the glass of the " Genuine Stunning."

At the end of Parliament Street we reach the Houses of Parliament, to the right of which is Westminster Hall.

In the preface to *The Pickwick Papers*, Dickens tells us how, when his first literary effusion " appeared in all the glory of print " he walked down to Westminster Hall and turned into it for half an hour because his eyes were " so dimmed with joy and pride that they could not bear the street and were not fit to be seen there."

It was here that a dramatic scene in *Barnaby Rudge* was enacted, when Mr. Haredale, after an angry meeting with Sir John Chester and Gashford, chided Lord George Gordon for " addressing an ignorant and exciting throng . . . in such injurious language," inciting them to riot and rebellion. Later, Lord George Gordon was tried here for high treason and found not guilty ; but his fate was to die in a Newgate cell some years later at the early age of forty-three.

In a building to the north of the old Hall the Law Courts were held until 1883, when the new buildings in Fleet Street were opened, and here the final scenes of the *cause célèbre* Jarndyce *v.* Jarndyce were enacted. The opening scenes in *Bleak House* dealing with this case were, of course, at Lincoln's Inn Hall (page 10), where the Lord Chancellor sat out of term time " in the heart of the fog." In the same book we read that during the long vacation when " the public offices lie in a hot sleep, Westminster Hall itself is a shady solitude where nightingales might sing, and a tenderer class of suitors than is usually found there walk."

Behind Westminster Hall rise the Houses of Parliament—but not the buildings of *Barnaby Rudge* time, where Lord George Gordon presented his famous No-Popery Petition. The present buildings were erected 1840–1857 after the old Parliament House was burnt down in 1834. Dickens entered the House as a reporter in 1831 and left it in 1836. Frequent references to the House of Commons and its Members are made in Dickens's books, particularly in the *Miscellaneous Papers*.

Westminster Abbey enshrines the body of Charles Dickens.

The stone placed upon the grave is inscribed ;

CHARLES DICKENS.
BORN FEBRUARY THE SEVENTH, 1812.
DIED JUNE THE NINTH, 1870.

Facing the grave, on its left and right, are the monuments of CHAUCER, SHAKESPEARE, and DRYDEN, "the three immortals who did most to create and settle the language to which CHARLES DICKENS has given another undying name." (*Forster.*)

A somewhat prophetic reference is made in *Little Dorrit* :

" Time shall show us. The post of honour and the post of shame . . . a peer's statue in Westminster Abbey, and a seaman's hammock in the bosom of the deep . . . only Time shall show us whither each traveller is bound."

In *Our Mutual Friend* we read that " Some waterside heads . . . harboured muddled notions that, because of her dignity and firmness," Miss Abbey Potterson who kept the Six Jolly Fellowship Porters at Limehouse, " was named after, or in some way related to, the Abbey at Westminster."

In *Great Expectations*, Pip and Herbert went to morning service at Westminster Abbey, and in the afternoon walked in the Parks, when Pip wondered who shod all the horses, and wished Joe did !

When David Copperfield and Peggotty, in the hope of news of Little Em'ly, followed Martha from Blackfriars to Millbank, " Westminster Abbey was the point at which she passed from the lights and noise of the leading streets."

They passed Old Palace Yard—but the Exchequer Coffee House there, at which Mr. Julius Handford was staying, according to the information he gave Mr. Inspector in *Our Mutual Friend*, was a myth—like his own name—for there is no trace of any such place. They continued along " the narrow water-side street by Millbank " ; Grosvenor Road is entirely different to-day from what it was then, and the Tate Gallery now occupies the site of the old Millbank Prison.

" There was, and is when I write, at the end of that low-lying street, a dilapidated little wooden building, probably an obsolete old ferry-house. Its position is just at that point where the street ceases and the road begins to lie between a row of houses and the river. As soon as she came here, and saw the water, she stopped as if she had come to her destination ; and presently went slowly along by the brink of the river, looking intently at it."

At Vauxhall, reached by crossing the bridge just beyond the Tate Gallery, Mr. Haredale took lodgings " in which to pass the day and rest himself ; and from this place, when the tide served, he usually came to London Bridge from Westminster by water, in order that he might avoid the busy streets."

Henrietta and the Pavement Artist, already referred to, used to walk on Vauxhall Bridge (the old one— not the present structure) and enjoy the cool breezes. On one occcasion, " after several slow turns, Henrietta gaped frequently, so inseparable from woman is the love of excitement, and said, ' Let's go home by Grosvenor Place, Piccadilly, and Waterloo '—localities, I may state for the information of the stranger and the foreigner, well known in London, and the last a bridge."

Bradley Headstone after meeting Lizzie Hexam at the house of the Dolls' Dressmaker—to which we refer later—crossed Vauxhall Bridge for South London, he " giving her his hand at parting and she thanking him for his care of her brother."

Vauxhall Station across the Bridge is opposite the site of Vauxhall Gardens ; one of the *Sketches by Boz* gives an account of these Gardens by day—" a thing hardly to be thought of ! " Vauxhall by daylight he likens to " a porter pot without porter, the House of Commons without the Speaker, a gas lamp without the gas." Yet what an amusing account Dickens makes of it !

Retracing our steps past the Tate Gallery and past Lambeth Bridge, we reach on the left at No. 48 Millbank, Dean Stanley Street, formerly known as Church Street, Smith Square. The Dolls' Dressmaker lived with her drunken father, her " bad boy," near " a certain little street, called Church Street, and a certain little blind square, called Smith Square, in the centre of which last retreat is a very hideous church, with four towers at the four corners, generally resembling some petrified monster, frightful and gigantic on its back with its legs in the air." The church still remains, but the " tree near by in a corner, and a blacksmith's forge, and a timber yard, and a dealer's in old iron " are things of the past. Jenny Wren's house was " at the point where the street and the square joined, and where there were some little quiet houses in a row."

Of the " hideous church," Jenny Wren told her visitors, " There's doors under the church in the square—black doors, leading into black vaults. Well, I'd open one of these doors and I'd cram 'em all in, and then I'd lock the door, and through the keyhole I'd blow in pepper."

Returning to Westminster Abbey, we turn to the right to cross Westminster Bridge. On the Embankment at the foot of the bridge is Westminster Station on the Underground, occupying the site of Manchester Buildings fully described in *Nicholas Nickleby* where Mr. Gregsbury, M.P., lived, to whom Nicholas applied for a situation.

The present Westminster Bridge was built in 1862. It replaced the older bridge which had existed for over a century, from which Barnaby and his mother saw the first rising of the Gordon Riots as " they sat down in one of the recesses of the bridge to rest."

Here Barnaby was spoken to by Lord George Gordon and enlisted in the cause, passing over the bridge, along the Bridge Road and so to St. George's Fields (page 159).

Later, when Barnaby and Hugh were rowing down the river under the bridge " they plainly heard the people cheering ; and, supposing they might have forced the soldiers to retreat, lay upon their oars for a few minutes, uncertain whether to return or not. But the crowd passing along Westminster Bridge soon assured them that the populace were dispersing."

Although properly speaking the Dover Road commences at the Surrey side of London Bridge and traverses the Borough (page 101) it is not incorrect to measure it over Westminster Bridge, the way some of the very earliest stage-coaches made the journey, according to an advertisement of 1751. That was the way the Pickwickians went to Rochester from the Golden Cross at Charing Cross in 1827. Mr. Peggotty on his first return to London after his search for Little Em'ly found " a traveller's lodging on the Dover Road," and David accompanied him over Westminster Bridge and parted from him on the Surrey side ; and, in the various ruses employed by Pip in *Great Expectations* to hide the tracks of his Uncle Provis, it was given out on one occasion that he had gone to Dover, for which purpose " he was taken down the Dover Road and cornered out of it." But what is undoubtedly the greatest memory associating itself with the Dover Road is that of little David's walk to his aunt's at Dover, when after being robbed at the outset of his luggage and his money, he was compelled to tramp the whole seventy odd miles of the road.

" There's milestones on the Dover Road," said Mr. F.'s aunt and Dickens must have known most of them intimately, for Rochester is on the Dover Road, and near by is Gad's Hill, his home for so many years ; and he often tramped the twenty-eight odd miles between London and Gad's Hill.

Dickens's earliest recollections of the Dover Road appear in the paper entitled *Dullborough Town*, in which he recalls leaving Chatham for London at the age of eleven. " As I left Dullborough in the days when there were no railroads in the land," he writes, " I left it in a state coach . . . melodiously called Timpson's Blue-eyed Maid. . . . Timpson's was a moderate sized coach office (in fact, a little coach office) with an oval transparency in the window, which looked beautiful by night, representing one of Timpson's coaches in the act of passing a milestone on the London road with great velocity."

In the concluding part of *The Seven Poor Travellers*, we get another personal touch. " As for me, I was going to walk by Cobham Woods, as far upon my way to London as I fancied. . . . Christmas begirt me, far and near, until I had come to Blackheath, and had walked down the long vista of gnarled old trees in Greenwich Park, and was being steam rattled through the mists now closing in once more, towards the lights of London."

Then, in *Travelling Abroad*, he writes enthusiastically of the joy of the road, recalling, as it does, so many historic associations. " Over the road where the old Romans used to march, over the road where the old Canterbury pilgrims used to go, over the road where the travelling trains of the old imperious priests and princes used to jingle on horseback between the Continent and this Island through the mud and water, over the road where Shakespeare hummed to himself, " Blow, blow, thou winter wind," as he sat in the saddle at the gate of the inn yard noticing the carriers ; all among the cherry orchards, apple orchards, corn-fields and hop-gardens ; . . . by Canterbury to Dover."

The progress along the Dover Road of the Dorrit Family on one of the occasions when they left London for the Continent after coming into their riches, is thus recorded :

" Next morning's sun saw Mr. Dorrit's equipage upon the Dover Road, where every red jacketed postillion was the sign of a cruel house, established for the unmerciful plundering of travellers. The whole business of the human race between London and Dover being spoliation, Mr. Dorrit was waylaid at Dartford, pillaged at Gravesend, rifled at Rochester, fleeced at Sittingbourne, and sacked at Canterbury."

Crossing Westminster Bridge we find ourselves in Westminster Bridge Road. Numbers 225/33 mark the site of Astley's, and with it go memories of the visit paid by Kit and his mother, and Barbara and her mother, to say nothing of little Jacob, so humorously described in *The Old Curiosity Shop*.

Hard by must have been the oyster shop into which, after the performance, Kit walked " as bold as if he lived there, and, not so much as looking at the counter or the man behind it, led his party into a box—a private box, fitted up with red curtains, white table-cloth, and cruet-stand complete—and ordered a fierce gentleman with whiskers, who acted as waiter and called him, him Christopher Nubbles, ' sir ' to bring three dozen of his largest-sized oysters, and to look sharp about it ! "

In *Bleak House* we read of Trooper George paying a visit to Astley's, and " being there, is much delighted with the horses and the feats of strength ; looks at the weapons with a critical eye ; disapproves of the combats, as giving evidences of unskilful swordsmanship ; but is touched home by the sentiments."

Through York Road on the left, we reach Waterloo Road. At the corner on the right is Waterloo Station mentioned more than once in *Our Mutual Friend*—one of the few books in which Dickens even mentions railways ! Passing under the railway arch we reach New Cut and Lambeth Marsh with the " Old Vic " on the left. This district is referred to more than once in *Sketches by Boz* and *The Amusements of the People* in *Miscellaneous Papers*.

It was in " a mean house situated in an obscure street, or rather court, near Lambeth " that Squeers rented a garret in the same house as Peg Sliderskew, and here his plans were thwarted by Nicholas and Newman Noggs.

Waterloo Road ends at St. George's Circus ; to

the right runs Lambeth Road ; a short way down on the left is the site of Bethlem Hospital, in front of which is the " Obelisk." This previously stood in the centre of St. George's Circus, formerly St. George's Fields, the scene of the massing of the Gordon Rioters as described in *Barnaby Rudge.* The " Obelisk " was— and still is—one of London's landmarks. In *Somebody's Luggage* Dickens humorously refers to it as the " Obstacle." But its chief claim to remembrance is the connection it has with David Copperfield's walk to Dover. Looking about him for somebody who could carry his box from his lodgings in Lant Street to the coach office, David found " a long-legged young man with a very little empty donkey-cart standing near the Obelisk in the Blackfriars Road," and bargained with him to do the job " for a tanner." How the long-legged young man not only ran off with the box, but with David's half-guinea too, is graphically described in chapter twelve. David ran after him as fast as he could, and had no breath to call out, or continue the chase ; so he tells us, " I left the young man to go where he would with my box and money ; and panting and crying, but never stopping, faced about for Greenwich, which I had understood was on the Dover Road : taking very little more out of the world, towards the retreat of my aunt, Miss Betsey, than I had brought into it, on the night when my arrival gave her so much umbrage."

There is a personal association with a house near the Obelisk, to which young Dickens had to go for an examination at the time his father was in the Marshalsea. It was a condition that the wearing apparel and personal matters retained were not to exceed twenty pounds sterling in value, and he tells us in his autobiographical fragment :

" It was necessary, as a matter of form that the clothes I wore should be seen by the official appraiser.

I had a half-holiday to enable me to call upon him, at his own time at a house somewhere beyond the Obelisk. I recollect his coming out to look at me with his mouth full, and a strong smell of beer upon him, and saying good-naturedly that ' that would do,' and ' it was all right.' Certainly the hardest creditor would not have been disposed (even if he had been legally entitled) to avail himself of my poor white hat, little jacket, or corduroy trousers. But I had a fat old silver watch in my pocket, which had been given me by my grandmother before the blacking days, and I had entertained my doubts as I went along whether that valuable possession might not bring me over the twenty pounds. So I was greatly relieved, and made him a bow of acknowledgment as I went out."

A little past the Obelisk we arrive in Kennington Road, off which is Walcot Square. Mr. Guppy, in proposing to Esther in Bleak House, informed her he had taken "a 'ouse . . . a hollow bargain (taxes ridiculous and use of fixtures included in the rent)." He added " I beg to lay the 'ouse in Walcot Square, the business and myself, before Miss Summerson for her acceptance."

At this end of the Blackfriars Road is the Surrey Theatre, where " Frederick Dorrit played . . . a clarionet as dirty as himself," and in the same theatre Fanny Dorrit used to dance.

Here it was that on November 19th, 1838, an unauthorised version of Oliver Twist was staged. Dickens attended it, and was so annoyed at the distortion of history that " in the middle of the first scene he laid himself down upon the floor in a corner of the box, and never rose from it until the drop-scene fell."

From St. George's Circus, London Road leads to the cross roads known as the Elephant & Castle, described in Bleak House as " that ganglion of roads from Kent and Surrey, and of streets from the bridges of London,

MEMORIAL IN DAVID COPPERFIELD'S GARDEN, NEW KENT ROAD

centring in the far-famed Elephant." To one of the
little shops in "a street of little shops" near here,
came Trooper George to visit Mrs. Bagnet, whom he
saw, "with her outer skirts tucked up, come forth with a
small wooden tub, and in that tub commence a whisking
and splashing on the margin of the pavement. Mr.
George says to himself 'She's as usual, washing greens.
I never saw her, except upon a baggage waggon, when
she wasn't washing greens.'"

Our way lies straight ahead down the New Kent Road.
On the left is Webb's County Terrace where David
rested after being robbed of his money and his box.

"I came to a stop in the Kent Road," he says,
"at a terrace with a piece of water before it, and a
great foolish image in the middle blowing a dry
shell. Here I sat down on a door-step, quite spent
and exhausted with the efforts I had already made,
and with hardly breath enough to cry for the loss
of my box and half-guinea."

The water and the "image" have disappeared from
the gardens some forty years. In their place, the
Dickens Fellowship recently erected a little statue to
connect the spot with history.

We bear to the right into the Old Kent Road. On
the right a new building has replaced the old Deaf
and Dumb Establishment to which Dr. Marigold
took his Sophy for tuition. Somewhere in the Old
Kent Road was the shop where David sold the first
portion of his wardrobe.

In this neighbourhood too was no doubt situated
Bradley Headstone's School in *Our Mutual Friend*,
described as being "down in that district of the flat
country tending to the Thames, where Kent and
Surrey meet and where the railways still bestride the
market-gardens that will soon die under them. The
schools were newly built, and there were so many like
them all over the country that one might have thought

11

the whole were but one restless edifice with the locomotive gift of Aladdin's palace."

It is some three or four miles to Greenwich, and we can take a conveyance the whole length of the Old Kent Road through New Cross and Deptford to Greenwich.

We alight at Greenwich Church, where Bella was married to John Rokesmith ; or, as Dickens puts it, " the church porch, having swallowed up Bella Wilfer for ever and ever, had it not in its power to relinquish that young woman but slid into the happy sunlight Mrs. John Rokesmith instead."

Church Street leads to the River, where, on the left is the Ship Hotel so full of memories of two delightful chapters in *Our Mutual Friend*, the first prior to the marriage, when Bella commanded Pa to " take this lovely woman out to dinner," and " they went to a hotel in Greenwich." " The little room overlooking the river into which they were shown for dinner was delightful. Everything was delightful. The park was delightful, the punch was delightful, the dishes of fish were delightful, the wine was delightful.

" And then, as they sat looking at the ships and steamboats making their way to the sea with the tide that was running down, the lovely woman imagined all sorts of voyages for herself and Pa."

At a later period of the story we read :

" The marriage dinner was the crowning success, for what had bride and bridegroom plotted to do, but to have and to hold that dinner in the very room of the hotel where Pa and the lovely woman had once dined together ! . . . What a dinner ! Specimens of all the fishes that swim in the sea had surely swum their way to it. . . . And the dishes, being seasoned with Bliss—an article which they are sometimes out of at Greenwich—were of perfect flavour. . . . Never-to-be-forgotten Greenwich ! "

Dickens and his friends often partook of the white-bait dinners for which both the Ship and the Trafalgar hotels were once so famous.

Returning to the Church, we turn left along Nelson Street, and then to the right into Greenwich Park, to which a chapter in the *Sketches* is devoted ; from this we learn that " the principal amusement is to drag young ladies up the steep hill which leads to the Observatory, and then drag them down again, at the very top of their speed, greatly to the derangement of their curls and bonnet-caps, and much to the edification of the lookers-on from below."

The road straight ahead takes us to the Observatory, from which the road to the right takes us out of the Park, across a small portion of the Heath into the Shooter's Hill Road, where we turn left.

Blackheath was very well known to Dickens, and, as the railway from London to Greenwich was the first one built in London it afforded him the opportunity of taking train for part of the journey, such as he describes in the concluding portion of the *Seven Poor Travellers*—in his walk from Rochester to London.

" Christmas begirt me, far and near, until I had come to Blackheath, and had walked down the long vista of gnarled old trees in Greenwich Park, and was being steam-rattled through the mists now closing in once more, towards the lights of London."

When little David Copperfield was sent to school it was to Salem House " down by Blackheath . . . a square brick building with wings, of a bare and unfurnished appearance." The identity of the school has never been discovered. After his mother died, David was taken from the school and put to work in the bottle warehouse ; from this he ran away and walked to Dover. After a hard day's work, he tells us how he " came climbing out at last upon the level of Blackheath. It cost me some trouble to find out

Salem House, but I found it, and I found a haystack in the corner and I lay down under it."

John Rokesmith and his wife, in *Our Mutual Friend*, had " a modest little cottage, but a bright and a fresh," on Blackheath.

The main road now ascends Shooter's Hill and we have thoughts of " that Friday night in November, one thousand seven hundred and seventy-five," when the Dover Mail " lumbered up Shooter's Hill . . . and the guard suspected the passengers, the passengers suspected one another and the guard, they all suspected everybody else, and the coachman was sure of nothing but the horses." For a full account of that spirited ride, the reader is referred to the second chapter of *A Tale of Two Cities.*

In *The Holly Tree* Cobbs informs us that " Master Harry Walmers's father lived at the Elmses, down away by Shooter's Hill there, six or seven miles from Lunnon," and in *Pickwick* we remember that the elder Weller retired on a handsome independence to " an excellent public-house near Shooter's Hill, where he is quite reverenced as an oracle."

A reference is made in *Sunday under Three Heads* to the ruined Severndroog Castle—built by Lady James in 1784—on the summit of the hill.

" Away they go . . . to catch a glimpse of the rich cornfields and beautiful orchards of Kent ; or to stroll among the fine old trees of Greenwich Park, and survey the wonders of Shooter's Hill and Lady James's Folly.'

The Dover Road continued takes us through Gravesend, Chalk, and Gad's Hill to Rochester, Canterbury, and Dover, with which places we deal in the remaining days' journeyings.

Our return from Greenwich can be made to follow our outward route until New Cross Gate is reached. Here a 'bus or tram to Camberwell Green takes us through Peckham, where Walter Gay went to a weekly boarding school. In the same book, *Dombey and Son*, we read that " Mr. Feeder spoke of the dark mysteries of London and told Mr. Toots that he was going . . . to board with two maidens ladies at Peckham."

It was in Camberwell that Mr. Pickwick made " unwearied researches." Oak Lodge, Camberwell, was the home of the Maldertons in that delightful humorous story in *Sketches by Boz*, entitled *Horatio Sparkins*, at the conclusion of which we read, " Years have elapsed since the occurrence of this dreadful morning. The daisies have thriced bloomed on Camberwell Green ; the sparrows have thrice repeated their vernal chirps in Camberwell Grove ; but the Miss Maldertons are still unmated."

The tragedy of George Barnwell, who lived in Camberwell, was a favourite with Dickens as a boy, for recitations, and several references to it are made in the novels.

In *Great Expectations* Camberwell figures in the amusing account of Wemmick's wedding.

" We went towards Camberwell Green, and, when we were thereabouts, Wemmick said suddenly : " ' Hallo ! Here's a church ! '

" There was nothing very surprising in that ; but, again, I was rather surprised when he said, as if he were animated by a brilliant idea :

" ' Let's go in ! ' . . .

" ' Hallo ! ' said Wemmick. ' Here's Miss Skiffins ! Let's have a wedding ! ' "

St. Giles's Church, Camberwell, near the Green, is pointed out as the church referred to.

Tom Pinch, and Mr. Pecksniff too, both visited the former's sister at a house in Camberwell, where she was a governess in a family, " in a house so big and fierce that its mere outside, like the outside of a giant's castle, struck terror into vulgar minds and made bold persons quail. There was a great front gate ; with a great bell, whose handle was in itself a note of admiration ; and a great lodge, which, being close to the house, rather spoilt the look-out certainly, but made the look-in tremendous."

In half a mile from Camberwell Green, we are in Walworth, but all trace is lost of the delightful cottage in which Wemmick lived.

It was " a little wooden cottage in the midst of plots of garden, and the top of it was cut out and painted like a battery mounted with guns.

" ' My own doing,' said Wemmick. ' Looks pretty, don't it ? '

" I highly commended it. I think it was the smallest house I ever saw ; with the queerest gothic windows (by far the greater part of them sham), and a gothic door, almost too small to get in at.

" ' That's a real flagstaff, you see,' said Wemmick, ' and on Sundays I run up a real flag. Then look here. After I have crossed this bridge, I hoist it up— so—and cut off the communication.'

" The bridge was a plank, and it crossed a chasm about four feet wide and two deep. But it was very pleasant to see the pride with which he hoisted it up and made it fast, smiling as he did so."

The " Walworth sentiments " of Mr. Wemmick are world famous : " my Walworth sentiments must be taken at Walworth ; none but my official senti- ments can be taken in this office."

Being in the proximity of Brixton, Clapham and Toot- ing, we cannot refrain from mentioning briefly their Dickens associations, although there are no places which can be identified as actual landmarks. At Brixton as well as at Clapham Mr. Pickwick made his " unwearied researches."

In the Clapham Road lived the Poor Relation who loved to build his castles in the air, in " a very clean back room, in a very respectable house, where I am expected not to be at home in the daytime—unless poorly."

Clapham Rise is mentioned in *The Haunted House*, but No. 2 Tuppintock's Gardens, Liggs's Walk, has never been discovered. Neither has Rose Villa, the residence of Mr. Gattleton, where the amateur theatricals took place, as described in *Mrs. Joseph Porter* in the *Sketches*, a slice of Dickens's own life at the age of about twenty-one.

Clapham Common was formerly known as Clapham Green. Mr. Cyrus Angelo Bantam at Bath thought he recognised in Mr. Pickwick " the gentleman residing on Clapham Green who lost the use of his limbs from imprudently taking cold after port wine."

Of Tooting we recall that Snagsby's maid Guster (*Bleak House*) " was farmed, or contracted for, during her growing time, by an amiable benefactor of his species resident at Tooting."

Guster had evidently been an inmate of the Children's Farm conducted by a certain Mr. Drouet at the *Paradise at Tooting* which Dickens exposed at about this time ; a full account of which is to be found in the *Miscellaneous Papers*.

Hall, the publisher lived in Norwood, and Dickens was a frequenter visitor to his house ; and in the same locality David Copperfield spent many an anxious and delightful hour at the house of Mr. Spenlow, in the garden of which he courted Dora.

" In the green and wooded country near Norwood " Dickens located the home of Carker.

When Mr. Pickwick announced the break-up of the club bearing his name, he informed his friends that he was retiring to a house in Dulwich, but we are given no clues as to its whereabouts ; the house there named " Pickwick Villa " must not be accepted other than as a tribute to the creator of the famous man.

" The house I have taken," said Mr. Pickwick, " is at Dulwich. It has a large garden, and is situated in one of the most pleasant spots near London. It has been fitted up with every attention to substantial comfort; perhaps to a little elegance besides; but of that you shall judge for yourselves."

At Dulwich Church Mr. Snodgrass was married to Arabella Allen, and in conclusion we read : " Mr. Pickwick is somewhat infirm now ; but he retains all his former juvenility of spirit, and may still be frequently seen contemplating the pictures in the Dulwich Gallery, or enjoying a walk about the pleasant neighbourhood on a fine day. He is known by all the poor people about, who never fail to take their hats off as he passes, with great respect. The children idolise him, and so indeed does the whole neighbourhood."

A little farther afield are a few river-side associations with Dickens which do not call for a special day being devoted to them, although the visitor will find much pleasure in Richmond Park and Hampton Court for an excursion, during which a few houses associated with Dickens can be seen.

At Chelsea, Dickens was married on April 2nd, 1836, at St. Luke's Church in Sydney Street.

At No. 11, Selwood Terrace, off Fulham Road, Dickens stayed for a time prior to his marriage, to be near the home of his future wife.

Quite a number of Dickens characters lived at Chelsea, Mr. Vincent Crummles was actually born there, and consequently was " not a Prussian." Mr. Bayham Badger in *Bleak House* " had a good practice at Chelsea " ; Miss Sophia Wackles, beloved of Dick

Swiveller, resided at Chelsea, and maintained there
" a very small day-school for young ladies of propor-
tionate dimensions."

In *Bleak House* Mr. Bucket announces his intention
to visit an aunt " that lives at Chelsea—next door
but two to the old original Bun House." The Chelsea
Bun House was demolished in 1839. It stood opposite
the Barracks. In *Barnaby Rudge* the Royal East
London Volunteers, in which Gabriel Varden was
a sergeant, "having displayed their military prowess
to the utmost in these warlike shows, they marched
in glittering order to the Chelsea Bun House, and
regaled in the adjacent taverns until dark."

Between the Barracks and Chelsea Hospital, now
incorporated in the Hospital grounds, were Ranelagh
Gardens. In *A Tale of Two Cities* " Mr. Stryver
inaugurated the Long Vacation with a formal proposal
to take Miss Manette to Vauxhall Gardens ; that
failing, to Ranelagh."

In *Reprinted Pieces*, Chelsea is mentioned more
than once as the home of some of the characters,
and in *Our Mutual Friend* Silas Wegg drops into poetry :

> Then farewell my trim-built wherry.
> Oars and coat and badge farewell !
> Nevermore at Chelsea Ferry
> Shall your Thomas take a spell.

In *Dombey and Son* we are introduced to Sir Barnet
and Lady Skettles, " very good people, who resided
in a pretty villa at Fulham, on the banks of the Thames;
which was one of the most desirable residences in the
world when a rowing match happened to be going
past, but had its little inconveniences at other times,
among which may be enumerated the occasional
appearance of the river in the drawing-room, and
the contemporaneous disappearance of the lawn and
shrubbery."

To Putney Dora went to live with her aunts after the death of her father, in consequence of which David Copperfield found time to haunt Putney and " contrived, by some means or other, to prowl about the neighbourhood pretty often."

When Traddles accompanied him to the house we remember how he was at such a discount in respect of his personal looks and presence of mind that Traddles proposed a gentle stimulant in the form of a glass of ale. " This having been administered at a neighbouring public-house, he conducted me, with tottering steps, to the Misses Spenlow's door."

At Hammersmith lived the Pocket family, in *Great Expectations* : the family that Dickens describes as " not growing up or being brought up, but tumbling up."

Whether or not Hammersmith was noted for schools in Dickens's day, we do not know, but his view of life encountered many there. Mrs. Nickleby tells Kate how " your dear papa's cousins' sister-in-law, a Miss Browndock, was taken into partnership by a lady that kept a school at Hammersmith and made her fortune in no time at all."

Clara Barley, in *Great Expectations*, was met by Herbert Pocket " when she was completing her education at an establishment at Hammersmith " ; in *Miscellaneous Papers* (*Gone to the Dogs,*) we read of a " Miss Maggigg's boarding establishment at Hammersmith," and in *Sketches by Boz*, under the title *Sentiment*, is a long account of Minerva House, Hammersmith, a " finishing establishment for young ladies, where some twenty girls of the ages of from thirteen to nineteen acquired a smattering of everything and a knowledge of nothing."

This way came Oliver Twist and Bill Sikes on the way to the burglary at Chertsey. " Kensington, Hammersmith, Chiswick, Kew Bridge and Brentford

were all passed," we are told " and yet they went on
as steadily as if they had only just begun their journey."

The river makes a big sweep here to our right,
through Brentford. In *Great Expectations* we read that
" Arthur lived at the top of Compeyson's house
(over nigh Brentford it was), and Compeyson kept
a careful account agin him for board and lodging."

The abode of Mrs. Betty Higden in *Our Mutual
Friend* was not easy to find, lying in such complicated
back settlements of muddy Brentford " that Robe-
smith and Mrs. Boffin left their equipage at the sign
of the Three Magpies and went in search of it on foot."

The Three Magpies is identified with the Three
Pigeons at Brentford.

" Mr. Tupman, when his friends married, and Mr.
Pickwick settled, took lodgings at Richmond, where
he has ever since resided. He walks constantly on
the Terrace during the summer months, with a
youthful and jaunty air which has rendered him the
admiration of the numerous elderly ladies of single
condition who reside in the vicinity."

In *Great Expectations* we are again introduced to
this Royal Borough.

" ' I'm going to Richmond,' Estella told Pip.
' Our lesson is that there are two Richmonds, one
in Surrey and one in Yorkshire, and that mine is the
Surrey Richmond. The distance is ten miles. . . .
I am going to live at a great expense with a lady
there who has the power—or says she has—of taking
me about, and introducing me,' . . .

" We came to Richmond all too soon and our
destination there was a house by the Green ; a staid
old house, where hoops and powder and patches . . .
had had their court days many a time. Some ancient
trees before the house were still cut into fashions as
formal and unnatural as the hoops and wigs and
stiff skirts."

At the top of Richmond Hill is a hospital on the site of the Star & Garter, the famous Hotel where Dickens celebrated the completion of *David Copperfield*. Thackeray and Tennyson were of the party.

At Elm Cottage (now called Elm Lodge), Petersham, Dickens lived during the summer of 1839. In a letter written at the time he referred to " those remote and distant parts, with the chain of mountain formed by Richmond Hill presenting an almost insurmountable barrier between me and the busy world."

He had previously stayed at Petersham for a time in 1836 whilst writing the *Village Coquettes*, as shown by a letter to the composer, John Hullah, from Petersham, suggesting that Hullah should pay him a visit there.

The duel in *Nicholas Nickleby* between Sir Mulberry Hawk and Lord Frederick Verisopht was fought in " one of the meadows opposite Twickenham by the river side."

Mr. Meagles and Pet had a cottage at Twickenham. " It was a charming place (none the worse for being a little eccentric) on the road by the river, and just what the residence of the Meagles family ought to be. It stood in a garden . . . and it was defended by a goodly show of handsome trees and spreading evergreens. . . . Within view was the peaceful river and the ferry boat."

Eel Pie Island lies a little beyond the ferry. It was one of the resorts of Dickens, and in *Nicholas Nickleby* he sends one of the Kenwigs family upon an excursion there " to make merry upon a collation, bottled beer, shrub and shrimps, and to dance in the open air."

At 4 Ailsa Park Villas, Twickenham, Dickens stayed for a time in 1838. The house is in the Isleworth Road near St. Margaret's Station.

GAD'S HILL AND DISTRICT

ALMOST midway between Gravesend and Rochester standing a little way back on the right, is the house that is familiarly and affectionately known to the innumerable band of Dickens devotees the world over as Gad's Hill, its full and correct name being Gad's Hill Place. This was Dickens's home from 1857 until his death in 1870.

But years before it became his home—indeed from his very earliest years when a small boy at Chatham—he conceived a great attachment to the house. He used to like to be taken out to see it by his father, and it was a cherished ambition of his life to be in a position to buy the house and live there.

He has confirmed this in his paper *Travelling Abroad* in *The Uncommercial Traveller*, in which as he is journeying along the road to Dover there crosses it a vision of himself :

" So smooth was the old high road, and so fresh were the horses, and so fast went I, that it was midway between Gravesend and Rochester, and the widening river was bearing the ships, white-sailed or black-smoked, out to sea, when I noticed by the wayside a very queer small boy.

" Holloa ! " said I, to the very queer small boy, ' where do you live ? '

" ' At Chatham,' says he.

" ' What do you do there ? ' says I.

" ' I go to school,' says he.

" I took him up in a moment, and we went on. Presently, the very queer small boy says, ' This is

Gadshill we are coming to, where Falstaff went out to rob those travellers, and ran away.'

"'You know something about Falstaff, eh?' said I.

"'All about him,' said the very queer small boy. 'I am old (I am nine), and I read all sorts of books. But *do* let us stop at the top of the hill, and look at the house there, if you please.'

"'You admire that house?' said I.

"'Bless you, sir,' said the very queer small boy, 'when I was not more than half as old as nine, it used to be a treat for me to be brought to look at it. And now I am nine, I come by myself to look at it. And ever since I can recollect, my father, seeing me so fond of it, has often said to me, 'If you were to be very persevering, and were to work hard, you might some day come to live in it.' Though that's impossible,' said the very queer small boy, drawing a low breath, and now staring at the house out of window with all his might.

"I was rather amazed to be told this by the very queer small boy; for that house happens to be *my* house, and I have reason to believe that what he said was true."

"When I was at Gravesend t'other day," wrote Dickens to W. H. Wills, his assistant editor of *Household Words*, early in 1855, "I saw at Gad's Hill a little freehold to be sold. The spot and the very house are literally 'a dream of my childhood,' and I should like to look at it before I go to Paris." That the dream of his childhood was not a mere phrase of the moment, it is confirmed in a letter to his Swiss friend de Cerjat, dated 17th January, 1856:

"Down at Gad's Hill, near Rochester, in Kent—Shakespeare's Gad's Hill, where Falstaff engaged in the robbery—is a quaint little country-house of Queen Anne's time. . . . It had always a curious interest for me, because when I was a small boy down in these parts I thought it the most beautiful house

CHARLES. DICKENS'S HOUSE, GAD'S HILL PLACE
FRONT VIEW (ABOVE) AND BACK VIEW SHOWING CONSERVATORY,
LAST ADDITION MADE BY DICKENS, (BELOW)

(I suppose because of its famous old cedar-trees) ever seen. And my poor father used to bring me to look at it, and used to say that if I ever grew up to be a clever man perhaps I might own that house, or such another house. In remembrance of which, I have always in passing looked to see if it was to be sold or let, and it has never been to me like any other house, and it has never changed at all."

Some years before (1843), he had pictured the house in *A Christmas Carol*, when the spirit of Christmas Past took Scrooge to the scenes of his childhood :

" ' Good Heavens,' said Scrooge . . . ' I was born in this place. I was a boy here.' . . .

" ' You recollect that ? ' enquired the Spirit.

" ' Remember it,' cried Scrooge. . . . ' I could walk it blindfold. . . .'

" They walked along the road, Scrooge recognising every gate and post and tree until a little market town appeared in the distance, with its bridge, its church and widening river. . . . They left the high road by a well-remembered lane and soon approached a mansion of dull red brick, with a little weathercock—surmounted cupola on the roof, and a bell hanging in it. It was a large house, but one of broken fortunes."

We can therefore well imagine the great joy with which he completed the purchase on the 14th March, 1856, writing to Forster :

" This day I have paid the purchase-money for Gadshill Place. After drawing the cheque (£1,790) I turned round to give it to Wills, and said, ' Now isn't it an extraordinary thing—look at the Day—Friday ! I have been nearly drawing it half-a-dozen times when the lawyers have not been ready, and here it comes round on a Friday as a matter of course." He had now arrived at his last harbour, the home of his dreams, after twenty years of fame and wandering through four London houses, two London apartments, some half-dozen different seaside lodgings at Broad-stairs and Brighton ; country houses in Genoa, Lausanne, and Boulogne ; apartments in Paris, and elsewhere. Gad's Hill at last—his haven of rest ; surrounded by his two grown-up daughters, his devoted sister-in-law, and his younger sons : but without his Catherine, from whom he had parted, an incompatibility of temper for which he was mostly to blame. How the subject affected him we have no record ; but it was bitterness and gall to him we have no doubt. The first series of public readings in 1858, before taking up full possession of Gad's Hill, is a proof of his desire to hide his anguish in a series of exciting encounters with a public which adored and worshipped him.

The many alterations necessary to make his new home habitable occupied the attention of Dickens in the summer of 1857, when he and his wife spent irregular intervals at Waite's Hotel in Gravesend, demolished in 1929. The sinking of a well was a long and costly job, " two pounds per day for wages. The men seem to like it very much," he wrote. " Five men have been looking attentively at the pump for a week, and (I should hope) may begin to fit it in the course of October. By the time it is finished, the cost of this water will be something absolutely frightful." That it increased the value of the property was his only comfort. While still engaged in the embellishment of the house, he again wrote to de Cerjat (July, 1858) :

" At this present moment I am on my little Kentish freehold (not in top-boots, and not particularly prejudiced that I know of), looking on as pretty a view out of my study window as you will find in a long day's English ride. My little place is a grave red brick house (time of George the First, I suppose), which I have added to and stuck bits upon in all manner of ways, so that it is as pleasantly irregular, and as violently opposed to all architectural ideas, as the most hopeful man could possibly desire. It is on the summit of Gad's Hill. The robbery was committed before the door, on the man with the treasure, and Falstaff ran away from the identical spot of ground now covered by the room in which I write. A little rustic ale-house, called the Sir John Falstaff, is over the way—has been over the way, ever since, in honour of the event. Cobham Woods and Park are behind the house; the distant Thames in front; the Medway, with Rochester, and its old castle and cathedral on one side. The whole stupendous property is on the old Dover Road, so when you come, come by the North Kent Railway (not the South-Eastern) to Strood or Higham, and I'll drive over to fetch you."

It was not until the autumn of 1860 that his furniture and books were sent from Tavistock House, London, and the occupation of the house begun in earnest. At this time we find him writing to Forster :

" When you come down here next month, we have an idea that we shall show you rather a neat house. What terrific adventures have been in action ; how many overladen vans were knocked up at Gravesend, and had to be dragged out of Chalk-turnpike in the dead of the night by the whole equine power of this establishment shall be revealed at another time."

Alterations and improvements to the property still continued and the younger daughter Kate, who was married in 1860, was often specially called down to Gad's Hill from London to witness the " latest improvement " her father had made at the house of his dreams. He would greet her with all solemnity and say, " Now, Katie, to behold your parent's latest and last improvement," which was a standing joke between them. Mrs. Perugini recalls the occasion when the walls and doors of the drawing-room had been lined with mirrors, saying to her father that she firmly believed that when he became an angel his wings would be made of looking-glass and his crown of scarlet geraniums : for Dickens had a great liking for mirrors to reflect the light (he had several in the chalet in which he did most of his writing in the later years) and for scarlet geraniums, two beds of which always graced the front of the house. The conservatory at the back of the house was the very latest improvement on which he was engaged at the time of his death.

On the opposite side of the road to the house is a vacant strip of ground connected with the main grounds of the house by a tunnel. In this Wilderness, as it was called, Dickens erected the Swiss chalet which Fechter the actor presented to him.

" It will really be a very pretty thing," he wrote in January, 1865, " and in the summer (supposing it not to be blown away in the spring), the upper room will make a charming study. It is much higher than we supposed." When erected it became a favourite resort in the summer months, and much of Dickens's work was done there. He was busy writing there the whole of the day before he died. " My room is up among the branches of the trees and the birds and the butterflies fly in and out, and the green branches shoot in at the open windows, and the lights and shadows of the clouds come and go with the rest of the company. The scent of the flowers, and indeed of everything that is growing for miles and miles, is most delicious."

After Dickens's death the chalet was presented to Lord Darnley and it has been in Cobham Park ever since. In 1929 it was announced for sale and its ultimate fate is in the balance.

In the entrance hall of Gad's Hill Place still hangs the original framed greeting with which Dickens welcomed his many friends to his new abode :

" THIS HOUSE, GADSHILL PLACE, stands on the summit of Shakespeare's Gadshill, ever memorable for its association with Sir John Falstaff in his noble fancy. *But, my lads, to-morrow morning, by four o'clock, early at Gadshill ! there are pilgrims going to Canterbury with rich offerings, and traders riding to London with fat purses : I have vizards for you all ; you have horses for yourselves.*"

It was the pride of Dickens's life to show the house to his friends and entertain them there. According to Forster, when he received visitors to whom he owed special courtesy, " he would compress into infinitely few days an enormous amount of sight seeing and country enjoyment, castles, cathedrals, and fortified lines, lunches and picnics among cherry orchards and hop-gardens, excursions to Canterbury or Maidstone and their beautiful neighbourhoods, Druid-stone and Blue Bell Hill."

When Longfellow paid him a visit which was necessarily brief, Dickens showed him all the neighbouring country that could be shown in so short a time. " I turned out a couple of postillions in the old red jacket of the old red royal Dover Road, for our ride," he wrote, " and it was like a holiday ride in England fifty years ago. Of course we went to look at the old houses in Rochester and the old cathedral, and the old castle, and the house for the six poor travellers who, ' not being rogues or proctors, shall have lodging, entertainment, and four pence each.' "

The villages of Shorne, Cobham, and Cooling represented the favourite objectives of Dickens for some of his shorter walks.

There is a lane by the side of Gad's Hill Place which takes us, in about a mile, into the road from Strood to Cobham. On reaching this road we bear to the right past the quaint Three Crutches Inn and then skirt the grounds of Cobham Hall on the left. In about a mile and a half, a road turns to the right and leads to Shorne, about a mile distant.

This delightful old-world village was a particular favourite with Dickens, Forster tells us that for a short summer walk he was " fond of going round the village of Shorne, and sitting on a hot afternoon in its pretty shaded churchyard " ; and according to the same authority, Dickens had expressed a wish to be buried here in what he described in *Pickwick* as " one of the most peaceful and secluded churchyards in Kent."

Not far from Shorne is the village of Cobham.

Again to quote Forster, " Round Cobham, skirting the park and village, and passing the Leather Bottle famous in the pages of *Pickwick*, was a favourite walk with Dickens . . . the Cobham neighbourhood was certainly that which he had greatest pleasure in ; and he would have taken oftener than he did the walk through Cobham park and woods, which was the last he enjoyed before his life suddenly closed upon him, but that here he did not like his dogs to follow." On the 7th June, 1870, the day before Dickens was seized with his fatal illness, he drove to Cobham Woods with Miss Hogarth, there dismissed the carriage and walked round the park and back home to Gad's Hill. It was old, familiar and dearly loved ground to him. Many a short holiday had he spent here at different times with Maclise, Douglas Jerrold and the beloved Forster. In 1845 he had celebrated a birthday there, " thus by indulgence of the desire which was always strongly urgent in him, associating his life with those earliest scenes of his youthful time," as his biographer remarks.

This love of Cobham finds reflection in an early chapter of *The Pickwick Papers*, when Mr. Pickwick, Mr. Winkle and Mr. Snodgrass walked from Rochester to seek the love-lorn Tracy Tupman at the " Leather Bottle " there, on a June day—a walk repeated by Dickens forty-three years later.

" A delightful walk it was : for it was a pleasant

afternoon in June, and their way lay through a deep
and shady wood, cooled by the light wind which gently
rustled the thick foliage, and enlivened by the songs
of the birds that perched upon the boughs. The ivy
and the moss crept in thick clusters over the old trees,
and the soft green turf overspread the ground like a
silken mat. They emerged upon an open park, with
an ancient hall, displaying the quaint and picturesque
architecture of Elizabeth's time. Long vistas of
stately oaks and elm trees appeared on every side ;
large herds of deer were cropping along the fresh
grass ; and occasionally a startled hare scoured along
the ground, with the speed of the shadows thrown
by the light clouds which swept across a sunny land-
scape like a passing breath of summer.

" If this," said Mr. Pickwick, looking about him,
" if this were the place to which all who are troubled
with our friend's complaint, came, I fancy their old
attachment to this world would very soon return."

A similar walk was repeated in the concluding
portion of the Christmas story of *The Seven Poor Travellers* when parting from the travellers Dickens tells us
that he was going to walk by Cobham Woods, as far
upon his way to London as he fancied. " When I
came to the stile and footpath by which I was to
diverge from the main road, I bade farewell to my last
remaining Poor Traveller, and pursued my way alone.
. . . Going through the woods, the softness of my tread
upon the mossy ground and among the brown leaves
enhanced the Christmas sacredness by which I felt
surrounded. As the whitened stems environed me,
I thought how the Founder of the time had never
raised his benignant hand, save to bless and heal,
except in the case of one unconscious tree. By Cobham
Hall, I came to the village, and the churchyard where
the dead had been quietly buried, ' in the sure and
certain hope ' which Christmas time inspired."

Returning to Mr. Pickwick, his opinion of Cobham is endorsed by all who know it : " this is one of the prettiest and most desirable places of residence I ever met with."

At the far end of the village we find the Leather Bottle Inn, a quaint and picturesque hostelry famous the world over for its connection with Pickwick.

The parlour where Mr. Tupman was discovered seated at the table " well covered with a roast fowl, bacon, ale and et ceteras . . . looking as unlike a man who had taken leave of this world as possible," is on the left, " a long, low-roofed room furnished with a large number of high-backed leather-cushioned chairs, of fantastic shapes, and embellished with a great variety of old portraits and roughly-coloured prints of some antiquity."

Opposite the Leather Bottle is the church, famed far and wide for its wonderful brasses. " Finish your dinner," said Mr. Pickwick to Mr. Tupman, " and walk with me ; I want to speak with you alone." And accordingly they sought the churchyard for the purpose. " For half an hour," we are told, " their forms might have been seen pacing the churchyard to and fro, while Mr. Pickwick was engaged in combating his companion's resolution."

There is another association with Cobham, " that immortal discovery," made by Mr. Pickwick, which was " the pride and boast of his friends, and the envy of every antiquarian in this or any other country . . . a small broken stone, partially buried in the ground in front of a cottage door " a little way down the village, inscribed :

+
BILST
UM
PSHI
S.M.
ARK

" ' This is some very old inscription, existing perhaps long before the ancient alms-houses in this place. It must not be lost,' " declared that emphatic gentleman. And, how his eyes " sparkled with delight, as he sat and gloated over the treasure he had discovered ! He had attained one of the greatest objects of his ambition."

A full account of the great controversy that raged round this discovery is to be found in the pages of *Pickwick*, including the researches of " the presumptuous and ill-conditioned Blotton " : who " with a mean desire to tarnish the lustre of the immortal name of Pickwick, actually undertook a journey to Cobham in person, and on his return, sarcastically observed in an oration at the club, that he had seen the man from whom the stone was purchased ; that the man presumed the stone to be ancient, but solemnly denied the antiquity of the inscription—inasmuch as he represented it to have been rudely carved by himself in an idle mood, and to display letters intended to bear neither more nor less than the simple construction ' BILL STUMPS, HIS MARK.' "

The ancient alms-houses in this place of which Mr. Pickwick made mention are to be seen at the far side of the Church. These are referred to as " Titbull's Almshouses " in *The Uncommercial Traveller* : " a charming rustic retreat for old men and women ; a quaint ancient foundation in a pleasant English country, behind a picturesque church and among rich old convent gardens."

In spite of the fact that it lies midway between Gad's Hill and Rochester, and was known to Dickens very well indeed, Gravesend finds but little mention in Dickens's novels.

It used to be a popular holiday resort in Dickens's day. In *Bleak House* we read how, in the long vacation, " all the young clerks are madly in love, and . . .

pine for bliss with the beloved object, at **Margate,** **Ramsgate** or **Gravesend,"** and in *The Tuggses at Ramsgate,* Mr. Joseph Tuggs suggested Gravesend as the place for the family holiday, but " the idea was unanimously scouted. Gravesend was *low*."

Gravesend was formerly an important port ; when Peggotty and Ham visited David at Salem House, we are told they came from Yarmouth to Gravesend by water, and when Peggotty and Micawber emigrated, their boat set sail from Gravesend. Jack Malden in the same book left for India by a steamer from Gravesend, and Dora and David went there to see him off, and some years later when David returned from a long tour abroad, he landed at Gravesend.

Some people assert that Gravesend was the Muggleton of *The Pickwick Papers,* but, although Muggleton is doubtless a compound of more than one town, it is not likely that the place through which the Pickwickians had passed *en route* for Rochester, would be treated later on as a new town hitherto unknown to Mr. Pickwick and his friends.

Dickens spent some time here during the repairs and decorations of Gad's Hill in 1857 when he stayed at Waite's Hotel, on the Gordon Promenade, demolished in 1929.

Chalk is about a mile from Gravesend. It was here that Dickens spent his honeymoon in 1836.

About twenty years ago two tablets were affixed on a house, one of gun-metal with the inscription :

> In this house Charles Dickens spent his honeymoon in 1836 ; here also some early chapters of " Pickwick " were written.

The other a marble plate, with bronze plaque of Dickens, executed and presented by Percy Fitzgerald, and placed over the doorway, with inscription similar to the above.

The tablet, however, has been placed on the wrong house. In a letter to Thomas Beard, published in *Dickens to his Oldest Friend* (Putnams, 1932), edited by the present writer, there is a letter written from Chalk, and headed " At Mrs. Nash's." This lady's cottage, a more suitable one in many respects than Mrs. Craddock's on which the tablet was placed close on a quarter of a century ago, is two doors from the " White Hart " on the east side. It is hoped the tablets will be removed to their proper position.

Dickens was very partial to putting his characters in the position he had once occupied, so we find that both Walter Gay in *Dombey and Son* and Tommy Traddles in *David Copperfield* spent their honeymoons in Kent.

Chalk Church is a landmark hereabouts ; over the porch is a curious carving which Forster tells us used to attract Dickens's attention when he walked this way from Gad's Hill : " He would walk through the marshes to Gravesend, return by Chalk Church, and stop always to have greeting with a comical old monk who for some incomprehensible reason sits carved in stone, cross-legged, with a jovial pot, over the porch of that sacred edifice."

The blacksmith's forge on the right-hand side of the road going in the direction of Rochester, with its adjacent wooden cottage, was the original of Joe Gargery's Forge in *Great Expectations*, although its actual location in the story was transferred by Dickens to the marshes near the river, a few miles away. Mullinder the blacksmith was well known to Dickens.

" I have discovered that the seven miles between Maidstone and Rochester is one of the most beautiful roads in England," wrote Dickens when living at Gad's Hill ; but the discovery was not new, because ten years before he had written to Forster : " The eight miles' walk from Maidstone to Rochester, and a visit to the Druidical altar on the wayside, are charming."

This " Druidical altar " is Kits Coity House, a Saxon cromlech in a field on Blue Bell Hill, a spot often frequented by Dickens, as his letters show, and where on more than one occasion he arranged picnic parties with his visitors.

Dickens had a good knowledge of most of this part of Kent, even in his young days ; nevertheless for some unknown reason he veiled in mystery the identity of Muggleton and Manor Farm, neither of which, according to the details given in *Pickwick*, could have been very far from Rochester.

Muggleton being a corporate town and some ten miles from Rochester, possessing also a jail, has been identified with Maidstone, and Manor Farm, Dingley Dell, with Cob Tree, Sandling, two miles away ; but Mr. S. J. Rust has argued, with great success, that the choice by Charles Dickens the younger of Town Malling as the original of Muggleton owing to its association with cricket, is a more sure one, and that Birling Place near by fits in better with Dickens's description of the journey of the Pickwickians to Mr. Wardle's hospitable roof.

In no way does the prospect around either place belie the description of Manor Farm given in Chapter Six.

" ' Delightful situation this,' said Mr. Pickwick.

" ' There an't a better spot o' ground in all Kent, Sir,' said the hard headed man with the pippin face."

A further description of the surroundings of Manor Farm is supplied on the morning after their arrival :

" ' Pleasant, pleasant country,' sighed the enthusiastic gentleman, as he opened his lattice window. ' Who could to live to gaze from day to day on bricks and slates, who had once felt the influence of a scene like this ? Who could continue to exist, where there are

no cows but the cows on the chimney pots ; nothing
redolent of Pan but pan-tiles ; no crop but stone-crop ?
Who could bear to drag out a life in such a spot ?
Who I ask could endure it ? ' and, having cross-
examined solitude after the most approved precedents,
at considerable length, Mr. Pickwick thrust his head
out of the lattice, and looked around him."

The marsh country between Gad's Hill and the river
Thames was another favourite objective with Dickens.
" To another drearier churchyard, itself forming part
of the marshes beyond the Medway," says Forster,
" he often took friends to show them the dozen small
tombstones of various sizes adapted to the respective
ages of a dozen small children of one family which he
made part of his story of *Great Expectations*, though,
with the reserves always necessary in copying nature
not to overstep her modesty by copying too closely,
he makes the number that appalled little Pip not more
than half the reality. About the whole of this Cooling
churchyard, indeed, and the neighbouring castle ruins,
there was a wierd strangeness that made it one of his
attractive walks in the late year or winter, when from
Higham he could get to it across country over the
stubble-fields." Although this same authority has
said in regard to the setting of Chapter One of that
fascinating story of *Great Expectations*, " It is strange,
as I transcribe the words, with what wonderful vivid-
ness they bring back the very spot on which we stood
when he said he meant to make it the scene of the
opening of his story—Cooling Castle ruins and the
desolate Church, lying out among the marshes seven
miles from Gadshill ! " and although George Dolby,
Dickens's manager for the reading tours, stated how
he and " the chief " took " many a misty walk to the
Marshes at Cooling that we might get a realistic
notion of the dreariness and loneliness of the scenes in

Great Expectations, made famous by Pip and the convict,"
my friend Mr. W. Laurence Gadd considers that
Higham Church itself—which is much more " on
the marshes " than Cooling—was actually the churchyard where the convict Magwitch, " one memorable
raw afternoon," surprised Pip in the act of deriving
from the shape of the letters on the tombstones an idea
of what sort of people his dead parents were.

" The shape of the letters on my father's," he says,
" gave me an odd idea that he was a square, stout,
dark man, with curly black hair. From the character
and turn of the inscription, ' Also Georgina wife
of the Above,' I drew a childish conclusion that my
mother was freckled and sickly. To five little stone
lozenges, each about a foot and a half long, which
were arranged in a neat row beside their grave,
and were sacred to the memory of five little brothers
of mine—who gave up trying to get a living exceedingly
early in that universal struggle—I am indebted for a
belief I religiously entertained that they had all been
born on their backs with their hands in their trousers-
pockets, and had never taken them out in this state
of existence."

Although these little stones—hardly lozenge shape
it must be confessed—are to be seen only in Cooling
Churchyard, Mr. Gadd, with much ingenuity, shows
how Higham Church fits Dickens's description of
the bleak churchyard bordering the marshes and of
the village where Pip lived with his sister who had
" brought him up by hand "—the village of Gore
Green. But of course, the whole description of the
village, forge, cottage, inn and church, is a composite
one of an artist's fancy, as even the forge and cottage
were admittedly imported from Chalk near Gravesend
(see page 185) where Mullinder's Forge still standing,
was a favourite stopping-place of Dickens in his walks
thereabouts.

ROCHESTER

THERE is no town in Great Britain—perhaps not in all the world—that has so fascinated a writer throughout his whole life as Rochester fascinated Dickens. Although not his actual birthplace, it was, as Forster says, " the birthplace of his fancy " ; and his thoughts always turned to it in his writings.

Dickens was only four years of age when the family came from Portsmouth to live in the adjacent town of Chatham—and, to quote Richard Doubledick in *The Seven Poor Travellers*, " if anybody present knows to a nicety where Rochester ends and Chatham begins, it is more than I do."

Here the family resided for seven years, and here, as his friend and biographer John Forster states, " the most durable of his early impressions were received ; and the associations that were around him when he died, were those which at the outset of his life had affected him most strongly."

There is preserved in the Eastgate House Museum at Rochester a letter written by Dickens in 1865 thanking a correspondent for a book entitled *Curious Visits to Rochester*. In it he says : " As I peeped about its old corners with interest and wonder when I was a very little child, few people can find a greater charm in that ancient city than I do."

In the preface to the cheap edition of *Nicholas Nickleby* in 1848 we find him speaking of being " a not very robust child, sitting in bye-places, near Rochester Castle, with a head full of Partridge, Strap, Tom Pipes and Sancho Panza " ; and when the time came for the father to fill a post in London, deep was his grief at parting with the city he had learnt to love so well.

"It was the birth-place of his fancy," says Forster, "and he hardly knew what store he had set by its busy varieties of change and scene, until he saw the falling cloud that was to hide its pictures from him for ever. He was to be taken away to London inside the stage-coach Commodore; and Kentish woods and fields, Cobham Park and Hall, Rochester Cathedral and Castle, and all the wonderful romance together, including a red-cheeked baby he had been wildly in love with, were to banish like a dream."

Rochester figures under its own name in *The Pickwick Papers, David Copperfield,* and *Christmas Stories.* As "Dullborough Town," "Mudfog," and "Great Winglebury" it appears in *Sketches by Boz.* In *Great Expectations* it is called "The Market Town" and referred to as "Up town" and "Our town," and in *Edwin Drood,* "Cloisterham."

Although Dickens often wrote of Rochester under a fictitious name, he made no concealment otherwise that he was referring to the city he loved so dearly. His earliest reference to Rochester is in "The Great Winglebury Duel" (*Sketches by Boz*), written in 1836, when he says:

"The little town of Great Winglebury is exactly forty-two miles and three quarters from Hyde Park Corner. It has a long straggling quiet High Street, with a great black and white clock at a small red Town Hall, half way up—a market place—a cage—an assembly room—a church—a bridge—a chapel—a theatre —a library—an inn—a pump—and a post office."

In January of the following year he contributed the first of the *Mudfog Papers* to *Bentley's Miscellany,* which he was editing, when he found another name for his much loved city—but hardly a complimentary one ; no doubt he had in mind the Chatham portion.

ROCHESTER CATHEDRAL AND CASTLE

THE POND AT MANOR FARM

" Mudfog is a pleasant town—a remarkably pleasant town—situated in a charming hollow by the side of a river, from which river, Mudfog derives an agreeable scent of pitch, tar, coals, and rope yarn, a roving population in oil-skin hats, a pretty steady influx of drunken bargemen, and a great many other maritime advantages. There is a good deal of water about Mudfog, and yet it is not exactly the sort of town for a watering place, either."

In the February number of *Bentley's Miscelleny Oliver Twist* commenced. Readers of that work, as subsequently printed, are unaware that Mudfog was the place of Oliver's birth ! Yet it was at Mudfog that the story opened in the magazine—to be altered when issued in volume form.

It is however in *Pickwick* that Rochester first appears under its real name ; and it is *Pickwick* that commenced the romance centred in it. With notebook and telescope Mr. Pickwick descended on the city, and a fund of genuine good humour, perennial in its freshness, was the result, and pilgrimages are made to Rochester, not so much to see its historic castle and ancient cathedral, as to see the places associated with " The Immortal Pickwick " and the other works of his equally immortal creator.

In *A Christmas Carol* the first of the three spirits takes Scrooge to the place where he was born, and he sees in the distance " A little market town . . . with its bridge, its church, and widening river." This was Rochester.

It was not until 1854 that Rochester again figured to any large extent in his stories. This time, the house known as Watts's Charity for Six Poor Travellers, was the subject of one of the Christmas numbers, which he entitled *The Seven Poor Travellers*, Dickens himself making the seventh traveller.

In 1860 *Great Expectations* appeared, and the " Market

Town " of that book was of course Rochester, near to which he had lately come to reside.

Ten years later came *Edwin Drood*, and his fancy again turned to the Cathedral city as the setting for the story ; and he called the city Cloisterham.

" For sufficient reasons, which this narrative will itself unfold as it advances, a fictitious name must be bestowed upon the old Cathedral town. Let it stand in these pages as Cloisterham . . .

" An ancient city, Cloisterham, and no meet dwelling-place for any one with hankerings after the noisy world. . . .

" A drowsy city, Cloisterham, whose inhabitants seem to suppose, with an inconsistency more strange than rare, that all its changes lie behind it, and that there are no more to come. . . . So silent are the streets of Cloisterham (though prone to echo on the smallest provocation), that of a summer-day the sunblinds of its shops scarce dare to flap in the south wind . . . " The streets of Cloisterham city are little more than one narrow street by which you get into it and get out of it ; the rest being mostly disappointing yards with pumps in them and no thoroughfare— exception made of the Cathedral Close, and a paved Quaker settlement, in colour and general conformation very like a Quakeress's bonnet, up in a shady corner."

" In a word, a city of another and a bygone time is Cloisterham, with its hoarse Cathedral-bell, its hoarse rooks hovering about the Cathedral tower."

His last description of Rochester and its Cathedral is as beautiful as any he ever penned.

" A brilliant morning shines on the old city. Its antiquities and ruins are surpassingly beautiful, with a lusty ivy gleaming in the sun, and the rich trees waving in the balmy air. Changes of glorious light from moving boughs, songs of birds, scents from gardens, woods, and fields—or, rather, from the one great

garden of the whole cultivated island in its yielding
time—penetrate into the Cathedral, subdue its earthy
odour, and preach the Resurrection and the Life.
The cold stone tombs of centuries ago grow warm ;
and flecks of brightness dart into the sternest marble
corners of the building, fluttering there like wings."

He was writing this in the Chalet at Gad's Hill
(now in Cobham Park, see page 178) on the afternoon
of the June day that was his last on earth ; a very
few more words and *The Mystery of Edwin Drood* was
laid aside for ever, to prove a mystery that is perhaps
unsolvable. A few days before he had been seen in
Rochester, " peeping about " the nooks and corners
he loved so much, and it was thought that this last
number would contain other word-pictures of the city ;
but no notes remained.

Forster gives an interesting account of a visit paid
to Rochester and district on the occasion of Dickens's
thirty-fourth birthday The party consisted of Mrs.
Dickens and her sister, Maclise, Jerrold, and Forster ;
" going over the old Castle, Watts's Charity, and Chatham fortifications on the Saturday, passing Sunday in
Cobham Church and Cobham Park ; having our
quarters both days at the Bull Inn made famous in
Pickwick ; and thus, by indulgence of the desire which
was always strangely urgent in him, associating his
new resolve in life with those earliest scenes of his
youthful time."

In the concluding remarks to *Dullborough Town* in
The Uncommercial Traveller Dickens writes :

" When I went alone to the Railway to catch my
train at night I was in a more charitable mood with
Dullborough than I had been all day ; and yet in
my heart I had loved it all day too. Ah ! who was I
that I should quarrel with the town for being changed
to me, when I myself had come back, so changed,
to it ! All my early readings and early imaginations

13

dated from this place, and I took them away so full of innocent construction and guileless belief, and I brought them back so worn and torn, so much the wiser and so much the worse ! "

So much for a brief survey of Dickens's association with Rochester and Chatham. We shall now proceed to take a ramble through the two towns, noting all the places of interest figuring in his books and in his life.

The most convenient starting place for a ramble through Rochester and Chatham is Rochester Bridge. This was the way most of Dickens's characters approached the Cathedral City. The railway was not mentioned until the last novel, *Edwin Drood*, in which we are told : " In those days there was no railway to Cloisterham, and Mr. Sapsea said there never would be. Mr. Sapsea said more ; he said there never should be. And yet, marvellous to consider, it has come to pass, in these days, that Express Trains don't think Cloisterham worth stopping at, but yell and whirl through it on their larger errands, casting the dust off their wheels as a testimony against its insignificance."

Old Rochester Bridge, the one Dickens always had in his mind's eye, was pulled down in 1859 ; the balustrades were used in the construction of the Esplanade in front of the Castle and one of them was presented to Dickens, who placed it on the lawn at Gad's Hill, adorned with a sun-dial.

The bridge in recent years has unfortunately undergone a further alteration, rendering it an eyesore, and obscuring the view of the Castle and Cathedral, which was formerly a very pleasing prospect.

It was by the bridge that the Pickwickians first caught sight of Rochester, its castle and Cathedral, which called forth the admiration of the Pickwickians " when they first came in sight of the fine old castle "

which probably interrupted the stories of the loquacious
stranger, Alfred Jingle, for we read : " In this strain . . .
did the stranger proceed until they reached Rochester
Bridge, by which time the note books, both of Mr.
Pickwick and Mr. Snodgrass, were completly filled."

" ' Magnificent ruin,' said Mr. Augustus Snodgrass
with all the poetic fervour that distinguished him. . . .

" ' What a sight for an antiquarian,' were the
very words which fell from Mr. Pickwick's mouth,
as he applied his telescope to his eye.

" ' Ah ! Fine place,' said the stranger, ' glorious
pile, frowning walls—tottering arches . . . old cathedral
too. . . .' "

On a later occasion, it will be remembered, Mr.
Pickwick was on the bridge wrapped in contemplation
of the scene before him, when he was interrupted
by the dismal man who made allusion to drowning
being a happiness on such a morning ; at which
Mr. Pickwick edged " a little from the balustrade,
as the possibility of the dismal man's tipping him
over, by way of experiment, occurred to him rather
forcibly "—maybe the balustrade presented to Dickens
was the identical one which supported Mr. Pickwick's
portly frame !

" Bright and pleasant was the sky, balmy the
air, and beautiful the appearance of every object
around, as Mr. Pickwick leant over the balustrades
of Rochester Bridge, contemplating nature, and
waiting for breakfast. The scene was indeed one which
might well have charmed a far less reflective mind,
than that to which it was presented.

" On the left of the spectator lay the ruined wall,
broken in many places, and in some, overhanging
the narrow beach below in rude and heavy masses.
Huge knots of sea-weed hung upon the jagged and
pointed stones, trembling in every breath of wind ;
and the green ivy clung mournfully round the dark

and ruined battlements. Behind it rose the ancient castle, its towers roofless, and its massive walls crumbling away, but telling us proudly of its own might and strength, as when, seven hundred years ago, it rang with the clash of arms, or resounded with the noise of feasting and revelry.

Little David Copperfield records in Chapter thirteen how he crossed Rochester Bridge at the end of the second day of his tramp to Dover " footsore and tired, and eating bread that I had bought for supper. One or two little houses, with the notice, ' Lodgings for travellers,' hanging out, had tempted me ; but I was afraid of spending the few pence I had, and was even more afraid of the vicious looks of the trampers I had met or overtaken. I sought no shelter, therefore, but the sky."

And Richard Doubledick in *The Seven Poor Travellers* " limped over the bridge here with half a shoe to his dusty foot."

There are one or two other incidents directly connected with Rochester Bridge, which we may mention here. We can see Pip after he had news of his Great Expectations, feeling uncomfortable in his resplendent dress as a gentleman, and being pursued across the bridge by Trabb's boy, who, when passing abreast of him " pulled up his shirt collar, twined his side hair, stuck an arm akimbo and smirked extravagantly by, wriggling his elbows and body and drawling to his attendants. ' Don't know yah, don't know yah, 'pon my soul don't know yah ! ' "

The river at Rochester is the Medway, and here came Mr. Micawber when, on the advice of some branches of Mrs. Micawber's family, he turned his attention to coals, being " induced to think, on inquiry, that there might be an opening for a man of his talent in the Medway Coal Trade. Then, as Mr. Micawber very properly said, the first step to be taken clearly was, to come and *see* the Medway. . . . We came, and saw the Medway," added Mrs. Micawber who gave it as her opinion that " It may require talent, but that it certainly requires capital. Talent, Mr. Micawber has ; capital, Mr. Micawber has not. We saw, I think, the greater part of the Medway ; and that is my individual conclusion."

Strange to say there is no description of Mr. Micawber's stay in Rochester.

The bridge leads straight into the High Street of which Dickens says in revisiting " Dullborough Town," " of course, the town had shrunk fearfully. I had entertained the impression that the High Street was at least as wide as Regent Street, London. I found it little better than a lane."

" The silent High Street of Rochester is full of gables with old beams and timbers carved into strange faces," says Dickens in *The Seven Poor Travellers*, and in " The Great Winglebury Duel " he describes it as " a long straggling, quiet High Street, with a great black and white clock at a small red Town Hall half way up."

Rochester High Street has many other memories. We can recall Alfred Jingle, having received the invitation of the Pickwickians to dine with them, marching off from the Bull. " Lifting the pinched-up hat a few inches from his head, and carelessly replacing it very much on one side, the stranger, with half the brown paper parcel sticking out of his pocket, walked briskly up the yard, and turned into the High Street."

We can conjure up a picture of that " curious little green box on four wheels with a low place, like a wine bin, for two behind, and an elevated perch for one in front, drawn by an immense brown horse, displaying great symmetry of bone," drawn up in front of the Bull ; and we can see Mr. Winkle endeavouring to mount the horse on the wrong side ; and the same horse, when ultimately mounted, " drifting up the street in the most mysterious manner, side first, with his head towards one side of the way and his tail towards the other."

We can see Rosa purchasing the Turkish Delicacy at " the Lumps of Delight Shop " ; we can picture the shop where Neville Landless bought the knapsack and the heavy walking-stick ; and the shop where Edwin went to have his watch repaired, when the jeweller told him how Jasper had said, " he had an inventory in his mind of all the jewellery his gentlemen relative ever wore." We can see the old Opium Woman wandering in the High Street, on the watch for the omnibus that is to bring Jasper from the railway station, and having her interview with Mr. Grewgious there. We can see Pip in *Great Expectations* visiting Mr. Trabb the tailor, the open window of whose parlour behind the shop " looked into a prosperous little garden and orchard, and there was a prosperous iron safe let into the wall at the side of the fireplace," and we can picture the collapse of the great but nameless character, Trabb's boy, as he was directed by his master to show—Door !

At the commencement of High Street, on the right is the Crown Hotel, once kept by Wright, referred to by Jingle, who was asked by the Pickwickians if he was stopping at the Bull Inn : " Here—not I— but you'd better—good house—nice beds—Wright's next house, dear—very dear—half-a-crown in the bill if you look at the waiter—charge you more if you dine at a friend's than they would if you dined in the coffee-room—rum fellows—very."

The Crown is also said to be the Crozier of *Edwin Drood*, where Mr. Datchery put up on his first arrival in Cloisterham, but Dickens may have had in mind the Mitre at Chatham (see page 221).

A few doors past the Crown is the Bull. This was

the destination of the Pickwickians, for after crossing the bridge " they arrived at the Bull Inn, in the High Street, where the coach stopped." On Mr. Winkle enquiring of Jingle if he stayed there the stranger replied, with this striking advertisement of the hotel, of which the subsequent proprietors have not failed to make use, " Here—not I—but you'd better—good house—nice neds."

In " The Great Winglebury Duel " (*Sketches by Boz*) there is a description of the Bull which is missing from any other references. It is then called the " Winglebury Arms " and described as situated " in the centre of the High Street, opposite the small building with the big clock. . . . The house is a large one with a red brick and stone front. A pretty spacious hall, ornamented with evergreen plants, terminates in a perspective view of the bar, and a glass case, in which are displayed a choice variety of delicacies ready for dressing, to catch the eye of the new-comer the moment he enters, and excite his appetite to the highest possible pitch. Opposite doors lead to the ' Coffee ' and ' Commercial ' rooms ; and a great wide, rambling staircase, three stairs and a landing— four stairs and another landing—one step and another landing—half-a-dozen stairs and another landing— and so on—conducts to galleries of bedrooms, and labyrinths of sitting-rooms, denominated ' private,' where you may enjoy yourself, as privately as you can in any place where some bewildered being or other walks into your room every five minutes by mistake, and then walks out again, to open all the doors along the gallery till he finds his own."

The whereabouts and identity of the Blue Lion and Stomach Warmer Inn also at Great Winglebury in the same story are not known.

In *Great Expectations* the Bull figures as the Blue Boar, where Pip's sister, becoming so excited by the twenty-five guineas which Pip had received from Miss Havisham on being bound 'prentice to Joe, that " nothing would serve her but we must have a dinner out of that windfall, at the Blue Boar," on which occasion, " Mr. Wopsle gave us Collins's ode, and threw his blood-stain'd ̇ sword in thunder down, with such effect that a waiter came in and said, ' The Commercials underneath sent up their compliments, and it wasn't the Tumblers' Arms.' "

Here too in later days Pip stayed with Mr. Jaggers, when his expectations warranted him living like a gentle-man ; but what a difference in the Boar's demeanour, when it was found that the rich and eccentric Miss Havisham was not the founder of his fortunes !

" I found the Blue Boar in possession of the intelli-gence, and I found that it made a great change in the Boar's demeanour . . . The Boar could not put me into my usual bedroom, which was engaged (probably by some one who had expectations), and could only assign me a very indifferent chamber among the pigeons and post-chaises up the yard. But, I had as sound a sleep in that lodging as in the most superior accommodation the Boar could have given me, and the quality of my dreams was about the same as in the best bedroom."

On the ground floor the present lounge was formerly the coffee-room, in which the amazed Winkle, wrapped in a travelling shawl and dressing gown, met Dr. Slammer's second and was challenged to the duel. From the coffee-room window Mr. Pickwick beheld the " curious little green box on four wheels with a low place like a wine bin for two behind and an elevated perch for one in front " that was to take them to Dingley Dell.

Here in this room we can see again the picture Dickens drew for us of the meeting in *Great Expecta-tions* between Pip and Bentley Drummle.

" As he pretended not to see me, I pretended not to see him. It was a very lame pretence on both sides ; the lamer, because we both went into the coffee-room, where he had just finished his breakfast, and where I had ordered mine. It was poisonous to me to see him in the town, for I very well knew why he had come there."

The staircase, on which Jingle insulted Dr. Slammer whilst dressed in Winkle's clothes, leads to the ball-room.

" ' Devil of a mess on the staircase, waiter,' said the stranger. 'Forms going up—carpenters coming down —lamps, glasses, harps. What's going forward ? ' ' Ball, Sir,' said the waiter."

The ball-room remains pretty much as it was when Dickens knew it, except that it is now used as a dining-room : " a long room, with crimson-covered benches, and wax candles in glass chandeliers. The musicians were securely confined in an elevated den, and quad-rilles were being systematically got through by two or three sets of dancers."

Bedroom No. 17 is pointed out as being the one " occupied by Mr. Pickwick," and Nos. 13 and 19 as the rooms of Messrs. Tupman and Winkle, these two being inter-communicating, for we are told that " Winkle's bedroom is inside mine," said Mr. Tupman, and this ensured the successful abstraction of the former's dress coat, and its subsequent replacement " without troubling him at all about the matter."

No. 17—Mr. Pickwick's room—Dickens himself occupied more than once. In *The Seven Poor Travellers*, we read how he went back to his inn to give the necessary directions for the turkey and roast beef, and, during the remainder of the day, could settle to nothing for thinking of the Poor Travellers, picturing them " advancing towards their resting-place along various cold roads, and felt delighted to think how little they foresaw the supper that awaited them. . . .

After the Cathedral bell had struck eight, I could smell a delicious savour of Turkey and roast Beef rising to the window of my adjoining bedroom, which looked down into the inn-yard just where the lights of the kitchen reddened a massive fragment of the Castle Wall." He then proceeded to make the Wassail " in a brown earthenware pitcher, tenderly suffocated, when full, with a coarse cloth." And on the stroke of nine, he set out for Watts's Charity, carrying the brown beauty in his arms. " I would trust Ben, the waiter, with untold gold; but there are strings in the human heart which must never be sounded by another, and drinks that I make myself are those strings in mine."

Opposite the Bull is the Town Hall, where Pip was bound an apprentice to his brother-in-law Joe Gargery.

" The Hall was a queer place, I thought, with higher pews in it than a church . . . and with some shining black portraits on the walls, which my un-artistic eye regarded as a composition of hardbake and sticking-plaister. Here, in a corner, my indentures were duly signed and attested, and I was ' bound.' "

A short distance beyond the Town Hall is the Corn Exchange described in *The Seven Poor Travellers* as being " oddly garnished with a queer old clock that projects over the pavement out of a grave red brick building, as if Time carried on business there, and hung out his sign.

In talking of his re-visit to " Dullborough Town " Dickens confuses this building with the Town Hall.

There was a public clock in the High Street, he says, " which I had supposed to be the finest clock in the world ; whereas it now turned out to be as inexpressive, moon-faced and weak a clock as ever I saw. It belonged to a Town Hall. . . . The edifice had appeared to me in those days so glorious a structure that I had set it up in my mind as the model on which

the Genie of the Lamp built the Palace for Aladdin.
A mean little brick heap, like a demented chapel, with
a few yawning persons in leather gaiters, and in the
last extremity for something to do, lounging at the
door with their hands in their pockets, and calling
themselves a Corn Exchange."

On the opposite side of High Street we see a quaintly
gabled house surmounting a gateway and leading to
the Cathedral Close. This is College Gate, but it is
better known through the medium of *Edwin Drood* as
Jasper's Gate House, and is so marked by a bronze
tablet with the City Arms and the following inscription :

College Gate
formerly called " Cemetery Gate "
and afterwards " Chertsey's Gate "
Jasper's Gate House, " Edwin Drood."

We are first introduced to it in Chapter II of *Edwin
Drood* as Jasper's " bachelor gatehouse " " an old
stone gatehouse crossing the Close, with an arched
thoroughfare passing beneath it. Through its latticed
window, a fire shines out upon the fast-darkening
scene, involving in shadow the pendant masses of ivy
and creeper covering the building's front."

On two subsequent occasions Dickens likens this
quaint piece of architecture to a lighthouse. " One
might fancy that the tide of life was stemmed by Mr.
Jasper's own gatehouse. The murmur of the tide
is heard beyond ; but no wave passes the archway,
over which his lamp burns red behind his curtain, as
if the building were a Lighthouse."

Inside the gateway on the left is the house of the
verger Tope, with whom the much-discussed Dick
Datchery came to lodge.

" Mr. Tope's official dwelling, communicating by
an upper stair with Mr. Jasper's (hence Mrs. Tope's

attendance on that gentleman), was of very modest proportions, and partook of the character of a cool dungeon. Its ancient walls were massive, and its rooms rather seemed to have been dug out of them, than to have been designed beforehand with any reference to them. The main door opened at once on a chamber of no describable shape, with a groined roof, which in its turn opened on another chamber of no describable shape, with another groined roof : their windows small, and in the thickness of the walls."

This house has a melancholy interest, as the last lines Dickens penned had reference to it :

'Mrs. Tope's care has spread a very neat, clean breakfast ready for her lodger. Before sitting down to it, he opens his corner-cupboard door ; takes his bit of chalk from its shelf ; adds one thick line to the score, extending from the top of the cupboard door to the bottom ; and then falls to with an appetite."

Rochester Cathedral Close naturally figures very largely in the story of *Edwin Drood*.

Edwin and Rosa " wandered discontentedly about the old Close " on the occasion of the first suggestion of their engagement being broken off, " and each sometimes stops and slowly imprints a deeper footstep in the fallen leaves."

Sir Luke Fildes' picture " Under the Trees " depicts a part of the Close.

When at length they really decided to part it was " among the quiet walks in the neighbourhood of the Cathedral and the river " that they said good-bye to each other :

" When they came among the elm-trees by the Cathedral, where they had last sat together, they stopped as by consent.'

Another description of the precincts is also given in *Edwin Drood*.

" Among those secluded nooks there is very little

JASPER'S GATE HOUSE, ROCHESTER

stir or movement after dark. There is little enough in the high tide of the day, but there is next to none at night. Besides that the cheerfully frequented High Street lies nearly parallel to the spot (the old Cathedral rising between the two), and is the natural channel in which the Cloisterham traffic flows, a certain awful hush pervades the ancient pile, the cloisters, and the churchyard, after dark, which not many people care to encounter."

In *Great Expectations* there is also a reference to the Cathedral Close, although no other mention of the Cathedral itself is made in that book.

" The best light of the day was gone when I passed along the quiet echoing courts behind the High Street. The nooks of ruin where the old monks had once had their refectories and gardens, and where the strong walls were now pressed into the service of humble sheds and stables, were almost as silent as the old monks in their graves. The cathedral chimes had at once a sadder and a more remote sound to me, as I hurried on avoiding observation, than they had ever had before; so, the swell of the old organ was borne to my ears like funeral music ; and the rooks, as they hovered about the grey tower and swung in the bare high trees of the priory-garden, seemed to call to me that the place was changed, and that Estella was gone out of it for ever."

The first reference to Rochester Cathedral is in *Pickwick* when the Pickwickians cross the bridge and view it before them ; and Jingle gives the following terse description :

" Old Cathedral too—earthy smell—pilgrims' feet worn away the old steps—little Saxon doors—confessionals like money-takers' boxes at theatres—queer customers those monks—Popes, and Lord Treasurers, and all sorts of old fellows, with great red faces, and broken noses, turning up every day—buff jerkins too—

match-locks—Sarcophagus—fine place—old legends too—strange stories : capital."

Cloisterham was but a thin disguise for Rochester ; and it was at the Cathedral that Jasper was lay precentor. The story opens with a vision of the doped Jasper in the opium den in the East End of London. "An ancient English Cathedral Tower ? How can the ancient English Cathedral tower be here ! The well-known massive grey square tower of its old Cathedral ? How can that be here ! "

And the close of the chapter tells us,

" That same afternoon, the massive grey square tower of an old Cathedral rises before the sight of a jaded traveller. The bells are going for daily vesper service, and he must needs attend it, one would say, from his haste to reach the open Cathedral door."

When Mr. Grewgious, Rosa's guardian, came down from London to visit her he afterwards sought Jasper at the Cathedral.

" And, crossing the Close, paused at the great western folding-door of the Cathedral, which stood open on the fine and bright, though short-lived, afternoon, for the airing of the place.

"'Dear me,' said Mr. Grewgious, peeping in, ' it's like looking down the throat of Old Time.' "

Mr. Sapsea, in showing Mr. Datchery the principal sights of Cloisterham, says :

" This is our Cathedral, sir. The best judges are pleased to admire it, and the best among our townsmen own to being a little vain of it. . . .

" Then Mr. Datchery admired the Cathedral, and Mr. Sapsea pointed it out as if he himself had invented and built it : there were a few details indeed of which he did not approve, but those he glossed over, as if the workmen had made mistakes in his absence."

The Crypt and the Tower both play important parts in the mystery that surrounds *Edwin Drood*.

Inside the Cathedral, is the tomb and effigy of Watts, the Philanthropist of Rochester, to which Dickens refers in *The Seven Poor Travellers*.

Below it is a tablet of brass to the memory of Dickens, bearing this inscription :

CHARLES DICKENS

Born at Portsmouth Seventh of February 1812 Died at Gadshill Place by Rochester Ninth of June 1870 Buried in Westminster Abbey.

—————

To connect his memory with the scenes in which his earliest and his latest years were passed and with the associations of Rochester Cathedral and its neighbourhood which extended over all his life This tablet with the sanction of the Dean and Chapter is placed by his Executors.

The little burial ground outside is where Dickens expressed a desire to be buried, but the greater claim to Westminster Abbey prevailed.

It bears a tablet, inscribed :

This Ground was originally part of the Castle Moat. Charles Dickens wished to be buried here.

Here was the Sapsea Vault which was doubtless meant to play an important part in unravelling the great mystery.

" When Mr. Sapsea has nothing better to do, towards evening, he often takes an airing in the Cathedral Close and thereabout. He likes to pass the churchyard with a swelling air of proprietorship, and to encourage in his breast a sort of benignant-landlord feeling, in that he has been bountiful towards that meritorious tenant, Mrs. Sapsea, and has publicly given her a prize. He likes to see a stray face or two looking in through the railings, and perhaps reading his inscription."

Beyond the west door of the Cathedral there is a road which takes us into Minor Canon Row described in *The Seven Poor Travellers* as " a wonderfully quaint row of red-brick tenements, which were inhabited by the Minor Canons. They had odd little porches over the doors, like sounding-boards over old pulpits ; and I thought I should like to see one of the Minor Canons come out upon his top step, and favour us with a little Christmas discourse about the poor scholars of Rochester ; taking for his text the words of his Master relative to the devouring of Widows' houses."

This was the Minor Canon Corner of *Edwin Drood*, where the Rev. Canon Crisparkle lived with his Ma, the " China Shepherdess "—" a quiet place in the shadow of the Cathedral, which the cawing of the rooks, the echoing footsteps of rare passers, the sound of the Cathedral bell, or the roll of the Cathedral organ, seemed to render more quiet than absolute silence. Red-brick walls harmoniously toned down in colour by time, strong-rooted ivy, latticed windows, panelled rooms, big oaken beams in little places, and stone-walled gardens where annual fruit yet ripened upon monkish trees.'

Leaving Minor Canon Row behind us on the left, we ascend Boley Hill, where is situated the one-time residence of Richard Watts, called Satis House.

When Queen Elizabeth visited Rochester in 1573, Watts entertained her here. To his expressions of regret at having no better accommodation to offer, the Queen replied " Satis," by which name the house was henceforth known. Dickens transferred the name of this house to Restoration House (see page 215) when giving a home to Miss Havisham in *Great Expectations*.

MINOR CANON CORNER, ROCHESTER

THE FORGE AT CHALK

From Boley Hill the Castle grounds are soon reached. We have already viewed it with the Pickwickians from the top of the Commodore coach as they entered the city, and with Mr. Pickwick as he contemplated nature and waited for breakfast (see page 195).

In *The Seven Poor Travellers* is a further description of Rochester Castle.

" Sooth to say, he (Time) did an active stroke of work in Rochester, in the old days of the Romans, and the Saxons, and the Normans, and down to the time of King John, when the rugged castle—I will not undertake to say how many hundreds of years old then—was abandoned to the centuries of weather, which have so defaced the dark apertures in its walls, that the ruin looks as if the rooks and daws had picked its eye out."

And prior to the dinner to the Poor Travellers at Watts's Charity, Dickens tells us how he " climbed to the top of the old Castle, and looked over the windy hills that slope down to the Medway," almost believing that he could " descry some of my Travellers in the distance."

In Dickens's time, before the present Castle grounds were planned, the Castle was rather inaccessible ; the following extract from Forster's *Life of Dickens* refers to a visit Forster, Longfellow, and Dickens paid to Rochester in 1842 :

" One day at Rochester, met by one of those prohibitions which are the wonder of visitors and the shame of Englishmen, we overleapt gates and barriers, and, setting at defiance repeated threats of all the terrors of law coarsely expressed to us by the custodian of the place, explored minutely the castle ruins."

Edwin and Rosa took their last walk together by the river when their engagement was broken off ; and on the night of his disappearance Edwin Drood walked this way after he had met the old Opium Woman in

14

the Vines, and prior to his repairing to his Uncle's gatehouse.

" And so *he* goes up the postern stair."

The athletic Minor Canon of *Edwin Drood*—Mr. Crisparkle, was very familiar with the Castle ruins and the river wall, " the Cathedral being very cold, he set off for a brisk trot after service ; the trot to end in a charge at his favourite fragment of ruin, which was to be carried by storm, without a pause for breath. He carried it in a masterly manner, and, not breathed even then, stood looking down upon the river." This was a favourite walk too with Helena Landless, whom he met here on one occasion.

A little beyond Jasper's Gatehouse, and on the opposite side of the way, is the quaintly gabled Watts's Charity, better known as the House of the Seven Poor Travellers after the Christmas story of that name.

Dickens visited it in company with Wilkie Collins in 1854, and the effect of his account of his visit was to remedy the abuse to which his attention was directed.

" Strictly speaking, there were only six Poor Travellers ; but, being a traveller myself, though an idle one, and being withal as poor as I hope to be, I brought the number up to seven. This word of explanation is due at once, for what says the inscription over the quaint old door ?

RICHARD WATTS, ESQUIRE,
by his will dated 22nd August, 1579,
founded this Charity,
for Six Poor Travellers,
who, not being Rogues or Proctors,
May receive gratis for one Night,
Lodging, Entertainment,
and Fourpence each."

Having seen over the house, Dickens hit upon the idea of entertaining the Six Poor Travellers :

WATTS' CHARITY, ROCHESTER
THE HOUSE OF THE SEVEN POOR TRAVELLERS

" It was settled that at nine o'clock that night a
Turkey and a piece of Roast Beef should smoke upon
the board ; and that I, faint and unworthy minister
for once of Master Richard Watts, should preside as
the Christmas-supper host of the six Poor Travellers."

With this in view he returned to the Bull Hotel,
and from his bedroom " could smell a delicious savour
of Turkey and Roast Beef rising to the window." Here
he " made a glorious jorum " of Wassail, in a brown
pitcher.

On the stroke of nine, he set out for Watts's Charity
carrying his " brown beauty " (the pitcher of Wassail)
in his arms . . . the supper following in procession.

> " Myself with the pitcher.
> Ben with Beer.
> Inattentive Boy with hot plates.
> Inattentive Boy with hot plates.
> THE TURKEY.
> Female carrying sauces to be heated on
> the spot.
> THE BEEF.
> Man with Tray on his head, containing
> Vegetables and Sundries.
> Volunteer Hostler from Hotel, grinning,
> And rendering no assistance.

" As we passed along the High Street, comet-like
we left a long trail of fragrance behind us which
caused the public to stop, sniffing in wonder. We had
previously left at the corner of the inn-yard a wall-
eyed young man connected with the Fly department,
and well accustomed to the sound of a railway whistle,
which Ben always carries in his pocket, whose instructions were, so soon as he should hear the whistle
blown, to dash into the kitchen, seize the hot plum-
pudding and mince-pies and speed with them to
Watts's Charity, where they would be received (he was

further instructed) by the sauce-female, who would be provided with brandy in a blue state of combustion.

"All these arrangements were executed in the most exact and punctual manner. I never saw a finer turkey, finer beef, or greater prodigality of sauce and gravy ; and my Travellers did wonderful justice to everything set before them. It made my heart rejoice to observe how their wind and frost hardened faces softened in the clatter of plates and knives and forks, and mellowed in the fire and supper heat."

A little farther along the High Street, on the same side as Watts's Charity, is a venerable brick edifice known as Eastgate House, which figured in *Edwin Drood* as the Nuns' House, the Seminary for Young Ladies kept by Miss Twinkleton at which Rosa was a pupil. "In the midst of Cloisterham stands the Nuns' House : a venerable brick edifice, whose present appellation is doubtless derived from the legend of its conventual uses. On the trim gate enclosing its old courtyard is a resplendent brass plate flashing forth the legend ; ' Seminary for Young Ladies. Miss Twinkleton.' The house-front is so old and worn, and the brass plate is so shining and staring, that the general result has reminded imaginative strangers of a battered old beau with a large modern eye-glass stuck in his blind eye."

The house is marked with an oblong bronze tablet bearing the City Arms and the following inscription :

EASTGATE HOUSE.

Built by the Right Worshipful Sir Peter Buck, 1590.
" Westgate House." *Pickwick Papers.*
" The Nuns' House." *Edwin Drood.*

In the porch is another bronze tablet with the City Arms and the the following inscription :

EASTGATE HOUSE.

The Nun's House of Charles Dickens's *Edwin Drood*.

Purchased by the Corporation in 1887 in the Mayoralty of Sir William Webb Hayward as a Diamond Jubilee Memorial of Her late Majesty Queen Victoria, opened as a Public Museum by the Right Honourable Earl Stanhope, Lord Lieutenant of the County, and President of the Kent Archaeological Society in the Mayoralty of William John McLellan, J.P., on March 30th, 1903.

One of the rooms is set apart as a Dickens Museum and contains many interesting items.

It is generally thought that Dickens had in mind Eastgate House, Rochester, when writing in *Pickwick* the account of Miss Tomkins's Establishment for Young Ladies at Bury St. Edmund's under the name of Westgate House. Indeed, we have only to stand in front of it to see in action the whole scene of Mr. Pickwick scaling the wall with the aid of Sam Weller prior to entering upon his adventure the other side.

"Over against the Nuns' House" was, we are told, the residence of Mr. Sapsea, auctioneer, "the purest jackass in Cloisterham"; and there, opposite us, is the pretty collection of gabled houses bearing a tablet reading :

"Mr Sapsea's House." *Edwin Drood.*
"Pumblechook's Premises." *Great Expectations.*

"Mr. Sapsea's premises are in the High Street, over against the Nuns' House. They are of about the period of the Nuns' House, irregularly modernised here and there, as steadily deteriorating generations found, more and more, that they preferred air and light to Fever and the Plague. Over the doorway is a wooden effigy, about half life-size, representing Mr. Sapsea's father, in a curly wig and toga, in the act of selling. The chastity of the idea, and the natural appearance of the little finger, hammer, and pulpit, have been much admired."

At one time a carved wooden figure of an auctioneer such as Dickens describes actually did grace the doorway.

In Dickens's time too the house was kept by John Bye Fairbairn, a seedsman, and as the " eminently convenient and commodious business premises situated within a hundred miles of High Street," of Uncle Pumblechook it actually appeared in *Great Expectations*.

" Mr. Pumblechook's premises in the High Street of the market town, were of a peppercorny and farinaceous character, as the premises of a corn-chandler and seedsman should be. It appeared to me that he must be a very happy man indeed, to have so many little drawers in his shop : and I wondered when I peeped into one or two on the lower tiers, and saw the tied-up brown paper packets inside, whether the flower-seeds and bulbs ever wanted of a fine day to break out of those jails, and bloom."

The next turning past Mr. Pumblechook's premises is the Maidstone Road. This was formerly known as Crow Lane. Here on the left, on the site now occupied by shops, once stood a low public-house known as The White Duck and later as Kitt's Lodging House. This is said to have been the Traveller's Twopenny in *Edwin Drood*, a " crazy wooden house of two low stories currently known as the Travellers' Twopenny :— a house all warped and distorted, like the morals of the travellers, with scant remains of a lattice-work porch over the door, and also of a rustic fence before its stamped-out garden ; by reason of the travellers being so bound to the premises by a tender sentiment (or so fond of having a fire by the roadside in the course of the day), that they can never be persuaded or threatened into departure, without violently possessing themselves of some wooden forget-me-not, and bearing it off.

" The semblance of an inn is attempted to be given to this wretched place by fragments of conventional red curtaining in the windows, which rags are made muddily transparent in the night-season by feeble lights of rush or cotton dip burning dully in the close air of the inside.

The vineyard referred to in the same description is a little farther along on the right. It is now a public garden called the Vines, and there is a pleasant walk across it into Minor Canon Row and the Cathedral.

In *Edwin Drood* it is called the Monks' Vineyard.

On the evening of his disappearance Edwin wanders in this direction and meets the old Opium Woman, who warns him that Edwin is a threatened name. " As dusk draws on, he paces the Monks' Vineyard. He has walked to and fro, full half an hour by the Cathedral chimes, and it has closed in dark, before he becomes quite aware of a woman crouching on the ground near a wicket gate in a corner. The gate commands a cross bye-path, little used in the gloaming ; and the figure must have been there all the time, though he has but gradually and lately made it out."

Opposite the Vines Gardens is an ancient house of striking picturesqueness, known as Restoration House ; but to Dickens readers it is the house of Miss Havisham, that figures so largely in *Great Expectations*.

Miss Havisham was " an immensely rich and grim lady," who lived " in a large and dismal house barricaded against robbers and who led a life of seclusion." Pip thus made his first acquaintance with it :

" Within a quarter of an hour we came to Miss Havisham's house, which was of old brick, and dismal, and had a great many iron bars to it. Some of the windows had been walled up ; of those that remained, all the lower were rustily barred. There was a court-yard in front, and that was barred ; so, we had to wait, after ringing the bell, until some one should come to open it. While we waited at the gate, I peeped in (even then Mr. Pumblechook said, ' And fourteen ? ' but I pretended not to hear him), and saw that at the side of the house there was a large brewery. No brewing was going on in it, and none seemed to have gone on for a long time."

Estella enlightened him further a few minutes later, by saying :

" As to strong beer, there's enough of it in the cellars already, to drown the Manor House."

" ' Is that the name of this house, miss ? '

" ' One of its names, boy.'

" ' It has more than one, then, miss ? '

" ' One more. Its other name was Satis ; which is Greek, or Latin, or Hebrew, or all three—or all one to me—for enough."

" Enough House ! ' said I : ' that's a curious name, miss.'

" ' Yes,' she replied ; ' but it meant more than it said. It meant, when it was given, that whoever had this house, could want nothing else. They must have been easily satisfied in those days, I should think.' "

The name of Satis House was taken by Dickens from the residence of Watts on Boley Hill, to which we have already referred on page 208.

A walk in this direction was a great favourite with Dickens. " He would turn out of Rochester High Street," says Forster, " through the Vines, where some old buildings, from one of which called Restoration House he took Satis House for *Great Expectations*, had a curious attraction for him."

It is on record that the day before his death he took this walk and was noticed resting near the spot, and so attentively engaged in observing the house that it was thought likely he would introduce it into the story. The chapter he did write on his return—the last—had reference to the spot.

In *The Seven Poor Travellers* he tells us how after entertaining them and leaving for his inn, "as I passed along the High Street, I heard the Waits at a distance, and struck off to find them. They were playing near one of the old gates of the city." He accompanied them "across an open green called the Vines, and assisted—in a French sense—at the performance of two waltzes, two polkas and three Irish melodies before I thought of my inn any more."

We now arrive at about the spot where Rochester ends and Chatham begins ; we will not attempt to define it, preferring to remain in the happy ignorance of Richard Doubledick, one of the *Seven Poor Travellers*. "If anybody . . . knows to a nicety where Rochester ends and Chatham beings, it is more than I do."

At the top of Star Hill, New Road branches off to the left, and we follow its course. To the right are the recreation grounds rented from the military authorities by the Corporation of Chatham. Across the recreation grounds to the right is Fort Pitt, and beyond it a meadow, the scene of the memorable duel that was to have taken place between Mr. Winkle and Dr. Slammer.

On the second night of his walk to Dover, David rested at Chatham, by the fortifications of Fort Pitt.

"I sought no shelter therefore but the sky and toiling into Chatham—which, in that night's aspect, is a mere dream of chalk, and draw-bridges, and mastless ships in a muddy river, roofed like Noah's arks—crept, at last, upon a sort of grass-grown battery overhanging a lane, where a sentry was walking to and fro. Here I lay down, near a cannon ; and, happy in the society of the sentry's footsteps, . . . slept soundly until morning."

It was at Chatham that he decided to sell his jacket. "It was a likely place to sell a jacket in ; for the dealers in second-hand clothes were numerous, and were, generally speaking, on the look-out for customers at their shop-doors. But, as most of them had, hanging up among their stock, an officer's coat or two, epaulettes and all, I was rendered timid by the costly nature of their dealings, and walked about for a long time without offering my merchandise to any one."

At length he made the unhappy selection of Mr. Dolloby's shop, struck a bargain, and had the greatest difficulty in getting the money out of the dreadful old man with his " goroo, goroo " " eyes and limbs " " lungs and liver," bidding him " go for fourpence more."

Leaving Fort Pitt and turning to the left we find ourselves in Ordnance Terrace. Here at No. 11 (then No. 2) Charles Dickens lived from 1817 for about three years. The house bears the following tablet :

In this house
Charles Dickens
lived
1817–1821

Dickens's first school, not reckoning the primary lessons he received at his mother's knee, was near the railway station, not far from Ordnance Terrace. Behind the school was the playing field of many pleasant memories, but also, like many other things, it has gone. Upon revisiting Dullborough Town, rambling about the scenes from which he had departed in a coach as a child, *en route* for the blacking factory, and which he did not revisit until he was a man—he made the discovery as soon as he had alighted from the S.E.R. engine No. 97, " that the station had swallowed up the playing field."

" It was gone," he continues. " The two beautiful hawthorn trees, the hedge, the turf, and all those buttercups and daisies, had given place to the stoniest of jolting roads ; while beyond the station, an ugly dark monster of a tunnel kept its jaws open as if it had swallowed them and were ravenous for more destruction. . . .

" When I had been let out at the platform-door, like a prisoner whom his turnkey grudgingly released, I looked in again over the low wall, at the scene of departed glories. Here, in the hay-making time had I been delivered from the dungeons of Seringapatam, an immense pile (of haycock), by my countrymen, the victorious British (boy next door and his two cousins), and had been recognised with ecstasy by my affianced one (Miss Green), who had come all the way from England (second house in the terrace) to ransom me, and marry me."

Such was one of the gentle games that the " very small and not-over-particularly-taken-care-of-boy " indulged in and such is one of his earliest memories.

The early impressions of the neighbours in Ordnance Terrace were transferred to his first book *Sketches by Boz*. In *Our Parish* the old lady was drawn from a Mrs. Newnham who lived at No. 5 ; and the Half-pay Captain was also a near neighbour. With the Stroughill family, who lived next door, young Charles was particularly friendly ; George is said to have stood for Steerforth, and Lucy with the golden hair was his earliest sweetheart and figured in *The Wreck of the Golden Mary*.

Leaving the station we find ourselves, by way of Railway Street, in High Street, Chatham, once again. Crossing the road, and continuing straight on down Military Road, we find on our right a street oddly called The Brook. A short way down this street, on the right hand, is a lodging-house—No. 18, St. Mary's Place—bearing a tablet inscribed :

In this house
Charles Dickens
lived
1821–1823

Next door is a factory, at one time a chapel presided over by a young Baptist minister, Mr. William Giles, who kept a school to which young Charles was forthwith sent. A great friendship sprang up between master and pupil, and when his father was called up to London, Charles, then only eleven years of age, had to leave his good master and the old place endeared to him by recollections that clung to him afterwards all his life long. " The night before we came away," he told Forster, " my good master came flitting in among the packing cases to give me Goldsmith's ' Bee ' as a keepsake, which I kept for his sake, and its own, a long time afterwards."

It was in this Chatham house that he made acquaintance with the books that had so great an influence on his later life : *Roderick Random, Peregrine Pickle, Humphrey Clinker, Tom Jones, The Vicar of Wakefield, Don Quixote, Gil Blas,* and *Robinson Crusoe* " a glorious host, to keep me company. They kept alive my fancy, and my hope of something beyond that place and time—they, and the *Arabian Nights,* and the *Tales of the Genii . . .* It is curious to me how I could ever have consoled myself under my small troubles (which were great troubles to me), by impersonating my favourite characters in them. . . . I have been Tom Jones (a child's Tom Jones, a harmless creature) for a week together. I have sustained my own idea of Roderick Random for a month at a stretch, I verily believe . . . Every barn in the neighbourhood, every stone in the church, and every foot of the churchyard, had some association of its own, in my mind, connected with these books and stood for some locality made famous in them. I have seen Tom Pipes go climbing up the church-steeple ; I have watched Strap, with the knapsack on his back, stopping to rest himself upon the wicket-gate ; and I *know* that Commodore Trunnion held that club with Mr. Pickle in the parlour of our little village alehouse."

Indeed, herein lies one of the secrets of Charles Dickens's success. He was an actor before he was an author and lived the parts he afterwards put into stories.

Chatham Lines are not far from The Brook. This was the scene of the " grand review " which Mr. Pickwick witnessed when he lost his hat, and found an acquaintance in the jovial Mr. Wardle and family. One of the favourite walks of Dickens when he came to live at Gad's Hill was " by Rochester and the Medway, to the Chatham Lines. He would turn out of Rochester High Street through the Vines, pass round by Fort Pitt, and coming back by Frindsbury would bring himself by some cross fields again into the high road."

The Mitre in the High Street has a personal association with the boyhood of Dickens. In the days when the Dickens family lived at Chatham the landlord of the Mitre was John Tribe and the two families were on visiting terms, as young Charles and his sister Fanny used to sing duets at parties held here.

In *The Holly Tree* is a distinct reference to the Mitre. " There was an Inn in the cathedral town where I went to school. . . . It was the Inn where friends used to put up, and where we used to go to see parents, and to have salmon and fowls, and be tipped. It had an ecclesiastical sign—the Mitre—and a bar that seemed to be the next best thing to a bishopric, it was so snug. I loved the landlord's youngest daughter to distraction—but let that pass. It was in this Inn that I was cried over by my rosy little sister, because I had acquired a black eye in a fight. And though she had been, that Holly-Tree night, for many a long year where all tears are dried, the Mitre softened me yet."

And there is a further reference to it in *Great Expectations* when Pip tells us that, " avoiding the Blue Boar, I put up at an inn of minor reputation down the town, and ordered some dinner. . . . My inn had once been a part of an ancient ecclesiastical house, and I dined in a little octagonal common-room, like a font."

It is probable, too, that Dickens had the Mitre in view when he referred to the Crozier in *Edwin Drood*, although by many it is thought he referred to the Crown in Rochester (see page 198).

Nearly opposite the Mitre stood the Mechanic's Institute, in aid of the funds of which Dickens gave a reading from his works prior to commencing his public readings, and several at later dates.

At the foot of Chatham Hill formerly stood an old inn called the Malt Shovel, whose sign bore the rhyme attributed to the Pegasus's Arms in Chapter six of *Hard Times* :

> " Good malt makes good beer,
> Walk in, and they'll draw it here ;
> Good wine makes good brandy,
> Give us a call and you'll find it handy."

Of the Thames and the Medway at Chatham, Dickens makes some interesting personal remarks at the opening of a paper on " Chatham Dockyard " in *The Uncommercial Traveller*. " There are some small out-of-the-way landing-places on the Thames and the Medway, where I do much of my summer idling. Running water is favourable to day-dreams, and a strong tidal river is the best of running water for mine." Then follows what is intended to be a vision of himself as a boy at Chatham.

From one of the landing-places near an old fort " emerges a boy, to whom I am much indebted for additions to my scanty stock of knowledge. He is a young boy, with an intelligent face burnt to a dust colour by the summer sun, and with crisp hair of the same hue. He is a boy in whom I have perceived nothing incompatible with habits of studious inquiry and meditation. . . . To him I am indebted for ability to identify a Custom-house boat at any distance, and for acquaintance with all the forms and ceremonies observed by a homeward-bound Indiaman coming up the river, when the Custom-house officers go aboard her. But for him, I might never have heard of ' the dumb-ague,' respecting which malady I am now learned. Had I never sat at his feet, I might have finished my mortal career and never known that when I see a white horse on a barge's sail, that barge is a lime barge. For precious secrets in reference to beer, am I likewise beholden to him, involving warning against the beer of a certain establishment, by reason of its having turned sour through failure in point of demand : though my young sage is not of opinion that similar deterioration has befallen the ale. He has also enlightened me touching the mushrooms of the marshes, and has gently reproved my ignorance in having supposed them to be impregnated with salt."

The end of the year 1822 witnessed the departure of the Dickens family to London ; but Charles did not join them there until the following year, remaining behind with his schoolmaster, Mr. Giles. He has recorded this event in *Dullborough Town.*

" As I left Dullborough in the days when there were no railroads in the land," he says, " I left it in a stage coach. Through all the years that have since passed, have I ever lost the smell of the damp straw in which I was packed—like game—and forwarded, carriage paid, to the Cross Keys, Wood Street, Cheapside, London ? There was no other inside passenger, and I consumed my sandwiches in solitude and dreariness, and it rained hard all the way, and I thought life sloppier than I expected to find it. . . . The coach that had carried me away was melodiously called Timpson's Blue-Eyed-Maid, and belonged to Timpson, at the coach office up street."

CANTERBURY, DOVER, AND FOLKESTONE

CANTERBURY is endeared to us through its association with Agnes Wickfield ; and *David Copperfield* is the only book in which it is referred to at any length.

Dickens must have been familiar with it, as he would probably have visited it from Broadstairs, where he spent his summer holidays for many years. But, strange to say, there is no record that Dickens actually visited the city prior to writing *David Copperfield* in 1849.

Dolby, in his interesting book, " Charles Dickens as I Knew Him," describes a visit to Canterbury paid by Dickens and a party of friends from Gad's Hill, and it serves to show the intimacy Dickens had with the city, and the thoroughness with which he entertained his friends :

" We drove into Canterbury in the early afternoon, just as the bells of the Cathedral were ringing for afternoon service. Entering the quiet city under the old gate at the end of the High Street, it seemed as though its inhabitants were indulging in an afternoon's nap after a midday dinner. But our entry and the clatter of our horse's hoofs roused them as it had done the people of Rochester, and they came running to their windows and out into the streets to learn what so much noise might mean.

" We turned into the bye-street in which the Fountain Hotel is situated, where the carriages and horses were to be put up while we explored the city. . . .

" Under his pleasant and instructive guidance, the afternoon passed only too quickly, and we stayed so long in the grand old Cathedral that we had but little time to spare for a ramble through the sleepy streets. Some of the Americans were rather disappointed at this, for, knowing the accuracy of Dickens's descriptions, they had shown an extreme curiosity to see and examine for themselves the very house where David Copperfield went to school.

" There are, however, many houses in Canterbury which would answer to Dickens's description of ' Doctor Strong's ' ; and in reply to one of the party who had asked him to point out the particular house, he said, laughingly, that ' there were several that would do.' We took tea at the hotel, and then at about six o'clock started on our homeward journey, Canterbury having by this time quite got over the effects of its day-sleep. The people were enjoying their stroll in the cool of the evening, and the streets presented a much more animated appearance than they had done on our arrival. In the interval between drowsiness and wakefulness, Canterbury had evidently summoned sufficient energy to make inquiries about our party ; and learning that no less a person than Charles Dickens was responsible for having disturbed their slumbers earlier in the day, the good people at once forgave us all, and were quite hearty in their salutations as we left the town."

With the exception of unimportant references in *Barnaby Rudge* and *Our Mutual Friend*, Canterbury's sole claim to Dickensian interest rests with *David Copperfield*.

We have already seen how little David left London on his long walk to his aunt's at Dover ; how he came to Rochester and Chatham, and at last passed through " the sunny street of Canterbury, dozing as it were in the hot light . . . with . . . its old houses and gateways, and the stately, grey Cathedral, with the rooks sailing round the towers."

When at length he reached his aunt's and it was decided to send him to school, he went to one in Canterbury. He lodged at the house of Mr. Wickfield, his aunt's lawyer, the original of which is said to be at No. 71 St. Dunstan's Street, near to the West Gate. It is described as " a very old house bulging out over the road ; a house with long low lattice-windows bulging out still farther, and beams with carved heads on the ends bulging out too, so that I fancied the whole house was leaning forward, trying to see who was passing on the narrow pavement below."

In the evening of his arrival he tells us how he went a little way across the street, that he might have another peep at the old houses, and the grey Cathedral ; and might think of his coming through that old city in his journey, and of his passing the very house, without knowing it.

Dr. Strong's School, to which David was sent by his aunt, is said to have had its prototype in the King's School, " A grave building in a courtyard with a learned air about it that seemed very well suited to the stray rooks and jackdaws who came down from the Cathedral Towers to walk with a clerkly bearing on the grass plot. . . . Doctor Strong looked almost as rusty as the tall iron rails and gates outside the house : and almost as stiff and heavy as the great stone urns that flanked them, and were set up, on the top of the red brick wall, at regular distances all round the court, like substantial skittles for Time to play at."

What stood for Dr. Strong's house is at No. 1 Lady Wootton's Green.

Uriah Heep's humble dwelling is said to have been situated in North Lane—now demolished.

The " county inn " at which Mr. Dick put up was no doubt the Fountain Hotel, at which Dickens stayed on the night of his reading in 1861.

" I saw Mr. Dick every alternate Wednesday, when

he arrived by Stage Coach at noon, to stay until next
morning. . . . Mr. Dick was very partial to Ginger-
bread. To render his visits more agreeable, my aunt
had instructed me to open a credit for him at a cake
shop, which was hampered with the stipulation that
he should not be served with more than one shilling's
worth in the course of any one day. This, and the
reference to all his little bills at the county inn where
he slept, to my Aunt, before they were paid, induced
me to suspect that he was only allowed to rattle his
money, and not to spend it."

The quaint little Sun Inn close to the Cathedral
has been identified as the hostelry where Mr. Micawber
stayed when he saw a " great probability of something
turning up in a Cathedral city."

" It was a little inn where Mr. Micawber put up,
and he occupied a little room in it, partitioned off
from the commercial room, and strongly flavoured
with tobacco smoke. I think it was over the kitchen,
because a warm, greasy smell appeared to come up
through the chinks in the floor, and there was a flabby
perspiration on the walls. I know it was near the bar,
on account of the smell of spirits and jingling of
glasses."

It was here that David, his aunt, Mr. Dick, and
Traddles stopped when they went down to Canterbury
to assist Mr. Micawber in the unmasking of Uriah
Heep. The preliminary appointment with Mr.
Micawber, was, to use his own words, " at the house
of public entertainment at Canterbury, where Mrs.
Micawber and myself had once the honour of uniting
our voices to yours, in the well-known strain of the
Immortal exciseman nurtured beyond the Tweed."

The party travelled " down to Canterbury by the
Dover Mail " and had some little trouble in getting
into the inn in the middle of the night. " After which,"
says David, "we went shivering, at that uncomfortable

hour, to our respective beds, through various close passages which smelt as if they had been steeped for ages in a solution of soup and stables."

At the Church of St. Alphege, in the High Street, Dr. Strong was married to Annie, a fact that Mrs. Markleham announced in Chapter XLV.

After Dickens's reading in 1861, he wrote to his daughter, " A word of report before I go to bed. An excellent house to-night, and an audience positively perfect. The greatest part of it stalls and an intelligent and delightful response in them, like the touch of a beautiful instrument. ' Copperfield ' wound up in a real burst of feeling and delight."

A few days later he paid a further compliment to the people of Canterbury in a letter to his sister-in-law, Miss Hogarth, by saying :

" The most delicate audience I have seen in any provincial place is Canterbury."

When David Copperfield at length came upon " the bare, wide downs near Dover " he was still not certain his aunt actually did live there. The answers of Peggotty to his enquiries had been rather vague ; " Miss Betsey lived near Dover, but whether at Dover itself, at Hythe, Sandgate, or Folkestone, she could not say." However, finding out that all these places were close together, he had set out for Dover, and had arrived there on the sixth day of his tramp. He enquired about his aunt among the boatmen first, and received various answers, mostly " jocose " and all " disrespectful." At length, worn out, he deliberated whilst " sitting on the step of an empty shop at a street corner, near the market-place."

This shop is claimed to be that occupied by a firm of bakers, Messrs. Igglesden and Greaves, who have fixed a tablet to their new premises, on the site of the old shop, worded as follows :

Here
is the site of the steps
on which
Charles Dickens
represents
David Copperfield,
as resting in his
search for his aunt
Betsey Trotwood

Through the help of a good-natured fly-driver he
became acquainted with his aunt's maid, and followed
her until he came to " A very neat little cottage with
cheerful bow-windows : in front of it, a small square
gravelled court of garden full of flowers carefully
tended, and smelling deliciously."

Here, he discovered his Aunt—busy with her donkey
scaring, and Phiz's excellent drawing of the meeting
will at once be called to mind, no less than Dickens's
description of the memorable scene.

There is no cottage at Dover that can be said to
have been the original of that of Miss Trotwood. It
is thought probable that Dickens simply transferred
the locale from Broadstairs, where the original of
David's aunt is said to have been a reality (see page 237).
Dickens wrote a portion of *David Copperfield* at Broadstairs, and although Dover was known to him, yet, so
far as we can trace, he had not stayed there for any
length of time prior to writing the story.

Dickens took up his residence in Dover for three
months in 1852, living at No. 10 Camden Crescent :
he was engaged on *Bleak House* at the time. His
opinion of the place expressed in a letter was that it
was not quite a place to his taste, being too prone to
itinerant music, and " infinitely too genteel." " But,"
he added, " the sea is very fine, and the walks are
quite remarkable. There are two ways of going to
Folkestone, both lovely and striking in the highest

degree : and there are heights and downs, and country roads, and I don't know what, everywhere."

The town undoubtedly attracted Dickens, for we find him writing from the Ship Hotel there in April and May, 1856, speaking of his walks to Deal and back, and "over the downs towards Canterbury in a gale of wind." Three years later *A Tale of Two Cities* was written, and with it an account of Dover, as viewed by Mr. Jarvis Lorry in a walk after breakfast :

"The little narrow, crooked town of Dover hid itself away from the beach, and ran its head into the chalk cliffs, like a marine ostrich. The beach was a desert of heaps of sea and stones tumbling wildly about, and the sea did what it liked, and what it liked was destruction. It thundered at the town, and thundered at the cliffs, and brought the coast down, madly. The air among the houses was of so strong a piscatory flavour that one might have supposed sick fish went up to be dipped in it, as sick people went down to be dipped in the sea."

The Royal George Hotel, where Mr. Lorry always stayed was undoubtedly the Lord Warden, and Dickens was on very friendly terms with the proprietor, Mr. Birmingham, and his wife. One letter from the Lord Warden Hotel—to Wilkie Collins—dated 24th May, 1861, is worth quoting :

"Of course I am dull and penitent here, but it is very beautiful. I can work well, and I walked, by the cliffs, to Folkestone and back to-day, when it was so exquisitely beautiful that, though I was alone, I could not keep silence on the subject. In the fourteen miles I doubt if I met twelve people."

On the 5th November, 1861, he gave a reading at Dover, after which he wrote :

"The effect of the readings at . . . Dover really seems to have outdone the best usual impression ; . . . they wouldn't go but sat applauding like mad . . . the audience with the greatest sense of humour certainly is at Dover. The people in the stalls set the example of laughing, in the most curiously unreserved way; and they laughed with such really cordial enjoyment when Squeers read the boys' letters, that the contagion extended to me. For one couldn't hear them without laughing too."

Although it was not until 1855 that Dickens spent a sea-side holiday at Folkestone, the place was well known to him before, and had often been visited during his holidays at Broadstairs.

In the summer of 1855 Dickens and his family took residence at No. 3 Albion Villas, Folkestone, and it was during his stay there that he decided to give a public reading from his works to assist the funds of the local institutes; this led to the idea of giving such readings for his own benefit, the first series of which was given three years later. In connection with this we find him writing to Forster from Folkestone on the 16th September, 1855 : " I am going to read for them here on the 5th of next month, and have answered in the last fortnight thirty applications to do the like all over England, Ireland and Scotland." And a week later : " I am going to read here next Friday week. There are (as there are everywhere) a Literary Institution and a Working Men's Institution, which have not the slightest sympathy or connection. The stalls are five shillings, and I have made them fix the working men's admission at threepence, and I hope that it may bring them together. The event comes off in a carpenter's shop, as the biggest place that can be got."

The " carpenter's shop " was a builder's saw-mills in the Dover Road, on the site now occupied by the Fire Station.

We cannot glean very much of Dickens's life at Folkestone from the published letters. The only references of importance to Folkestone in the works are to be found in *Reprinted Pieces*. The following extract is from " A Flight," describing the journey by train from London to Folkestone to connect with the steamer for Boulogne. The paper originally appeared in *Household Words*, 30th August, 1851.

" Now fresher air, now glimpses of unenclosed Downland with flapping crows flying over it . . . now the sea, now Folkestone. . . . We are dropped slowly down to the Port, and sidle to and fro (the whole train) before the insensible Royal George Hotel for some ten minutes. The Royal George takes no more heed of us than its namesake under water at Spithead, or under earth at Windsor, does. The Royal George dog lies winking and blinking at us, without taking the trouble to sit up ; and the Royal George's ' wedding party ' at the open window (who seem, I must say, rather tired of bliss) don't bestow a solitary glance upon us. . . . The first gentleman in Folkestone is evidently used up, on this subject."

There is no Royal George Hotel at Folkestone. Some years later, in writing *A Tale of Two Cities* Dickens calls the Ship Hotel at Dover the Royal George.

To *Household Words* of 29th September, 1855, Dickens contributed an article on Folkestone under the title of " Out of Town." In it he called the place Pavilionstone. This was subsequently published in *Reprinted Pieces*.

" Sitting on a bright September morning, among my books and papers at my open window on the cliff overhanging the sea-beach, I have the sky and ocean framed before me like a beautiful picture. . . . The name of the little town, on whose shore this sea is murmuring . . . is Pavilionstone. Within a quarter of a century, it was a little fishing town, and they do say, that the time was, when it was a little smuggling town. I have heard that it was rather famous in the hollands and brandy way, and that coevally with that reputation the lamplighter's was considered a bad life at the Assurance offices. . . . Now, gas and electricity run to the very water's edge, and the South Eastern Railway Company screech at us in the dead of night.

" But, the old little fishing and smuggling town remains. Let nobody with corns come to Pavilion-stone, for there are breakneck flights of ragged steps, connecting the principal streets by back-ways, which will cripple that visitor in half an hour. . . . In connection with these breakneck steps I observe some wooden cottages, with tumble-down out-houses, and back-yards three feet square, adorned with garlands of dried fish. . . . The South Eastern Company have brought Pavilionstone into such vogue with their tidal trains and splendid steam packets, that a new Pavilion-stone is rising up. . . . We are sensibly laid out in general ; and with a little care and pains (by no means wanting, so far), shall become a very pretty place. We ought to be, for our situation is delightful, our air is delicious, and our breezy hills and downs, carpeted with wild thyme, and decorated with millions of wild flowers, are, on the faith of a pedestrian, perfect."

The following year Dickens wrote another sea-side article, " Out of the Season," for *Household Words*. Folkestone was probably the " watering-place out of the season " that he had in his mind, although no mention is made of it by name.

TWELFTH DAY

BROADSTAIRS

DICKENS was admittedly of a restless disposition and loved change : to his favourite haunts, however, he was fairly constant, and so we find his English summer holidays were for the most part taken at Broadstairs, easily reached from Canterbury, nineteen miles away.

The little town of Broadstairs owes much to Dickens, who may well be said to have discovered it, and the house that stands on a projection of land overlooking the harbour, is known far and wide as " Bleak House," and as the house that Dickens occupied. However, the Dickens interest is by no means confined to this one house where he lived only two out of the dozen or more summers spent at Broadstairs.

A very apt description of Broadstairs was given by Dickens in a letter to his American friend Felton : " This is a little fishing-place ; intensely quiet ; built on a cliff, whereon—in the centre of a tiny semi-circular bay—our house stands ; the sea rolling and dashing under the windows. Seven miles out are the Goodwin Sands (you've heard of the Goodwin Sands ?) whence floating lights perpetually wink after dark, as if they were carrying on intrigues with the servants. Also there is a big lighthouse called the North Foreland on a hill behind the village, a severe parsonic light, which reproves the young and giddy floaters, and stares grimly out upon the sea. Under the cliff are rare good sands, where all the children assemble every morning and throw up impossible fortifications, which the sea throws down again at high water.

"Old gentlemen and ancient ladies flirt after their own manner in two reading-rooms and on a great many scattered seats in the open air. Other old gentlemen look all day through telescopes and never see anything.

"In a bay-window in a one-pair sits, from nine o'clock to one, a gentleman with rather long hair and no neckcloth, who writes and grins as if he thought he were very funny indeed. His name is Boz. At one he disappears, and presently emerges from a bathing machine, and may be seen—a kind of salmon-coloured porpoise—splashing about in the ocean. After that he may be seen in another bay-window on the ground floor, eating a strong lunch ; after that, walking a dozen miles or so, or lying on his back in the sand reading a book.

"Nobody bothers him unless they know he is disposed to be talked to ; and I am told he is very comfortable indeed. He's as brown as a berry, and they *do* say is a small fortune to the innkeeper who sells beer and cold punch. But this is mere rumour. Sometimes he goes up to London (eighty miles, or so, away), and then I'm told there is a sound in Lincoln's Inn Fields at night, as of men laughing, together with a clinking of knives and forks and wine-glasses."

It was in the autumn of 1837 that Dickens and his wife spent their first holiday at Broadstairs, then quite a retired spot and nothing approaching the importance it has since achieved. They stayed at No. 12 (now No. 31) High Street, and here a part of *The Pickwick Papers* was written, as recorded by a tablet on the wall reading :

Charles Dickens
lived here
And wrote part of " The Pickwick Papers "
1837

From this date until 1851 he was a regular summer

visitor to the town ; only two summers, 1844 and 1846, was he missing, and in nearly all cases his visits extended into several weeks.

For four years rooms at No. 40 Albion Street were taken ; this house was, later on, incorporated with the Albion Hotel, where Dickens also stayed in 1845, 1849 and 1859—as a tablet bears witness :

> Charles Dickens
> stayed here
> 1839, 1840, 1842, 1843, 1845, 1849, 1859,
> and wrote part of " Nicholas Nickleby "

According to a letter to Thomas Beard, Dickens was staying at No. 37 Albion Street in June, 1840. In September of the same year he was again at the little watering-place. " The residence he most desired there, Fort House, stood prominently at the top of a breezy hill on the road to Kingsgate, with a corn-field between it and the sea, and this in many subsequent years he always occupied ; but he was fain to be content as yet with Lawn House, a smaller villa between the hill and the corn-field " (*Forster*). " I have been at work of course," wrote Dickens to Forster on September 2nd, " and have just finished a number. I have effected a reform by virtue of which we breakfast at a quarter before eight, so that I get to work at half-past, and am commonly free by one o'clock or so, which is a great happiness."

Lawn House is marked with the following tablet :

> Here
> Charles Dickens
> lived and wrote
> Part of " Barnaby Rudge," 1841

This is hardly ample enough, as Dickens stayed in Lawn House also in 1840 and wrote part of *The Old Curiosity Shop* there.

In 1847 his stay lasted from June until October; he lived in Chandos Place; of the exact house we are not certain, it was probably No. 1 or No. 6; he occupied the same house the following year.

It was during the visit of 1847 that he first began to complain of the great noise in the streets, which rendered writing rather difficult. To Forster he wrote : " Vagrant music is getting to that height here, and is so impossible to be escaped from, that I fear Broadstairs and I must part company in time to come. Unless it pours of rain I cannot write half-an-hour without the most excruciating organs, fiddles, bells, or glee-singers. There is a violin of the most torturing kind under the window now (time, ten in the morning) and an Italian box of music on the steps—both in full blast."

However, in spite of this the charm of Broadstairs still continued to hold him. In 1848 he spent " an idle summer " there, with only *The Haunted Man* to finish.

The following year Dickens was in the throes of *David Copperfield ;* he was unsettled as to summer holidays and sought a change from Broadstairs. A visit to the Isle of Wight was arranged ; but he found the air too relaxing ; his daughter Maimie was taken ill, so in the September the family returned to their old favourite Broadstairs. As soon as he was in Broadstairs, he became more settled in his mind about the book and decided to put into it a great part of the MS. of his own life, on which he had been busy some time previously, into Number 4 of the story ; this was Chapter Eleven, which is mostly autobiographical.

The location of Betsey Trotwood at Dover was purely imaginary, as the original was a Broadstairs woman, one Mary Strong, who lived in the house in Nuckell's Place, now called Dickens House and marked with a tablet to the effect that in the house "lived the original of Betsey Trotwood in *David Copperfield* by Charles Dickens, 1849."

The gardens in front of the house facing the sea were meadow-land in those days, and Miss Strong, it is said, had the same decided antipathy to donkeys as Miss Betsey.

In July, 1850, Dickens was at last able to secure Fort House from the July for a few months, and here *David Copperfield* was completed.

The house has undergone several alterations since then, including the altogether unnecessary change of name to "Bleak House"—a tribute to Dickens, no doubt ; but it was not the Bleak House of the story, nor was any portion of *Bleak House* planned or written there.

On an outer wall of the house is a granite tablet bearing a bronze bust of Dickens, encircled by a wreath bound with ribbons upon which are inscribed the names of some of the works. It is a pity that *Barnaby Rudge* and *The Old Curiosity Shop*, both partly written at Broadstairs, should be omitted, and *Bleak House* and other works having no association with the place included.

The early summer of 1851 saw him again at Fort House, where he stayed until the October. An early letter (1st June) to Forster said : " It is more delightful here than I can express. Corn growing, larks singing, garden full of flowers, fresh air on the sea.—O it is wonderful ! Why can't you come down next Saturday (bringing work) and go back with me on Wednesday for the Copperfield banquet ? "

This was his last regular visit to Broadstairs ; the growth of the place, and " the plague of itinerant music," as Forster puts it, made it impossible for him to find there the seclusion he sought for his more important work.

With so large a house at his disposal, Dickens was able to invite many visitors to share in his joy and love of the district, and his large circle of friends from London and elsewhere ensured many delightful week-ends. The following extract from a letter to Charles Knight is typical of many of his hearty invitations : " You say you are coming down to look for a place next week. Now, Jerrold says he is coming on Thursday, by the cheap express at half-past twelve, to return with me for the play early on Monday morning. Can't you make that holiday too ? I have promised him our only spare bed, but we'll find you a bed hard by, and shall be delighted ' to eat and drink you,' as an American once wrote to me. We will make expeditions to Herne Bay, Canterbury, where not ? and drink deep draughts of fresh air. Come ! They are beginning to cut the corn. You will never see the country so pretty. If you stay in town these days, you'll do nothing. I feel convinced you'll not buy the ' Memoirs of a Man of Quality.' Say you'll come ! "

We have shown how, over a period of fourteen years, with only a year or two's interval, Dickens was faithful to the little Kentish coast town, and he took a fond farewell of it in a paper in *Household Words* for 2nd August, 1851, entitled *Our Watering Place* : " Half awake and half asleep, this idle morning in our sunny window on the edge of a chalk-cliff in the old-fashioned watering-place to which we are a faithful resorter, we feel a lazy inclination to sketch its pictures, its commerces."

He then goes on to paint a word sea-scape of " the ocean winking in the sun-light like a drowsy lion " and " the fishing boats in the tiny harbour all stranded in the mud " and the two colliers, sole representatives of the maritime trade, " exhausted on their sides, like faint fish of an antideluvian species " . . . We have a pier—a queer old wooden pier, fortunately without the slightest pretensions to architecture, and very picturesque in consequence. Boats are hauled up upon it, ropes are coiled all over it ; lobster-pots, nets, masts, oars, spars, sails, ballast, and rickety capstans, make a perfect labyrinth of it."

His last visit was some eight years later ; he was far from well at the time, as he wrote to Forster, " I have an instinctive feeling that nothing but the sea will restore me." His friend, Wilkie Collins, and his brother, were at Broadstairs at the time, and to them he wrote, " Nothing but sea air and sea water will set me right. I want to come to Broadstairs next Wednesday by the midday train and stay till Monday." Accordingly, Broadstairs welcomed him once again, and again he stayed at the Albion Hotel, from which place he wrote a very characteristic gossipy letter to his two daughters, commencing : " I have been ' moved ' here, and am now (Ballard having added to the hotel a house we lived in three years) in our old dining-room and sitting-room, and our old drawing-room as a bedroom."

INDEX

INCLUDING BOOK REFERENCES